JOHN GALSWORTHY

By Catherine Dupré

John Galsworthy

A BIOGRAPHY

Catherine ⌊Dupré

Coward, McCann & Geoghegan, Inc. New York

Illustrations follow page 160. All these photographs are reproduced by kind permission of Mr. Rudolph Sauter.

First American Edition 1976

SBN: 698-10715-2

Library of Congress Cataloging in Publication Data
Dupré, Catherine.
  John Galsworthy.

  Bibliography: p.
  Includes index.
  1. Galsworthy, John, 1867–1933—Biography.
PR6013.A5Z5655 1976 823'.9'12 [B] 76-13473

Printed in the United States of America

With love
This book is dedicated
to the memory of my husband
Desmond Dupré

Contents

Acknowledgments

My thanks are in the first place due to Mr Rudolf Sauter who has so generously made available to me all the papers and letters in his possession, and has patiently given up hours to talk to me about his uncle and aunt, John and Ada Galsworthy. Without his help and friendship, and that of Mrs Pat Scrivens, this portrait of Galsworthy, which I hope will enable readers to see him as the very human person he was, would never have been possible. I have also to thank Mr Hubert Galsworthy and Miss Muriel Galsworthy for recalling their memories of their uncle; Mrs Dorothy Ivens (née Easton) who has kindly lent me her unpublished memoir of John Galsworthy and personal letters; and Mr E. L. Sanderson for generously allowing me to use the memoirs of his father and aunt (Agnes Ridgeway). It would be impossible to mention all those who have helped me by lending letters and recording their reminiscences, but I must record my thanks to Miss Margaret Morris, Mrs Ada Hankinson (née Mottram), Mr Michael Hornby, Sir Kenneth Buckley, Dame Rebecca West, Sir Rupert Hart-Davis, Mr Dwye Evans, Mr John Detmor and Mr Charles Pick of Heinemann, Mrs Joan Dean and the late Mrs Minnie Green, for the help they have given me. I am also indebted to the Librarian and staff of Birmingham University Library for making available to me the large collection of Galsworthy papers in their possession, and their assistance to me in my work, to the Archivist of Norwich Public Record Office for allowing me to read their collection of letters from Ada Galsworthy to R. H. Mottram. Especially my thanks are due to Messrs Heinemann for allowing me to quote so liberally from the works of John Galsworthy, whose works they published from 1906 until the end of his life.

Until his death in 1974, my husband listened patiently to my growing obsession with the life of Galsworthy, shared my interest and criticized my work. For the latter part of the work I have been dependent on the help and encouragement of my family and friends; most especially I am indebted to Rivers Scott, who first suggested to me the possibility of writing about John Galsworthy, and who has criticized the manuscript at various stages, to Margaret Guido, and to my editor, Philip Ziegler, who has befriended and encouraged me throughout, and whose enthusiasm and help has never failed me. Lastly I have to thank my daughter, Caroline Hartnell, for reading and sorting out the manuscript and preparing the final typescript.

'a queer fish, like the rest of us. So sincerely weighed down by the out-of-jointness of things socially . . . but outwardly a man-about-town, so neat, so correct – he would go to the stake for his opinions but he would go courteously raising his hat. The other day he was flung out of a hansom and went as gracefully as if he were leaving his card. That is him today but has been all its opposites. I think he was once a cowboy, I have hopes he has been a pirate. He has been everywhere and has done most things and what turned him from one man into the other I don't know. He used to care for nothing but frivolity, shooting big game, and now so serious and could not put a pin into a butterfly.'

J. M. BARRIE
(*letter to Millicent, Duchess of Sutherland*)

Chapter 1

The Parents

In 1867 a little girl of three years old with a miniature silver trowel laid the foundation stone of a new mansion that was to be built in Coombe in Surrey. This almost regal occasion was, so the father hoped, the founding of a new dynasty: the child was Lilian Galsworthy, the first-born of John Galsworthy, a solicitor in the city of London. This John Galsworthy was not a young man; he had waited until his late forties, when he was well established in life, before selecting Blanche Bartleet, a woman some twenty years his junior, to be his wife. All seemed to bode well for the couple as they watched their attractive little daughter so ceremoniously inaugurate the building of their first country home. And Blanche was pregnant with her second child, who was to be a son, the novelist, John Galsworthy.

'We were four,' Galsworthy wrote in a short autobiographical note, 'Blanche Lilian (Lily), born September 1st 1864, myself, born August 14th 1867 (in a thunderstorm – I still have the penholder carved by our butler out of an oak struck in Richmond Park close by during that storm); Hubert born February 18th, 1869; Mabel Edith born October 7th, 1871.'[1] The thunderstorm is significant, for it seems at first sight almost the only event in John Galsworthy's childhood that was not ordered, that was violent, that was remarkable in any way.

Galsworthy's father, the model for old Jolyon of *The Forsyte Saga*, held first place in his children's affections. He was an admirable person, a great deal older than his children; he did not marry until he was forty-five, thus by the time his children were adult he was an old man. Most of the portraits show him as a very old man. Nevertheless he lived to see his grandchildren; in fact Rudolf Sauter, Lilian's son, was nine years old when he died in 1904.

John Galsworthy senior came from several generations of Devonshire yeomen. The family tree is traced back to one Edmund Galsworthy, who died at Plymstock in 1598, and following him there were no less than six male Galsworthys who lived and died in the region of

Plymstock and Wembury. It was John Galsworthy, the grandfather of the novelist, who first left Plymstock and settled in London in 1833. Like the Forsytes he invested prudently and widely in property at a moment when the city was expanding fast, and was thus able to leave his son, Galsworthy's father, a wealthy man.

This John Galsworthy had by now become completely urbanized; moreover his family were beginning to rise in the social world. He was a professional man, a solicitor, the head of a firm who had their offices in the city. His marriage in 1862 to Blanche Bailey Bartleet, a woman of twenty-five coming from a well-connected family, further improved his social standing. Blanche was the daughter of Charles Bartleet, a Justice of the Peace and a man highly considered in Worcestershire; living in the village of Redditch, the Bartleet family had for several generations been the leading family in the district. The Bartleets had brought prosperity not only to their own family but also to the community of Redditch by founding a successful business, a needle factory. This Charles Bartleet had married as his second wife Francis Lavinia Bayley, and though she died when Galsworthy was only ten years old he remembered his grandmother as 'an admirable, if somewhat irritating woman, and very fastidious in her standards of gentility'.[2]

Francis Lavinia had passed on to her daughter much of her own petty character, and Blanche was extremely conscious of the fact that she had married beneath her, and that the Galsworthys were poor stuff when compared to her own genteel ancestry. What she failed to appreciate was the rugged strength, determination and intelligence of these newly rich Galsworthys, qualities which her own family so conspicuously lacked.

It must have been a grievous disappointment to Blanche to see that her children, and particularly her daughters, took after their father rather than herself. In fact the children were constantly irritated by their mother's pettiness, while for their father they had boundless affection and admiration. 'My father really predominated in me from the start, and ruled my life,' John Galsworthy wrote in a long autobiographical note on his parents. 'I was so truly and deeply fond of him that I seemed not to have a fair share of love left to give to my mother.'[3]

By the time of his marriage John Galsworthy the elder was a man established in life and in his profession, and moreover a man of considerable personal fortune; it became at once his object to provide in a truly generous fashion for his young wife and the family they hoped to have. Possibly because of his own origins in the Devonshire country-side, John Galsworthy felt his children needed as much of country life as was compatible with his own work in the city. At any rate, soon after the birth of Lilian the Galsworthy parents moved with their small daughter to a house then pleasantly out of the town, Parkfield on Kingston Hill. The area was an exceedingly agreeable one; the suburban sprawl of London had not yet consumed the surrounding country, it was still a rural place of open fields and woods. Parkfield was a typical Victorian middle-class family house, a long low building with many round-arched windows standing in a large garden. But John Galsworthy was a man rich enough to build for himself exactly the house he wanted in a site of his own choosing, and having found that the area around Kingston suited him well he purchased a large piece of land in the neighbouring village of Malden, known as Coombe. Selecting a fair and high locality not too far away from London, he set himself at once to make a country place.[4]

To modern eyes the first house he built at Coombe, Coombe Warren, was a considerably less attractive house than the one he was leaving. A building of red brick, tall and angular, reminiscent of St Pancras Station with spiky, narrow windows, even a small tower, this great Victorian Gothic monstrosity must, one would imagine, have been dark and passagey to live in. Of course the fact that it was difficult and inconvenient to run would have been of no importance to the Galsworthys, who maintained a large staff of servants to deal with such problems. This grand and pretentious house was later renamed Coombe Court, and became the fashionable home of the Marquis of Ripon. It is not difficult to see it as the house, Robin Hill, built by Galsworthy's character Soames, the 'Man of Property', a house built to satisfy the ostentatious taste of its fictional owner.

John Galsworthy senior was to build two more houses on his piece of land at Coombe, Coombe Croft and Coombe Leigh; the family moved from one property to the other. In a notebook Blanche Galsworthy has noted that in 1868 they moved to Coombe Warren, in 1875 Coombe Leigh, 1878 Coombe Croft and in 1881 back to Coombe Leigh, and in the same year they left Coombe for good.

Coombe Warren was ready to move into soon after John's birth, and it was at Coombe, in one or other of these properties, that he and his sisters and brother spent most of their childhood. John Galsworthy certainly succeeded in giving to his children the life he so much desired for them, 'fresh air, new milk and all the fruits of the earth, home-grown round them.' And his children were fully aware of how much they owed to his foresight and care: 'Quite wonderful was the forethought he lavished on that house and little estate stretching down the side of a hill . . .'[5]

But there was more to this John Galsworthy than the sense of family which led him to provide so well and prudently for his four children. In a biographical essay entitled 'A Portrait', his son describes him as a highly cultured man devoted to all the arts, and particularly having a great sensitivity to all forms of beauty:

> A pretty face, a beautiful figure, a mellow tune, the sight of dancing, a blackbird's song, the moon behind a poplar tree, starry nights, sweet scents, and the language of Shakespeare – all these moved him deeply, the more perhaps because he had never learned to express his feelings. His attempts at literature indeed were strongly naïve and stilted; his verse, in the comic vein, rather good, but all, as it were, like his period, ashamed to express any intimate feeling except in classical language.

This love of nature his eldest son inherited to a marked degree; what was only to become evident much later, and increasingly as the years passed, was that he also shared the inhibitions which had proved a total stumbling block to his father's abortive efforts at creative writing.

Though John Galsworthy the elder did not write he was extremely well-read; among his favourite reading were the poets Milton and Byron, the novelist George Eliot, and towards the end of his life, surprisingly, like his son he came to admire the works of Turgenev as they were translated into the English language. His tastes extended to music and the theatre, Mozart, Beethoven and Wagner, and the acting of Irving, though he compared the actors of the present day unfavourably with those he had seen in his youth, such as Edmund and Charles Kean.

Like his son he was fastidious in his appearance, though avoiding eccentricity of any kind: 'he never abandoned very well made side-spring boots with cork soles, greatly resenting the way other boots dirtied his hands, which were thin and brown with long polished nails, and blue veins outstanding.'[6]

Galsworthy's essay on his father is almost too eulogistic; it is hard to

Blanche Galsworthy with
the infant John.

John Galsworthy senior.

Combe Warren, where John Galsworthy spent his childhood.

The Harrow XI, 1885. John Galsworthy, the captain, is in the front row with his foot resting on the ball.

Snarks Club, New College, Oxford in 1888. John Galsworthy is one from the right of those standing, wearing a bowler hat.

An early family group probably taken in Scotland. Lilian and Mabel are in the back row with John on the right. John Galsworthy senior is seated in the centre.

John Galsworthy at the time he met Ada.

Ada Nemesis Cooper.

A shooting party. John Galsworthy is seated while Ten Sanderson stands to his right.

John Galsworthy writing in the garden with his spaniel Chris.

Margaret Morris in 1910.

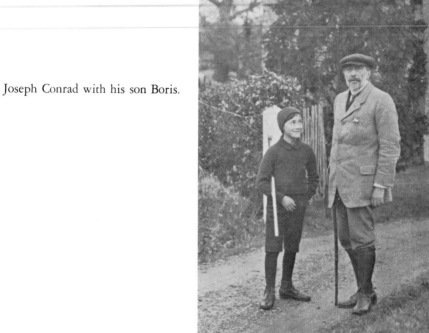

Joseph Conrad with his son Boris.

The Heinemann cricket team. John Galsworthy is seated and wearing a hat.

John Galsworthy's sister Lilian, later Mrs. Sauter.

A group at Wingstone. *From left to right:* Granville Barker, Ada Galsworthy, Bernard Shaw, Mrs. Shaw, John Galsworthy, Lilla McCarthy.

Journey into the Desert. Egypt, 1914. John and Ada Galsworthy on their camels; H. V. Massingham and his wife on donkeys.

John and Ada Galsworthy c. 1930.

believe in such a paragon, a man so well-educated and cultured, yet at the same time shrewd and prudent in matters of business, a successful solicitor, and above all an ideal parent. Yet all his children saw him in this light; and Galsworthy in his novels was to portray again and again the picture of an idyllic father and child relationship.

But mothers come off badly in the novels. They appear as fussy, tiresome individuals, with one notable exception: Mrs Pendyce in *The Country House*. Blanche Galsworthy too was a difficult and trivial woman, and though her children tried to be dutiful and loyal it is not difficult to see that they found her an exceedingly trying person.

Mrs Galsworthy was not in any sense an intellectual woman nor indeed a very intelligent one. Her world centred round her household and her family; it centred too in an essentially small and trivial way. She positively enjoyed littleness in things; she had her own set of little tools, she had her own almost doll-sized dust-pan and brush. She irritated her daughters by the way she fussed them, constantly adjusting their clothes, or fidgeting with their hair. 'She had the most exact standards of dress and appearance of any one I have known,' Galsworthy wrote of her. Yet she had the accomplishments common to a lady of her day. She spoke French well, sang and played a little, was a good needlewoman, rode well and 'could hold her own at archery'. But she seldom read, and what her son found most irritating in her was that she 'had no speculation in her soul'.[7] One cannot help sympathizing a little with Blanche, with her two blue-stocking daughters, reading Emerson, endlessly discussing questions of philosophy and religion. She must sometimes have felt very much of an outsider in her own family circle; the things which she took entirely for granted, they were constantly arguing about. The royal family, the Church, the structure of society: to Blanche they were just part of the world she lived in; she could not imagine, or see any point in imagining, a world that was in any way different.

The philosophical Lilian, trying to work out why she and her mother were so different, came to the conclusion that her mother's mind was an 'external mind . . . it *excels* in domestic duties of housekeeping and dressmaking; the arrangement of rooms, dresses and dinners, and the management of servants etc . . .' and 'is infinitely pained by untidiness and attaches the greatest importance I have noticed to the following details; threads and pins being left about, books, papers, etc. not put away, mistakes in grammar, spelling or etiquette, above all small points crooked, or wrong in personal appearance.'[8]

John and Blanche Galsworthy were not a well-matched couple, and after the first few years their marriage was not a happy one. They were both strong-willed people, and neither partner was prepared to give in to the other. But in the large Victorian establishments at Coombe and later at Cambridge Gate near Hyde Park, there was space and room for a couple to disagree and yet live a tolerable life together. They were not on top of each other as people so often have to be in modern homes; they might have met only at meals or for social and family gatherings; they would certainly never have expected the 'togetherness' that modern couples strive for.

Nevertheless the final incident of this married life is exceedingly strange, almost farcical: two years before his death, when her husband was well on in his eighties, Blanche decided that he had become overfond of one of her grandchildren's nursery governesses. Without considering whether her suspicions were justified or not, she packed her bags and left her husband, to whom she had now been married for more than forty years. She took a flat at Kensington Palace Mansions, and John spent his last year in the home of one or other of his married daughters, where he ultimately died.

Was this perhaps a final *cri de coeur* after a married life during which she must have felt so unappreciated? Her last fifteen years were spent travelling, seeing new places and new people, making friendships that did not last, and at home 'making a collection of the fashion plates of modern women's hats, cutting them out of the papers and pasting them into a book'.[9] At last she could be herself, and enjoy, uncriticized, the trivial things that pleased her.

Chapter 2

The Children

John Galsworthy, the father, certainly succeeded, as he so much wished, in establishing a home that had everything that could make happy his children's early days. In the spacious grounds at Coombe they could wander to their heart's content; they could play their games and ride their ponies; they even had a private cricket pitch, on which during the school holidays family matches were played, and the boys could practise their bowling and batting. The young John's enthusiasm for the game, though he was never very good at it, lasted all his life, and as an adult he seldom missed the Eton and Harrow Match at Lord's.

Everything that Galsworthy later wrote about childhood has an almost sentimental nostalgia for those early days at Coombe, *Awakening*, which describes the childhood of Jon Forsyte, the child of Irene and young Jolyon Forsyte, or the short essay 'Memorable Days'. It was a childhood in which nannies or governesses held first place in the young child's world and affections, in which the mother was still only a shadowy, comparatively unimportant figure in the background. Thus Blanche Galsworthy, with her fussy and irritating ways, was not yet to impinge seriously on the lives of her young children.

The small boy could watch fascinated the charade of his parents' lives, the formal social world of an opulent Victorian middle-class family; like a play he could observe its happenings, wonder at the way each character played his part:

First I had to attend the head gardener in the hothouse and the vinery, selecting pineapples and grapes; or from the south wall picking the peaches and nectarines; nor could I on any account be absent when Henry the butler, with two wicker baskets, and my Father, opened the door which kept in that half-nice, funny smell, as of gas and mushrooms . . . I had also constantly to be in the kitchen, to see exactly what was going to be eaten; and be told: 'Now, Master Johnny, don't touch.' I found it advisable, too, to watch the special polishing which George, the groom, would give his buttons, in order that he might take charge of – I forget exactly what.[1]

Then at last the great hour of the evening came, his mother 'Beautiful with ear-ring and a curl coming down each side of her neck', the carriages of the guests driving up, 'Henry, walking across the hall with a lady and gentleman behind . . . General and Mrs Grim . . .' But his mother had said, 'Now, Johnny darling go along to bed,' and the little boy, sitting at the top of the stairs, had had to dodge the vigilant eye of Mademoiselle or Nurse. Then at last, looking through the banisters, 'Dinner is served . . . It was like the Noah's Ark, only the gentlemen were black and shiny white in front, and the ladies had ever so much more skin than Mrs Noah, and were wider below . . .'[2]

But that was the world of the grown-ups, seen only from a distance; for the child, life was lived in the nursery and schoolroom, and the people who mattered were those who governed these dominions. 'Da' (the nanny in *Awakening*) left her charge when he was eight – ' "to be married" of all things – "to a man" ' – and it is at the age of eight that the new governess came (identified in *Awakening* with 'Auntie' June Forsyte): 'That was a year bathed in the glamour of the imagination, fighting and – love for the new governess.'[3]

It was while he had measles and was under the influence of this governess that books, fictional heroes and heroines suddenly awakened the young child's imagination. 'He read voraciously at an early age,' his sister, Mabel Reynolds, recorded, 'all sorts of books of adventure, travel and history, and made himself short-sighted by generally doing this face downwards on the floor. The battles, naval and military, about which he read were worked out afterwards by means of a boy's usual paraphernalia: lead soldiers, spring-cannon, boats, bricks etc. . . .'[4]

From the beginning John played a leading part in the lives of his sisters and brother and was their 'chief in all the wild games we played about the house and grounds on holidays; captain of the pillow fights, and of the ships we built of beds and chest of drawers . . .' But, 'though willing enough to profit by our "fagging", his rule was mild and his teasing good humoured . . .' Mabel commented.[5]

Of his family circle John was closest to his sister Lilian. Three years his senior, Lilian, exceptionally small in build, gave the appearance of being a fragile and delicate person. Such an impression would be misleading. She was a person of extraordinary character and will-power, and of quite outstanding intellectual ability. She had too a gentle and sympathetic nature, and an ability to communicate with those with whom she came into contact.

The companionship of this sister during school and university holidays was for John his first experience of a really stimulating mind, at that time more mature and developed than his own. It was with her that he first exchanged ideas on philosophy and religion, first began to consider questions of social justice, and even whether his own affluent circumstances, in a world where so many were poor and suffering, were tolerable. Very much later Lilian's marriage to the Austrian painter, Georg Sauter, a man of even more determined and radical views than herself, brought yet another formative influence to the young John Galsworthy.

Mabel Galsworthy, four years younger than John, hardly figured at all in those pre-school days at Coombe; by the time he was nine years old, like most boys born into prosperous families in the latter part of Queen Victoria's reign, John had left the nursery and schoolroom for good to be taken by his father's clerk, Joseph Ramsden, to Bournemouth to a small preparatory school, Saugeen, run by a Dr and Mrs Brackenbury. Galsworthy must have been thinking of this journey when his character Soames Forsyte is reminded by his clerk Gradman of a similar trip: 'It seems only the other day since I took you down to school at Slough.'

The Victorian preparatory school was often a small family affair, in which the headmaster's wife, according to her nature and inclination, mothered the little boys placed under her husband's care. It should also be remembered that the freedom of children in their own homes was far less than it is today; they were accustomed to living according to a strict routine, therefore the contrast between school and home was not so great. Ford Madox Ford even went so far as to say: 'There can scarcely have been at any stage of the world's history a happiness greater than that say of the schoolboy during the decades of the eighties and nineties.'[6]

Though this must be seen as an exaggeration characteristic of its writer, John Galsworthy was by all accounts happy at Saugeen. Bournemouth was at that date a pleasant and unspoilt town, with 'open sands, pinewoods and clean bright sea'.[7] The family visited Johnnie, as he was then called, at regular intervals, walking across the cliffs to the Church of St Swithins, where John with the other Saugeen boys sang in the church choir. Two or three cousins, and later his brother Hubert, also attended the school, so these family gatherings were happy ones, the children digging for buried treasure and building sandcastles on the beach.

There were only eighteen months between John and Hubert, and now that the two brothers were both at Saugeen they became much closer. Hubert was in many ways the odd-man-out in the Galsworthy family, an extrovert who excelled at sport and outdoor activities, less intellectual than his sisters and brother. Mabel tells us that Hubert was quicker and more 'wiry' than John (and also quicker-tempered), so that despite the age difference the two were well-matched in the singles tennis matches they played in the holidays at Coombe Leigh. They also had 'fierce billiard contests' during which the younger sister was dragooned into marking for her brothers.[8]

At Saugeen John was already a child likely to find favour with both masters and boys. He was good at games and keen to join in with enthusiasm all the activities of his school; he was what one would now term an easy child, well-mannered and obedient and able to get on well with his contemporaries. As a small boy he had read unusually widely not only in literature but also in history; he had especially a great admiration for Andreas Hofer and the role he had played in the Napoleonic Wars. 'At his prep. school the boys were asked to name their favourite hero, and to write an essay on the spot about him. Young Johnnie electrified his fellows by declaring Andreas Hofer [a Tyrolean freedom fighter], a name of which they had apparently never heard, and by writing the essay accounted the best.'[9] But though he devoured books and played all manner of imaginative games he said later of himself that these were the only signs he ever gave in his youth of becoming a writer of fiction.[10]

Chapter 3

Harrow

Harrow! For the soldier, the traveller, the scout
Whether it be victory, or whether it be rout!
And when the fight is lost or won, and the dark camp is still
There shall be thought of the old songs and dreaming of the Hill.

JOHN GALSWORTHY
(published in the Harrovian *Dec.* 21, 1929)

In the summer term of 1881 Galsworthy left Saugeen for Harrow. The graduation from preparatory to public school in the life of a young boy is a serious matter; he must shed all vestiges of childhood, at the same time as entering a hierarchy in which he, the new boy, will be the least significant, the most subservient, member. 'We're not sent here at enormous expense to learn only Latin and Greek,' says a character in Horace Vachell's *The Hill* (a novel written about Harrow in 1905). 'At Eton and Harrow one is licked into shape for the big things: diplomacy, politics, the Service.'*

John, now nearly fourteen years old, was certainly entering a strange world, but his time at Saugeen would have taught him what to expect. It was a *preparatory* school, and its function was exactly that, to prepare boys for the public school that would follow. To the school boy, raw and wet behind the ears, this world may not have seemed so strange as it does to an adult looking back. In a speech given in America in 1919 Galsworthy recalled some of the taboos of the public school:

> In that queer life we had all sorts of unwritten rules of suppression. You must turn up your trousers; must not go out with your umbrella rolled. Your hat must be worn tilted forward; you must not

* Galsworthy expressed interest in *The Hill* when it was sent to Garnett for review: 'I wish you had sent Vachell's book to me – he was in my house at Harrow before my time, I knew his younger brother there.' J. G. to Edward Garnett, 3 March 1905.

walk two abreast till you reached a certain form; nor be enthusiastic about anything, except such a supreme matter as a drive over the pavilion at cricket, or a run the whole length of the ground at football. You must not talk about yourself or your home people; and for any punishment you must assume complete indifference.[1]

All this had to be learnt by the new boy – at his peril should he be so forgetful as to do something that was not 'done'. The hero of Vachell's novel, John Verney, soon realizes that to display family photographs is in bad taste and not 'done'; he learns too the duties of a 'fag' (a system by which a new boy becomes virtually the servant of a senior boy): he had to see that his fagmaster's 'toast was always done to a turn, that his daily paper was warmed, as John had seen the butler at home warm *The Times*, that his pens were changed, his blotting paper renewed, and so forth'.[2]

Such would have been the duties of John Galsworthy as a new boy during his first terms at Harrow. In his turn he would reap the benefit of the system and have his own fag – at one time Hubert Galsworthy was his brother's fag. But during those early days life was hard-going for the new boy: it was difficult to keep up in form, it was even harder to make his pocket money go round. Nevertheless, on his arrival he was placed well in the school and wrote at once to his father to tell him how he had fared in the examination:

May 6th 1881   *Harrow.*
Dear Father, The result of the exam was known this morning at 8 a.m. I was placed in the *Upper Shell* high I believe for a new boy. I think I shall be able to keep up but I don't know. I was 7th from bottom at 1st School, 32nd from bottom at 2nd School, and top or 35th from bottom at last School. There are 36 fellows in our form. I suppose you know what Schools are, they are divisions of time when we are in the class rooms. Please send my hat box as soon as possible, because I must wear it on Sunday. I hope Mother is not the worse for her exertions on Wednesday.

I am beginning to shake down into the ways of the school now. I tried on my jacket to-day it was all right except being a little tight under the arm which Stevens said he would alter.

And now good-bye dear Father (as I have six sums of Colenso's arith to do now) with best love to all. I am your very loving boy,
                                       Johnny.

Money, as for most schoolboys, features a great deal in the letters that John wrote home to his parents: 'The subscriptions are very heavy here so Father must not be surprised if my money goes at a good rate . . .'[3] Then a few weeks later in a letter to his mother there is a careful account of his expenditure: £1 os od is for 'Grub', which he justifies: 'I'll tell you what I get under the heading grub on whole schooldays we have dinner over at 1.30 tea 6.30 at tea we only have bread and butter the latter article is not supplied in sufficient quantity, so I get rather hungry in between as it is 4 hours to wait. I generally have 1 cup of chocolate and a muffin which is the usual thing that comes to 6d. On half-holidays we have tea at 5.30 so nothing is required between dinner and tea but nearly everybody gets something for tea such as sausages . . .' Few mothers could resist such an appeal for cash to buy her hungry child a muffin!

The schoolboy at Harrow shared a room with one or two others, and this room they furbished with tables, chairs and ornaments, these things either brought from home or purchased from other boys; such a room is described in *The Hill*: 'charmingly furnished, gay with chintz, embellished with pictures, Japanese fans, silver cups and other trophies.' So John had to write to his mother asking her to remind 'dear Father to send me the money he promised me for my armchair. The armchair is 12/9. The cushions for it 12/9 . . .'[4]

Once established at Harrow, John did well, and his progress through the school can have given his parents nothing but satisfaction. He was first placed in one of the smaller houses, that of a Mr C. Colbeck, but by the end of the year he was transferred to Moreton's, where he ultimately became head of the house.

But in the public school world of the 1880s the accolades went to the sportsman rather than to the scholar; it was getting your colours that was important, the 'fez' (the cap of honour worn by the house football eleven) or your 'flannels', signifying that you were truly a 'Blood', a member of the Cricket XI, able to take part in that vital contest at Lord's, the Eton and Harrow Match.

Moreton's House kept a House Book in which the achievements of the house and its members are chronicled, trophies won largely on the playing field or in the gymnasium. The list of John's triumphs must make monotonous reading to anyone outside that small élite, but a few should be mentioned: in his first term in Moreton's House he won his 'fez', the following term he played for the house in Torpids (the junior football matches); he also won the house mile. In 1884, the last year of his school career, he reached the pinnacles of the schoolboy world, head of the house, captain of House Football XI, member of the School XI. His first biographer, H. V. Marrot, peppers his pages with photographs of the young Galsworthy in football shirts and running vests, and one cannot fail to be struck by these portraits. He is disarmingly handsome at this period of his life, with his straight regular features, a somewhat stern mouth, and eyes that gaze unflinchingly from the page.

It is not surprising that H. E. Hutton, the housemaster of Moreton's, wrote in an early report to Galsworthy's father: 'Your elder boy gives me great satisfaction. His tone, character, temper and manners are all thoroughly good; and if only he was not so weak in composition he might really distinguish himself at Harrow.'[5]

Outwardly Galsworthy appears to have been a very normal schoolboy, doing well but not brilliantly at his schoolwork, but covering himself with honours in the athletic field, and becoming, as he entered his last years at school, a monitor in the school and head of house, Moreton's. 'I can honestly say to you that I never expect to be able to replace your loss; and I have never had amongst many good heads one who was at once more easy to work with than yourself, and so completely to my heart in every respect. I shall always look back to you, therefore, as my ideal head, without exaggeration; . . .' his housemaster wrote to him when he left the school.[6]

But John Galsworthy as a boy of eighteen was already an extremely serious young man, serious almost to a fault, lacking the light-heartedness or sense of humour that would have made him more approachable to his contemporaries. Though he was a member of the school debating society, one is not surprised to learn that his 'voice was seldom or never heard'. He was known by the nickname 'T.G.', owing to his inability to pronounce the letter 'J'; other friends called him 'Galer', with a long 'a'; this nickname persisted into his Oxford days, and it was not until considerably later that he adopted the present pronunciation of Galsworthy.

The indefatigable Marrot collected many personal reminiscences of the young Galsworthy for the purposes of his biography: the ex-headmaster of Harrow, Dr J. E. C. Welldon, wrote, in an amazingly pompous account that reads like a school report, that 'He was a quiet, modest, unassuming boy . . . he was a strictly honourable boy who made his mark both in work and in play, without affording any notable promise of his distinction in after-life.' His school contemporaries appear to have found him distant and remote: one wrote that he was 'a quite unassuming fellow who took life seriously even then. He was always kind and considerate, and it was not a disagreeable duty to act as his fag.' Another commented that he was 'reserved and dignified; he was practically too much on a pedestal for any of the younger boys to mix with or become in any way intimate with'.

From his family we have a slightly less solemn account of the school-boy in his last term at Harrow. The entire family came down to Harrow for John's final speech day in 1886, and Mabel Reynolds recalled that even in the awe and solemnity of the great occasion they 'laughed to see "Galer", as they called him, seated in state in the front row on the platform of "Speecher", carefully flicking with his handkerchief at the dust on his patent leather shoes!'[7]

Chapter 4

The Undergraduate

John Galsworthy, who arrived at Oxford in the Michaelmas term of 1886 to read law, taking up residence at New College, was a meticulously and fashionably dressed young man. This interest in clothes was a characteristic which remained with Galsworthy throughout his life; few people who have described him have not commented on his good looks and well-turned-out appearance. H. A. L. Fisher, the historian, and a contemporary of Galsworthy at New College, describes him as being 'tall and slim, well-built, strikingly handsome; and always, I should say, the best dressed man in College . . .'[1]

Oxford was for Galsworthy a happy, almost frivolous, interlude in a life that was lived in general with the greatest solemnity. The responsibilities of the schoolboy were in due course to be replaced by the cares of adult life, cares which lay on Galsworthy's shoulders as an almost unendurable burden, for no cause was too trivial to attract his concern, no effort great enough to alleviate the misery he saw everywhere around him. But all this lay in the future. In 1886, fresh from the successes of his school career, he was ready to enjoy Oxford; he was rich, good-looking, and able enough to take an adequate degree without taxing himself unduly.

His career at Oxford was for the most part singularly undistinguished and conventional; as H. A. L. Fisher's account attests:

> For the most part he associated with Etonians and Harrovians, and though he did not, so far as I can recall, come into conflict with the authorities, he often climbed in after hours and led the conventional life of the well-to-do, not very intellectual under-graduate from a great Public School . . . I do not recall that he belonged to any of the intellectual coteries in College or that he ever read a paper to an Essay Society, or contributed to a debate. He moved among us somewhat withdrawn, saying little, and that in a gentle voice, a sensitive, amused, somewhat cynical (as we thought) spectator of the human scene.[2]

28

He does add, with perception, that he had felt that Galsworthy was 'a very clever fellow with reserves of power'. At the age of twenty-one, however, Galsworthy still lacked the confidence to be himself; even in his family circle, where he was most at ease, he was quiet and reserved and far less vociferous than either of his sisters.

In his early novel *The Island Pharisees*, the character Shelton, whose experiences are drawn largely from Galsworthy's own, remembers his own time at Oxford:

> They now entered the Bishop's Head, and had their dinner in the room where Shelton had given his Derby dinner to four-and-twenty well bred youths; here was the picture of the racehorse that the wine glass, thrown by one of them, had missed when it hit the waiter; and there, serving Crocker, with anchovy sauce, was the very waiter. When they had finished, Shelton felt the old desire to patrol the streets with arm hooked in some other arm; the old eagerness to dare and do something heroic and unlawful; the old sense that he was of the finest set, in the finest college, of the finest country in the finest world.

Racing was in fact Galsworthy's main and most absorbing preoccupation at this time. 'His knowledge of racing was, or seemed to us, to be extensive,' H. A. L. Fisher commented in his account; and when playing 'Confession', a favourite Victorian parlour game in which the subject noted a list of characteristics concerning him or herself, under the heading 'My Favourite Study' John entered *Ruff's Guide to the —*. But horse-racing was not Galsworthy's only form of gambling; the son of Galsworthy's friend, St John Hornby, says that his father often referred to Galsworthy as a 'compulsive gambler' and describes an incident on a train journey when the two undergraduates were travelling together, and Galsworthy became involved in a card game with a doubtful character who was in the same carriage. He lost every penny he had on him, and more, and then had to turn to his friend to settle the debt for him. Ford Madox Ford, who first met Galsworthy in a Sporting Club, tells a similar story, but his anecdote is, as one would expect, much more elaborate. He names Galsworthy's companion as Lord Bathurst and states that on this occasion John staked 'his watch and chain, tie-pin, signet ring'.[3] Whatever the truth of these tales there can be no doubt that John was much addicted both to the race-course and to gambling.

But there were other activities to engage the attention of the young student: he joined the OUDS, the flourishing dramatic society at Oxford; he himself wrote plays for his friends the Sandersons, the large family whose father, Lancelot Sanderson, ran the preparatory school at Elstree. At Oxford he wrote a play called *Guddirore*, a skit on Gilbert and Sullivan's *Ruddigore*, and in it he himself played the part of Spooner, then a don and notorious eccentric at New College.

Amateur theatricals also played an important part in country house life. The young Galsworthys and their friends produced plays; in fact it was while acting in an amateur production of *Caste* that he later met the first woman he was to fall in love with, Sybil Carlisle. For the moment his attentions were not seriously engaged; nothing more than the most trivial flirtation had stirred his heart. From New College, in a round unformed hand, he is writing to a Miss Blanche Buckley: 'I suppose the arts have been flourishing like a green bay-tree in your part of the world, my two and only two, (the she-ing and the he-art) have been withering away during the prolonged period that has passed since I set eyes on yer (again pardon the vulgarism)', and he signs himself 'Yrs. for ever and a day, John Galsworthy'.

During the vacations, while with his family, a more serious atmosphere prevailed. Lilian and Mabel Galsworthy had by now grown into two intelligent and thoughtful young women; had they been born fifty years later they would most certainly have graduated from Girton or Somerville. To their own generation these young intellectuals were almost alarming: 'At first we were nervous of them,' Agnes Sanderson wrote in her memoirs, 'they were well educated and very "Arty". They wore at that time immense beaver hats with ostrich feathers drooping on to their shoulders. Long seal-skin coats enveloped their small figures, and the effect was unfamiliar to us. They scarcely spoke above a whisper, and were very serious. They were good linguists, and never used slang.'[4] But the Sanderson family was a very different one from the Galsworthys; an extremely large middle-class family (there were fourteen of them), they had, as all large families do, their own lore and customs. To them the young Galsworthys seemed almost over-genteel and well-bred. As Agnes Sanderson said, at first they made them feel 'extremely gauche and raw', though later the girls of the two families became close friends.

If not conventionally beautiful, Lilian and Mabel were extremely attractive girls: 'Lily like a little moth, so tiny and gentle, the other

Mabel, more like Jack, but with the most marvellous golden hair.'[5]

A photograph of the family, probably taken in the summer of 1888, still survives. John Galsworthy, senior, is seated in the centre of the family group, his enormous Father Christmas beard covering his face, a bowler hat on his head; beside him is his wife, Blanche, a small well-dressed woman, elderly in appearance for her fifty-one years. Around them are clustered the younger members of the family, sitting at their feet or standing 'casually' posed behind their elders. There is John, exceptionally handsome and always well-turned-out, wearing unusual, sometimes rather bounderish clothes. As an undergraduate he adopted the habit of wearing an eyeglass, which though necessary to counteract a weakness in his right eye also appealed to his flamboyant style of dressing. His features are so regular as to defy description. In his twenties he wore a moustache, which gave him a somewhat military appearance, especially as he carried himself rather stiffly. Already there is a shy diffidence about the way he is usually to be seen slightly apart from the others, and, on looking more closely, a sadness about the eyes; one senses criticism and a non-identification with the Victorian family who were to become his Forsytes. Lilian and Mabel are unusually good-looking girls. In Lilian's face there is the same over-sensitive tension that we see in her brother; even more so, because she was the first to rebel, to flout openly the many petty strictures that Mrs Galsworthy attempted to impose on her children.

John Galsworthy the elder would whenever possible rent large country houses where he could take his family to spend the summer months; there they would be joined by friends and cousins, and it was in this house party atmosphere of picnics, excursions, amateur theatricals or music-making, and above all long hours of conversation, that Jack and Hubert, back from school or college, grew to know their sisters. In the summer of 1888 the house chosen by the Galsworthys was Dalnabreck in Perthshire, a house that was, according to the detailed diary that Lilian kept of this holiday, 'small and *very* plainly furnished'. However, it turned out to be large enough to accommodate a fairly large party and to afford a great deal of pleasure to the holidaymakers. The boys shot grouse, hares and rabbits. On 14 August it was John's twenty-first birthday. Nothing is said of any particular celebration; as usual the 'boys shot' and the rest of the party picnicked.

Lilian's diary, written with perception and liveliness, paints a vivid picture of the Galsworthy family life. It also gives considerable insight into her own remarkable character, which was to have such an enormous influence on John's development. 'It was she who brought to us three younger ones the greater part of such mental stimulus as our very normal, ordinary lives ever knew,' Mabel Reynolds wrote of her sister. 'Always quietly busy herself with her painting, reading, needlework or writing, it was she who would start interesting subjects for discussion; she who told us stories when we were little; she who opened our eyes and minds to beautiful things to be seen or heard or read.'[6] And as she grew older 'She read deep philosophical books in German, and could discuss philosophy with experts.'[7] One can see from these accounts that the companionship of Lilian would have been both stimulating and demanding, and it is not surprising to read in her diary that during the holiday they were reading Emerson's essay on Friendship, and the others (Charlie Vaughan and Mabel) 'came to me for an elucidation. It is no easy task to read Emerson to any one else,' she concludes.

The house at Dalnabreck must have echoed with the endless conversations of the young people, often serious, but sometimes lighthearted. 'Argumentative dinner – Discussion of good breeding – refinement . . . Question started, does fine breeding give pluck? Jack maintained for argument's sake that a well and low bred boy brought up in ignorance of their station would have an equal amount of gentleness of manner – or lack thereof . . .' Or on another occasion: 'She [a young lady called Gertie Fair] had many talks with Jack of a serious nature I should judge. He likes her, but not so much as Maud [one of the guests].'[8] John's fancy seems to wander pleasantly and without serious involvement among the female members of the party.

Considering that the date is 1888, and the family one as conventionally reared as the young Galsworthys, it is surprising to note the freedom and lack of supervision with which the sexes mixed. We find Lilian having a long discussion on celibacy with a young man she refers to as G. 'He maintaining that on *personal* grounds it was he thought better for him – but he was undecided – I urge arguments to contrary, but had not much to say in a case where a man thought it would personally interfere with his work.' And later in the same holiday: 'We all made a compact to call each other by our Christian names and immediately broke it,' but two days later Charlie Vaughan took the plunge and coming into the drawing-room said, 'Good morning, Lily,

I have been screwing my courage up to saying it all the way down the stairs.'[9] (Twenty years later Virginia and Vanessa Stephen considered themselves advanced when they moved on to Christian-name terms with Lytton Strachey.)

Life was not all so serious at Dalnabreck; a great deal of time was spent in preparing a tableau, and we find Jack and Maud 'improvising tails to be red jackets for hunting coats'. On 27 August there was a dress rehearsal for the servants, and on the 28th the 'Grand day came at last', and was considered by all to be a great success. The evening ended with songs 'uprising from the porch to my window produced by the three Oxford men'. Music-making was in fact a great feature of the holiday; in the evenings they sang 'glees and songs, notably our "Columbine's dear" ', and also danced 'to our own playing'.[10]

One small calamity clouded what was otherwise an almost perfect holiday. John Galsworthy senior was bitten by a dog, but 'Mother promptly cauterized it, having a little bundle of useful things in her bag.' The incident seemed to cause his family an inordinate amount of worry – though one has to remember that by now Galsworthy's father was quite an old man (seventy-one), and Lilian notes that it was some days before the family recovered their high spirits. That evening 'Jack came and sat on a cushion by my side with his head in my lap and was very comforting and sweet. I said "I wish it had been anyone but F." "So do I," said he.'[11]

I have dwelt at some length on this Scottish holiday because no other document gives so complete a picture of the family from which Galsworthy came. It is well known that the background of many of Galsworthy's novels was taken from that branch of society to which his parents belonged, newly rich middle-class people, with considerable vested interests in property and business. But equally important were the close relationships within that family group, the small intellectual world which they created for themselves, and which had already begun to criticize so sharply the values of their parents. Lilian and John were both preoccupied with religious ideas, and Lilian had already decided that she could no longer accept the Church of England faith of her parents. She had confessed her situation to her mother – 'she put direct questions and drew out all my heresies'[12] – and had long discussions on religion with her brother. Together they had read Matthew Arnold's *Literature and Dogma* and studied Emerson, and in the end both were to discard conventional Christian teaching.

Whether alone, without the constant spur and stimulation of Lilian's active mind, John would have arrived at what was then unconventional and generally unacceptable, is doubtful. Nor do we know at what point he finally discarded Christianity in favour of the humanistic view of life that was to dominate his thinking and his writing for the rest of his life. It is futile to attempt to pinpoint the time or place of a man's conversion, for that in fact is what it was. The barometer of Galsworthy's philosophy swung dramatically away from any orthodox religion or creed: good was here and now, suffering was here and now, and a man's work, and most particularly his, was to crusade against suffering; the poor were no longer to be poor, prisoners were to be happy in their prisons, wives content in their marriages; animals were no longer to be ill-treated, even cage birds, liberated, were to sing for ever in a new freedom. It was a naïve conception; nevertheless it was one that was deeply felt, and it was during those long vacations from Oxford – perhaps during that summer at Dalnabreck – that it began to take so strong a hold on the mind of the young John Galsworthy.

But though the much more serious ideas of Lilian were beginning to make their impression on John, it would be wrong to envisage him at the age of twenty-two, just down from Oxford, as anything other than a rather immature young man with almost no idea of what he was going to do with his life. To illustrate this point it is worth quoting the 'Confession' which he gave to one of his cousins, though this should not be taken as an entirely serious document.

CONFESSION

My Ideal Virtue	Unselfishness.
My Idea of Beauty in Nature	A Scotch grouse moor at its best.
My Idea of Beauty in Art	Turner.
My Favourite Study	*Ruff's Guide to the* . . .
„ Flower	Carnations, well wired.
„ Colour	The colour of Queenie's hair.
„ Qualities in Man	Stoicism.
„ Qualities in Woman	Sympathy.
My Greatest Happiness	A 'Right and Left'.
„ Misery	Ear-ache.
My Favourite Amusement	Grouse-driving.
„ Residence	Anywhere away from London.
„ Authors	Thackeray, Dickens, Whyte Melville.

„	Poets	Lewis Caroll [*sic*].
„	Musical Composer	Beethoven.
„	Instrument	Piano.
„	Heroes in Real Life	Bayard. Damien.
„	Heroines in Real Life	Only heard of Florence Nightingale, so suppose it is she.
„	Actors and Plays	Edward Terry. Fred Leslie. *Caste.*
„	Animal	Horses. Setters.
„	Names	Ethel. Grace. Claud. Hubert.
„	Quotation	'Harry no man's cattle.'
My present State of Mind		Embarrassed to a degree.
My Motto		Never do to-day what you can put off till to-morrow.
My Signature		John Galsworthy. Dec. 29th 1889.[13]

The one thing in his life Galsworthy was serious about was his love for Sybil Carlisle, though she did not return his feelings. Sybil Carlisle (sometimes referred to as Sybil Carr) was the daughter of Mrs Carlisle Carr, who for a short while taught singing. The pair met at a house-party given by Colonel Randall at his country house in the Wye Valley. At this house-party there were the inevitable theatricals and Sybil played the part of 'Polly' to Galsworthy's 'Sam' in T. W. Robertson's play *Caste*. The play had its repercussions for both the young actors: Jack Galsworthy fell in love with Sybil, and Sybil fell in love with the stage. (She did in fact become a professional actress and J. M. Barrie wrote the part of Mrs Darling in *Peter Pan* for her, which she played for many years.) But for Galsworthy she felt only affection, not love.

The Galsworthy family did not approve of their son's choice. Lilian, writing in her diary in October 1888, wrote that her father 'suffered great anxiety and trouble about Jack, who accepted an invitation to the Rowlands contrary to all wishes of F. & M. at the beginning of the long vac'.[14] Galsworthy, looking back at this long-drawn-out affair – for it was to engage his attentions for several years – also dismissed it as trivial. In 1906 he wrote to the young writer Ralph Mottram, who was himself unhappily in love, 'I thought myself absolutely certain off and on from nineteen to twenty-four about someone who wouldn't have done at all, and can only thank my stars humbly that preserved me for *Her*.'

Chapter 5

The Lawyer

The years that followed Galsworthy's coming down from Oxford were a period of indecision. He graduated in 1889 with a second-class degree in law; according to Marrot he only narrowly missed getting a first. But though he had worked conscientiously at it, the subject of law seemed to have aroused little enthusiasm in him, and it was only because of his father's wish that his son should be a barrister (a profession he would have liked to have followed himself[1]) that John was admitted to Lincoln's Inn and called to the Bar in the Easter Term, 1890.

Galsworthy's romantic attachment to Sybil Carlisle may well have had some part in his complete failure to find any enthusiasm for his new career in the law. During the two years that followed his coming down from Oxford John applied himself to his new profession half-heartedly: 'I read in various Chambers, practised almost not at all, and disliked my profession thoroughly.'[2]

By now the Galsworthy family had left their 'country' houses at Coombe and moved into London; now that their three elder children wished to study in London it was an obvious and sensible arrangement. With his usual business acumen John Galsworthy senior had entered into a partnership with his brother Fred and bought land on the site of the old Colosseum in Regent's Park. Here they had built a row of ten houses, calling the row Cambridge Gate. It was into number 8 that the Galsworthy family moved in 1887, and it was from here that John Galsworthy, now a fashionable young man about town, set out each day to his chambers, eating his 'dinners' in the evening, and no doubt also finding plenty of time to amuse himself at the theatre or on the racecourse.

His progress was a disappointment to his father, who attributed his son's unsatisfactory development entirely to his attachment to Miss Carlisle. Such a judgement was certainly an over-simplification: John was not happy studying law; he couldn't envisage a life devoted to a

36

profession with which he had so little sympathy. It is likely that he already had yearnings – though yearnings that he felt to be quite hopeless – towards writing.

It was at this point that a new personality became part of the Galsworthy circle, the painter Georg Sauter, who both by the strength of his personality and by the fact that he was himself an artist must have made the idea of devoting oneself to the arts suddenly more imaginable. Georg Sauter was a young man only a year older than John Galsworthy himself. By 1890 he had begun to establish a modest reputation for himself as a portrait painter in London. He was commissioned to paint the portrait of the older John Galsworthy and in this connection was first admitted to the Galsworthy household. Georg became intimate with the younger members of the family and he and Lilian fell in love. If one considers that the older Galsworthys had been doubtful as to the propriety of inviting him to lunch at their own table between sittings for the portrait – a situation which Lilian soon and unequivocally resolved – one will realize that he was the last person they would have welcomed as a future son-in-law: he was foreign, he was not a gentleman (his parents were Bavarian peasants), and he was an artist. But Lilian was determined enough to overcome her parents' opposition, though it must have been a painful process, and in 1894 the couple were married.

Georg has described the first impression he had of John. He burst into the billiard-room while Georg was painting: 'an exceedingly well-dressed young man stood on the threshhold. He wore a small light moustache, and a rather formidable-looking monocle on a black ribbon fixed in his eye . . . He moved towards me, and as he did so the eye-glass fell from his eye, while a very kindly and gentle smile spread over his face.'[3] At first their conversations had to be carried on with Lilian as interpreter, for Georg was entirely German-speaking, but the painter realized that he was probably the first person John had come across outside his own circle, Harrow, Oxford and the law, the first person with ideas that were independent of the customs and conventions of an Englishman of his own class. 'It is my inward conviction,' he said, 'that, at that period of his development, the presence of one like myself – from another country, and with such totally different ideas from those of the conventional middle-class English family such as his – did serve, indirectly, perhaps, but most definitely, to give him that "push" which was necessary to make him choose a career so unusual, from the family standpoint, as that of a novelist and writer.'[4]

From his point of view old Mr Galsworthy had many good reasons for removing his eldest son from England at that moment. New scenes and a new country might distract him from his infatuation for Miss Carlisle; it would remove him from the Bohemian influence of Georg Sauter; it might in fact settle the young man down, get the wildness (if such a word could ever be applied to Galsworthy) out of his hair, and bring him back steadier and more ready to apply himself to law.

It was arranged that John should join his brother Hubert in America, ostensibly to investigate the affairs of a certain coal mining company at Nanaimo, Vancouver Island. He sailed in the SS *Circassian*, leaving England on 16 July 1891. His fellow passengers he found 'rather so-so', and by 8.30 p.m. on the day he sailed he found he was 'Not sea-sick but very sick of the sea already. There is something very depressing about the sea at all events about one's first acquaintance with it.' But worse was to follow; two days later he noted, 'When I am not sea-sick I am homesick, which is curious for me, I think.'[5]

On 26 July he landed at Quebec; with curiosity and ultra-Englishness he observed the behaviour of the natives of the French town: 'Saw some French people parting from each other. The kissing was something awful.'[6]

John joined Hubert on 9 August at Nanaimo and devoted the next week to inspecting and touring the mines there. The brothers then set out on a camping expedition to the lakes, which John describes in great detail in a long letter to his family in England. They set out on horseback, taking with them an Indian guide called Louis Goode – '(for very little)', Jack adds in his letter. And later: 'Louis and I went out hunting and before very long succeeded in losing ourselves, a gruesome sensation in those immense woods; the fool of an Indian, not knowing the country, had come without taking bearings or anything.' At last, wet through, having tramped 'up to your knees in water and over your head in thick growth', they found their camp, determined to be more cautious in the future.[7]

'The next day, which was gloriously fine, we devoted to making a raft (hard work), composed of three logs of cedar split, 20 feet long and very heavy, joined together by pegs and cross beams, and which, launched at 4.30, provided us with a capital boat. We went up the lake fishing from her and caught about 15 trout, and I shot a couple of ducks, but one got off. I tumbled in and had to spend the greater portion of the evening fishing in a shirt alone.'[8] Hubert has left a rather more colourful account of this ducking: 'Old Jack bobbed up to the surface again in an upright position and looking as cool as a cucumber, with his rod still in his hands, and his eye-glass still in his eye!'[9]

On another day Jack, in search of better hunting, set off on his own. 'I started off to the head of the second lake – about five miles (fearful walking) – and took a couple of blankets, a rifle-gun and fishing-rod, and camped under a cedar tree, where I had seen lots of deer marks the day before when out hunting that way. I waited up most of the night as it was very moonlight and they sometimes came down to the water to feed then; alas, no result, and I had a very uncomfortable night, being slightly mosquito- and other animile-bitten [*sic*].'[10] In his diary of 22 August he wrote: 'Queer sensation being all alone amongst those woods, and a little of it goes a long way. I fear I am too socially inclined to repeat the experiment.' The brothers continued their trip to Comox and from there to Denman Island in search of better shooting, returning in the middle of September to Vancouver where they parted, Jack making his way back to England.

Chapter 6

Journey to Australia

It was at this time that Galsworthy became intimate with Ted Sanderson, the son of Lancelot Sanderson, headmaster of Elstree Preparatory School. Like so many preparatory schools Elstree was a family school; in time Ted was to succeed his father as headmaster, and after him his own son took over. Elstree was the preparatory school for Harrow, so inevitably Ted Sanderson went on to that public school, where he had a career as distinguished as his friend and contemporary, John Galsworthy.

From his sister Agnes's memoirs one has a picture of a young man of almost alarming perfection of both character and appearance, with eyes of such a 'deep blue as only to be found in the sea'. He was scholarly and athletic, a person, she says, 'who did things in the right way'.[1] As the eldest child of such an enormous family he was groomed from the start to take authority, first over his younger brothers and sisters, and later over his father's school. But this virtuous behaviour seemed to be largely the characteristic of the older brother only, and the younger members of the family were from Agnes's description an unruly tribe. When the dapper young John Galsworthy first appeared in their midst they treated him in a barbarous fashion.

He arrived, immaculately dressed complete with monocle. Without his monocle he was practically blind and it was a real necessity, and not merely worn for swank as we thought. His manner so gentle and refined, and his voice soft and weak, we mistook for feebleness. We summed him up as 'Impossible'.

Ted sometimes brought friends we thought 'No good' and this must be one of them. We let him settle down, before we began our treatment of teasing and ragging. He was introduced to hockey in the Dining Hall, a very strenuous game with canes and a tennis ball. It was no joke to be whacked on the legs with a biting cane or across the toes if you had slippers on . . . We dropped his monocle in the tadpole bowl when we wanted him to be completely at our mercy. Even Monica took part in this treatment and actually asked if she might hit him hard with a knotted bath towel? He was very obliging and bent down so that she could get at his back, which she did with some hefty blows . . .[2]

It is not surprising that after such treatment Agnes says, 'We pretty soon changed our opinion of Jack and became attached to him . . .' Even so he was not quite safe from their teasing: the Sanderson children encouraged him to sing, 'a breathy sound with little timbre . . . We loved listening to him so that we could imitate him in private . . .'[3]

It is a tribute to Galsworthy's character – and good nature – that he could accept, and be accepted by, a family so different from his own. He 'was adopted into our way of life', Agnes graciously comments, as of one who has passed the formidable process of initiation. 'He gradually gave up wearing town-looking clothes and took to home spun, and was more like one of us.'[4] (Here I think she exaggerated the family influence.) The whole family, financially much less well-off than the Galsworthys, was impressed by the generosity of their new friend, who showered them with presents and largesse. One incident particularly struck Agnes: 'One summer's day he and Gerry [another Sanderson sister] were riding through a hay field when something happened to Jack's horse, which threw him. Gerry said that sovereigns flew in all directions, and could not be found in the thick hay. She said, Jack didn't seem to mind, and would be quite pleased to think the hay makers would benefit.'[5]

The young Sandersons, when introduced into the Galsworthy home, were equally bewildered:

Before us lie acres of red pile carpet, a thousand gold chair legs dance across this gory desert. From recesses of grandeur emerges a minute dame, a veritable French Marquise, with silver fluff piled on top of her proud little head. She smiles without showing her teeth, holds out a quarter sized hand, greets Monica by pulling her head down level with her own and pecks at her cheek, and does the same to me. I forget whether she kissed Murray, but I do remember seeing her go over the carpet where we had entered with a toy dust pan and brush sweeping up Murray's foot marks! He *did* look a fool. Why hadn't he wiped his shoes. That was Mrs Galsworthy . . .[6]

Though treated so differently the Sanderson children at 8 Cambridge Gate were having almost as testing a time as John had had at Elstree: 'the atmosphere of Victorian propriety, the dumb immaculate servants, the low flannelety Galsworthyian voices, killed all life in us . . .' Agnes concluded her account of the visit.[7]

By the summer of 1892 John Galsworthy senior was again making plans to send his eldest son abroad: John was still not making the progress at the Bar that his father hoped for, and he was still infatuated with Sybil Carlisle. A further period of travel might at last make his son more resolute in his profession; it was also considered sensible for him to take the opportunity of a long sea voyage to study navigation and maritime law. It was during this same summer that Ted Sanderson joined the Galsworthys at their holiday rendezvous, Vorsindae in Scotland. Ted had suffered a minor breakdown from overwork and was planning to go abroad to recuperate, and almost inevitably the two friends decided to join forces and travel together. They were both passionate admirers of the writer Robert Louis Stevenson; they would go to Australia and New Zealand and the South Seas, where at Samoa they hoped to meet him.

Galsworthy and Ted Sanderson left England in November 1892 on the Orient liner *Oruba*. The voyage 'isn't half bad in spite of many drawbacks, chief of them being the fact that I don't care about leaving England much just now', Jack wrote on the 26th to one of his sisters. Presumably he was thinking wistfully of the beautiful, but uncaring, Miss Carlisle.

The two travellers seemed undecided as to how their journey should proceed: 'I never knew two people who had more ideas and changed them more frequently than we two.'[8] They spent half a day en route at Colombo, and John found it a:

charming place, and one's first glimpse of Indian life is ripping. I am smitten with a desire to spend a year at Ceylon and India and see the country peoples and life thoroughly . . . We dined at the hotel, punkahs going, and sat out on the verandah afterwards watching the Indian jugglers growing [throwing] mangoes and doing other rather feeble tricks. We had a drive round in the afternoon through the cinnamon gardens and the native markets. The people seemed all very contented and happy – much more so than the lower classes of the so-called civilised countries. I want to get a book on Buddhism and study the teaching that produces such a self-contented character . . . Ted and I have wild ideas of going out on stations as rabbiters – i.e. professional slayers of rabbits at so much a hundred – or going up to the gold diggings.[9]

They arrived in Australia at Albany on 23 December, and a few days later proceeded to Sydney. Here they were frustrated in their original plan of going to Samoa, and took instead a 'rather dirty little ship', a tramp steamer bound for New Caledonia and the Fiji islands. On the way the ship called at Noumea, a South Sea island used as a French convict settlement. Here they 'sat under Flamboyant trees and listened to the Convict Band; and most beautifully those convicts played. The day or two we spent there made a great impression on Jack, who afterwards made use of some of the stories we heard there.'[10] This must have been Galsworthy's first encounter with human beings in captivity; sitting under the Flamboyant trees with Ted Sanderson in a heat that was of 'the hot-house order', the contrast between his own life as a rich young man, free to travel where he would, with that of these wretches imprisoned forever in this faraway island struck him forcibly. It was an experience that must have begun to crack the Forsyte complacency, that would bring him later to Dartmoor to study at first hand the conditions there, to write *Justice*, and ultimately to campaign against the conditions of prisoners and particularly the appalling inhumanity of solitary confinement.

From Noumea they continued their journey, arriving at Levuka, a place which enchanted them with its natural beauty: 'The chief attraction to us was a waterfall in the bush, of immense height; a tree grew out over the fall near the top and the natives used to jump over this tree into the deep pool below. They swam with us and gave us milk from the green coconuts.'[11] Ted was inclined to stay in this paradise, but Galsworthy, who was perhaps rather a stickler for timetables, insisted that they proceeded to Ba, where his cousin Bob Andrews had a sugar plantation. So on 20 January the travellers set off in 'a Ketch or small schooner' to Ba – where in fact Andrews, having only the day before received notification of their visit, was quite unprepared for them. There was no food and only one narrow bed for the two of them, the mosquitoes were awful, and 'sleeping head and tails, J & I kicked each other in the face periodically from the chagrin of mosquito poison'. The visit continued to be eventful: the guests were taken a ride round

the plantation; their mounts were to be a horse and a mule. Ted con-
siderately took the latter, 'thinking Jack would never recover his self-
respect if he mounted a mule'. His unselfishness was rewarded; Jack's
horse was swept down a river they were crossing and Ted thought 'he
was lost for a cert; but some Fiji men entered the river and turned him
and he was none the worse'.[12]

From Ba they planned to continue their journey on foot, to travel
some thirty or forty miles through jungle country to Fort Carnavon,
where they would take a boat to Suva. 'We shall be doing a very
unusual thing in going across,' Galsworthy wrote to his mother, 'but
there is no danger from the natives, and living among them, as we shall
do for nearly a fortnight, will be a new experience well worth having.'[13]

They set out on their expedition, Jack insisting they keep to a rigid
timetable:

> Brooks and rivers had to be crossed every mile or less and we just
> squelched through them in our shoes. Jack occasionally would pause
> and poise himself on a stone for a moment and would say 'I'll jump
> I think.' He invariably slipt and tumbled in. At 12 I cried out for
> food. Jack said wait till we get to a certain river at 1, which will end
> the first 10 miles. I weakly assented. From various reasons my lunch
> didn't get inside me till 2: and then I was too cooked to eat it. Besides
> Jack had forgotten to ask M for plates and also said there was no salt.
> I had two mouthfuls of sodden fly-covered beef, a little biscuit and
> marmalade . . .
>
> After our meal we went down stream and bathed in a rapid which
> carried me down to a shady pool. There, under the shadow of a big
> rock and a clump of Bamboo, I tried to sleep. We were not allowed
> to rest a moment. About ½ dozen natives rushed across the stream and
> crowded round us, examining everything and asking for everything,
> specially my Perfection Umbrella which is a marvel to them. One
> of them with long hair went through curious antics in the water.
> Then they carried us across the stream to their village which was not
> inviting. I wanted to have a meal about 4. Jack for some reason
> objected. He is in mortal terror of being late, though we have lots of
> time to reach Naborga by dark.[14]

They reached the village after a long trek over the mountains and were
taken to the chief's hut, which was like a 'haystack built not quite on
the ground'. By that time 'We were too much in want of our dinner

to make a fuss over our meal, we just hauled out a tin of soup and put it on the logs to melt, opened a bag of biscuits and "blomey" sausage and sat down to our rather piggish meal just as we were. I wanted to bathe and wash and change, but Jack said "food first, cleanliness after", which order prevailed.'[15]

The next day, as they walked on through the wild country, Ted became increasingly ill with a violent attack of fever, and on their arrival at the next native village he collapsed completely. During the following days of acute sickness and dysentery Sanderson owed his survival and safe return to Ba to Galsworthy's care and organization. It is a humorous and also touching picture Ted gives of his friend in the journal he wrote afterwards, that of a young man totally impractical when it came to such matters as preparing food or packing luggage, but with a natural gift for looking after people.

> Jack was awfully sweet to me and as tender as a woman . . . Poor old Jack over the billy and smouldering logs was a touching sight. He hates cooking and all the discomfort of a picnic. But if there is one thing which he detested and is utterly incapable of doing – it is opening a tin of meat or jam. If it has to be opened at the side he opens at the top, wrenching the case apart and tearing at the contents through the jagged opening. Imagine a 2 lb ox tongue treated in this fashion. Poor old Jack; poor old Ox. I didn't know whether to laugh or cry. If the tin contained jam, poor Jack was sure to put it back in the packing case upside down, so that the contents flowed in a sticky stream into anything which could least stand contact with the sticky.[16]

The two Englishmen excited immense curiosity among their native hosts, who crowded round to observe and touch them. The girls were particularly fascinated by the whiteness of Ted's legs and arms, but the success of the evening was his undressing: 'yells of delight arose' at the removal of each garment, and 'when I pulled off my trousers I fairly brought the house down'. Later their attention became almost too much of a good thing and Galsworthy sat at the door of the hut mesmerizing them with his eyeglass and only letting in a few of the crowd who besieged him for admittance.

At last, a message having been sent to the coast for help, relief came, and Sanderson was carried back to the station at Ba, a journey of some twenty-eight miles, by a party of native bearers. We have a last picture of Galsworthy packing up the luggage of the two travellers, after one or two further minor disasters.

> Jack was without an eyeglass having packed all his spare ones in his leather pocket with a pile of loose silver. The loss of the glasses is not so strange as he thought it. Whenever he took off his belt he threw it on the ground, soft or strong as the case might be. Anyway silver is hard enough to crack thin glass which it did effectually.
>
> Well in spite of his blindness things got packed – or rather shovelled into tins and 'holdall' by the carriers. Of course most of the sticky provision found the closest proximity to clothing whether in packing tins or holdall. Jack elected to fill my hautboy case with a bag of powdered sugar – which had several holes and also contained biscuits. To this he added a large bottle of medicine and a flask. These were, he said, the necessaries of life so must be kept handy – ready to be consumed at any moment. So they were – but in an indistinguishable mass of sticky filth. This also surprised Jack. At one time he would exclaim – 'Good Heavens. The sugar has got all over the bag and bottles and everything. How annoying'. At another 'By Jove, the cork has come out of your medicine and there's the devil of a mess.'[17]

After their dramatic experiences in Suva their journey proceeds comparatively uneventfully. By the middle of February Sanderson was sufficiently recovered to take the boat for Auckland, New Zealand, but still under doctor's orders he opted for a fishing holiday in the South Island while Galsworthy set off on his own to explore 'the hot lakes and the curious but infernal regions of the North Island'. While at Auckland he received letters from home, including news of his sister Lilian's engagement to Georg Sauter. In his letter of congratulation to her he comments on his own affair. 'Nothing will ever come of this matter between me and Sybil; I am too vague, and she doesn't care; all the better, really you know, because I am not cut out for domesticity at first hand.'[18]

On his return he reported to Ted that 'the scenery amounted to a maximum of the marvellous and a minimum of beauty'.

The two travellers proposed to return to England by the SS *Torrens*, one of the most famous sailing ships of her time, a clipper of 1276 tons. It was a journey that was to have far-reaching consequences for Galsworthy, for on that ship he made a new friend: the first mate was

Joseph Conrad. As yet he had published nothing, but he was already working on his first novel, *Almayer's Folly.*

> It was in March 1893 that I first met Conrad on board the English sailing ship *Torrens* in Adelaide Harbour. He was superintending the stowage of cargo. Very dark he looked in the burning sunlight, tanned, with a peaked brown beard, almost black hair, and dark brown eyes, over which the lids were deeply folded. He was thin, not tall, his arms very long, his shoulders broad, his head set rather forward. He spoke to me with a strange foreign accent. He seemed to me strange on an English ship. For fifty-six days I sailed in his company.
>
> Many evening watches in fine weather we spent on the poop. Ever the great teller of tales, he had already nearly twenty years of tales to tell. On that ship he talked of life, not literature. At Cape Town on my last evening he asked me to his cabin and I remember feeling that outweighed for me all the other experiences of that voyage. Fascination was Conrad's great characteristic – the fascination of deep expressiveness and zest, of his deeply affectionate heart and his far-ranging subtle mind. He was extraordinarily perceptive and receptive.[19]

The standard of living caused the young travellers some misgivings at first: 'the worst breakfast I have ever sat down to,' Galsworthy wrote home. But they need not have worried: the great sailing ship carried 'a cow and calf, and a good many sheep, geese, turkeys, ducks, hens, pigs and cabbages', as well as (presumably not for eating) 'a kangaroo, two wallabies, five parrots, a dog, two cats, several canaries, and two laughing jackasses – in fact we are exceedingly suggestive of the Ark'.[20]

During the voyage Galsworthy was given regular lessons in navigation and seamanship by the captain: 'He says I get on very fast, and I do begin to know something about the game,' he wrote home.[21]

Galsworthy left the *Torrens* at Cape Town, and after a short visit to certain mines in High Constantia he returned to England on the *Scot*, making the journey in the record time of fifteen and a half days.

These two long journeys abroad, and a shorter one to Russia to inspect yet another mine, had been intended by his father to have a settling influence on his son. As it turned out all this travelling had quite the reverse effect; John returned home even more restless and loath to turn his attention to his work at the Bar. If there had ever been any hope that he would settle down to a career in the law, now there was none. His mind wandered uncertainly from one idea to another, from aesthetic searchings to ridiculous ideas of adventure abroad. 'I always want to get inside beautiful things and feel more in touch with them; and somehow one can never get far enough . . .' he wrote to Monica Sanderson, and in the same letter: 'Have you read the accounts of the gold finds in Western Australia? If it wasn't for my governor I should like to join two or three fellows and have a shy at them. It does seem to me so beastly dull to go on grinding at a profession or business just to make money, when one might make as much in two or three years . . .' And he ends his letter: 'I do wish I had the gift of writing, I really think that is the nicest way of making money going, only it isn't really the writing so much as the thoughts that one wants; and, when you feel like a very shallow pond, with no nice cool deep pool with queer and pleasant things at the bottom, what's the good? I suppose one could cultivate writing, but one can't cultivate clear depths and quaint plants.'[22] He wrote this letter from Craig Lodge in Scotland, gazing out across the sea, which he found made him 'restless'. It also made him think of their mutual friend Joseph Conrad – for Ted Sanderson had brought his new friend back to Elstree, where he had been riotously received, and he soon became a greatly loved family friend. That these vague ideas at last crystallized and he began to work with determination at writing, Galsworthy himself attributes almost entirely to one person, his cousin's wife, Ada Galsworthy. Biographers too have taken his account of his meeting with Ada at the Gare du Nord in Paris as the moment at which the momentous decision was taken: 'the encounter, in Easter Week 1895, at the Gare du Nord in Paris, when, as he was seeing her and her mother off, she spoke the fateful words: "Why don't you write? You're just the person".' This is Marrot's rather naïve account, but it would seem obvious that this was not in fact a shaft from the blue, a piece of telepathy on the part of Ada; she and John must already have discussed his tenuous hopes, and now, as they parted, she wished to leave with him words that would act as a spur and encouragement, words that would stay in his mind (as indeed they did for the rest of his life), that would inspire him in moments of despair and hopelessness.

In two short sentences Ada had placed herself in his life forever; now for always she would be his amanuensis, the inspiration for all his work, the companion on whose constant presence and support his life and work was to depend. This, however, is leaping ahead into the future; the present was far less hopeful, for Ada was still the wife of Major Galsworthy, John's first cousin.

Chapter 7

Ada

Ada Nemesis Pearson Cooper was a most remarkable woman, and the part she played in the life of John Galsworthy cannot be overestimated. From the moment they grew to know each other until his death in 1933 the figure of Ada dominated Galsworthy. To the young man, newly returned from his travels, she gave inspiration and direction; that he would never have written without her is an absurd proposition; that he would have written differently is certain. Throughout the years of their lives together Ada was always the first object of John's compassion and care; it was her wishes that were his first consideration, and her interests that dictated the type of life they led together. Finally to the dying man she was once again his support and strength; he became afraid both for her and himself – how would they survive apart, she without him who had always shielded and protected her, he alone in the darkness that is death? One hears the voice of the sick man echoing through the mansion at Bury, where he spent his final years, 'Where's Auntie?' For Ada, the lover of 1865, had become, by 1933, 'Auntie' not only to John's nephews and nieces but to John also.

Ada's background and early life provide many of the clues to her enigmatic character, and particularly the place she held in John's life. The circumstances of Ada's childhood are not easy to establish; these were facts that she herself wished to forget, and certainly facts that she did not wish her biographers to know. That this first period of her life was extremely unhappy is obvious, so unhappy that it seems probable that the scars of her childhood, rather than her notoriously unsuccessful marriage to Arthur Galsworthy, made her the frail and emotionally unstable person that she was.

The only fact that Ada Galsworthy gave to her husband's first biographer, H. V. Marrot, was that she was the daughter of Emanuel Cooper, MD, of Norwich, and in the family tree at the beginning of his book her date of birth is given as 21 November 1866. In fact even this very small amount of information appears to be inaccurate; the will of Emanuel Cooper, which recently appeared among her papers, states that Ada was the *adopted* daughter of Dr Cooper. Her mother was an Anna Julia Pearson (almost certainly never the doctor's wife) and the will, dated 24 August 1866, mentioning the existence of Ada, was drawn up three months before her supposed birth. Now further documents have shown conclusively that Ada was born on 21 November 1864. The assumed birthday two years later would have made it possible for her to have passed as Emanuel Cooper's daughter, and it seems probable that it was for this reason that she changed the date rather than in an effort to conceal her age.

From these bare facts it is possible without being too fanciful to surmise at least some of the circumstances of Ada's early life. The name Ada *Nemesis*, which her mother gave her, indicates the appalling state of mind in which Anna Pearson gave birth to her child; Nemesis – 'the goddess of retribution; hence one who avenges or punishes' is the definition of the word given in the Oxford English Dictionary. Who was the father of this child, and where was she born? The only answers to these questions that can be established are negative ones; Ada was not the child of Emanuel Cooper (in legal documents she is described as a 'stranger in blood' to Cooper) and she was not born in Norwich. This Emanuel Cooper was a noted obstetrician practising in Norwich; he was the fashionable doctor who was called upon to deliver the children of well-to-do ladies in the district; it seems probable that it was in the course of his professional duties that he came across Ada's mother and decided to make her children his heirs.

The first we hear of Ada is in Cooper's will of 1866, when she was two years old and living with her mother and her brother, Arthur, in 36 Victoria Street, Norwich, a house which was the property of Emanuel Cooper and in which by the terms of his will Mrs Pearson could remain until such time as the children came of age or married. Victoria Street is a small road in the outer perimeter of the city; it is a shabby, characterless street and the small terraced houses, built not long before Ada's birth, are typical Victorian working-class dwellings. Here Mrs Pearson and her children, supported by the doctor's patronage, must have felt keenly aware of their degrading circumstances; in Emanuel Cooper's will Anna Pearson is 'allowed a liberal but not extravagant sum for their board and clothing' and presumably during the doctor's lifetime a similar allowance was made. They probably felt themselves to be superior to their neighbours, and anyhow Anna

Pearson's peculiar circumstances would have made her unwilling to associate with them.

Ada must have been a lonely child, becoming increasingly aware as she grew older that she was not the same as other children, and that she did not have a mother and father as they did. The extremely eccentric Dr Cooper must have seemed more like an elderly uncle than a father. He certainly took an interest in his adopted children, and probably had some affection for the attractive little girl that he had made his heiress, for in 1875 he added a codicil to his will leaving her a further £10,000 specifically for her own use; her brother did not receive a similar legacy. R. H. Mottram, who must have known at least some of the facts of Ada's situation (though in his biography he is deliberately vague), describes how Ada's earliest recollection of her 'father' was being driven out in his carriage when he was visiting his wealthy patients. She also remembered going into the kitchen of '*his* house [the italics are mine] and taking salt in mistake for sugar, and on being told by one of the maids, "Never you do that again, you might die of it," she fell down in a dead faint.'[1] This story is another indication that she never actually resided in the doctor's house.

At the time of drawing up his will Emanuel Cooper was much concerned as to how he could perpetuate his name and memory; in this will he described the mausoleum he proposed to build for himself and for his adopted family, and made provision for its proper maintenance. This mausoleum became an obsession; when completed it was a magnificent and pretentious monument, which may still be seen in the Rosary Cemetery at Norwich. During what was left of his lifetime, we are told by Mottram, the doctor spent many hours sitting in the cemetery, smoking his pipe and contemplating his final memorial. It may well have been this obsession with perpetuating his name that led him to make Ada and Arthur Pearson his heirs, who would adopt the name of Cooper.

After the doctor's death on 26 January 1878, when Ada was fourteen years old, new pressures must have made life almost intolerable for an abnormally sensitive child. His will made no provision for the children's mother, except in so far as she needed to be supported in order to care for her children; even the house in Norwich was only hers during Ada and Arthur's minority. The trustees were however empowered to see that the children should receive a 'liberal education at such University and Schools as the Trustees or Trustee for the time being shall think proper and that such education shall include music singing drawing dancing and other accomplishments'.[2] Soon after the doctor's death, Mrs Cooper, as she now called herself, taking with her her two children, embarked on the most incredible programme of travelling; these journeys could be seen as being educative and beneficial for the children, and thus came within the terms of the will. Ada recorded that during the years 1883-5 she and her mother and brother visited no less than forty-four different places, and between 1887 and 1889 thirty-three more. It has been suggested that at least one motive for this travelling was that a suitable husband should be found for Ada. It seems possible that quite the reverse was the case, that while permanently on the move Ada was *less* likely to find a husband (she was after all an attractive and wealthy young girl in her own right). Her mother had no reason to wish her daughter married; when that happened she would lose any rights she had to Emanuel Cooper's money. Whatever the reason, these years of claustrophobic companionship increased the friction between mother and daughter (a situation so well described a few years later by Galsworthy in his novel *Jocelyn*). In the end Ada's marriage to Arthur Galsworthy, first cousin to John, in April 1891 may have seemed her only means of escape from this unhappy situation.

It was at one of the family wedding parties to celebrate the marriage that Ada first met her husband's cousin, John. She was, as we now know, twenty-six years old, three years older than John, and at this time of her life a strikingly handsome woman, with large brown widely spaced eyes and a classically beautiful nose, though the hard lines of her mouth showed that this was a woman who already knew the meaning of suffering.

As a young child the facts of Ada's birth would certainly have been concealed from her; at what stage of her life was she told, and how much was she told? These questions seem relevant when we see her marrying Arthur Galsworthy, a man of good family, and moreover an ambitious man with a career to make in the army. This marriage, Marrot tells us, presumably informed by Ada herself, was 'a tragic mistake. Blameless and helpless, she was living in extreme unhappiness.'[3] Soon the young bride was confiding the miseries of her marriage to her new cousins, Lilian and Mabel Galsworthy, who in their turn reported these harrowing tales to their brother, John. On him they made such an impression that unhappily married heroines were to people his novels from Irene in *The Man of Property* to Clare Corven, in his last novel *Over the River* (who is incidentally the first woman to give any indication as to the nature of her suffering – a riding whip was 'the last straw').

But was Major Arthur Galsworthy such an unpleasant man? Those who remember him say he was agreeable and very easy to get on with. This is certainly the picture that his second wife, Wilhelmine Galsworthy, gave to Dudley Barker when he questioned her about her late husband.[4] She told him that Ada and Arthur had very little in common, they did not get on together, and were sexually incompatible. But what she seems to have been most emphatic about was that her husband's over-riding interest in life was the army, and this was an interest that Ada did not share. Wilhelmine also told Dudley Barker that her husband had always seen himself as a failure, in his family, at school; looking at his career one cannot help seeing that he failed as a soldier also. He belonged to the Essex Yeomanry, and was never a professional soldier, but when war broke out, first the Boer War and then the Great War, it became his sole object to be involved in the conflict. With his wife's background, however, would a distinguished military career be possible? If exposed would not the fact that his wife was illegitimate give rise to unsavoury gossip? The year was 1881, a time when a Guard's officer who married an actress would be expected to resign his commission. What hope could there be for Arthur Galsworthy to rise in his chosen profession with such a wife as Ada? So it may well have seemed that Ada's 'nemesis' was once again catching up with her, that she was still doomed to a life without happiness, to a situation from which there was no escape.

For a man of Galsworthy's imaginative temperament the thought of such misery was unbearable; it was almost inevitable that love would follow hard on the heels of his compassion. The first occasion on which the couple met after Ada's wedding celebrations was the Eton and Harrow Match in 1893. After that they met frequently in the company of John's sisters, though the encounter at the Gare du Nord in the Easter week of 1895 was a turning point in their relationship, and by September of that year they had become lovers. (On 3 September 1916, John noted in his diary, 'Our wedding day of twenty-one years ago; *de facto* if not as yet *de jure* then.')

It is impossible not to feel some admiration for Ada's courage in embarking on a second relationship that was outside the social pale. Now, at the age of thirty, Ada as a married woman agreed to become the mistress of John Galsworthy; to become once again the object of 'nice' people's scorn and pity. Perhaps worst of all she was doing what her mother had done; 'Like mother, like daughter,' the old saying must have come into Ada's mind. But then John was to Ada all she could wish for in a man, handsome, well-bred, intelligent, but above all courteous and kind to a most exceptional degree. This was a man who would never hurt her, who would never betray her, who would shield her from the hurts and jibes of a cruel world.

Moreover John's love for Ada was intensely romantic; it was a love that almost belonged to the age of chivalry:

TO ADA (1895) ✔

Lady, who in the yew shades lie,
Glancing up as I go by –
Lady! Long long will I love you!
Truer than the blue above you,
Softer than the South Wind blowing,
Sweeter than the roses glowing,
Deeper than this dark yew tree,
So for you my love shall be.
Lady! You *you* are my Lady!

FOR A

God of the daylights, love her,
And guard her tender ways!
Make gentle skies above her,
And give her sunny days!

God of the dark defend her,
And keep well in thy sight
Her happy feet, and send her
The kiss of sleep at night.

The intensely private nature of these two hitherto unpublished poems is emphasized by the fact that they were hidden away in a small locked jewel case that had belonged to Ada. Not for prying eyes were these love poems, the only personal communications that remain of the love of John and Ada – Ada destroyed all John's letters to her during her widowhood. They were in fact only discovered long after her death, still locked in their little box, with only two other things, John's eye-glass, a little chipped and still threaded through with its black silken cord, and the ribbon of the Order of Merit.

Chapter 8

Beginning to Write

From 1894, for the next ten years, Galsworthy was, to use his own phrase, a man 'in chains'. He was committed to two things, his writing and his love for Ada, but could either venture succeed? It was doubtful – in fact extremely doubtful – whether he would ever be able to make writing his career; his situation with Ada was equally uncertain and unsatisfactory.

In the meantime he was still officially working towards a career at the Bar. In 1894 he had his own chambers at 3 Paper Buildings in the Temple. In the draft of his speech to be delivered at the awarding of the Nobel Prize many years later, he recalls 'the little narrow room in the Inner Temple in London, dignified as "my Chambers" and endowed with the services of some small portion of a clerk, whose name I remember was George. In that somewhat monastic room did I pen the first pages, and curiously enough, the remaining pages of my first story.'

It was about this time that Galsworthy ceased to live in the family house at 8 Cambridge Gate (though he returned there from time to time, possibly between flats, during the next few years). His first rooms were at 3 Palace Street, Buckingham Gate, and were shared with a former Oxford contemporary, George Montagu Harris. Harris, writing a recollection of Galsworthy for Marrot, says that he already showed what was then an unusual interest in the lives of working people; he had 'a fondness for wandering about at night in the poorer districts, listening to the conversations of the people, sometimes visiting doss-houses'. He also commented on his complete lack of interest in political matters, to such an extent that even though his room-mate was standing for the parliamentary election of 1895 as a Liberal candidate, 'he [Galsworthy] gave me no help, and showed so little interest in the whole affair that the night of the Election, when J returned to our rooms, I found him sitting reading a book, and he did not even ask what was the result of the poll'.[1] Understandably, even after the passing of time Harris still felt a certain affront at what can only be seen as aloofness on the part of Galsworthy.

George Harris would have had no idea of the personal difficulties that Galsworthy was having to face at this time. Eighteen ninety-five was the year in which his relationship with Ada reached a decisive point: they became lovers. To take such a step would for both of them have been a total and binding commitment, more binding in fact than marriage. Galsworthy never ceased to be aware of the immense trust Ada had put in him in taking so unorthodox a step; it was a trust that was sometimes in the future to weigh heavily on his shoulders.

It was not a coincidence that this same year he gave up the legal chambers that had been his for so short a time; his career at the Bar was over. It is recorded that he had only one brief, and that from the family firm of solicitors at the request of his father. It was an undefended petition and the case was over in a few minutes; nevertheless old Mr Galsworthy appeared in court to see his son's one moment of legal glory. The Galsworthy parents accepted with disappointment John's decision to abandon the law. Writing, Blanche Galsworthy felt, was not nearly so 'nice' a career as the law; in fact she told Georg Sauter in reply to a question of his that she did not want her son to be a famous author.

It was the presence of Ada in John's life that made this momentous decision possible. From now onwards he would devote all his time and energy to writing. He had a small but adequate private income from his father, and on this, and what he might ultimately earn, he could manage – though he managed, it must be said, in a fairly comfortable way.* Ford Madox Ford described Galsworthy as being 'moderate in everything', but again it sounds a very agreeable moderation: 'a little bachelor establishment; kept a small stable; drank very moderately and dressed with the careful negligence that was then required of you.' Ford, in common with other contemporaries, was not a little jealous of Galsworthy's lack of financial worries.

Ada had almost a vocation to foster and encourage talent in others; it was not only Galsworthy who came to depend on her for sympathy

* Ford Madox Ford, in *It was the Nightingale*, describes Galsworthy reading a newspaper cutting which told of his (Galsworthy's) early struggles with poverty, the bitter sufferings he had gone through. 'He smiled – the real smile coming out over the one that was always there . . . "Considering that I never had less than several thousand a year I can't be said to have suffered . . ." '

and understanding, for in the course of her life several other writers came under her wing. Notably, the son of her trustee, Ralph Mottram, whose poems she, and later John also, criticized and praised; 'let me see a little bit of your work – for if I am to believe all they tell, I have something of the critic in my composition . . .'[2] and later, 'I only hope I may be of some use – that I think is my aim in life to be of use – quite big enough too, for me.'[3] Conrad also found her a helpful critic and friend, and later they worked together on translations of Maupassant short stories.

But of course *her* writer, her first concern, was, from the beginning of their intimate friendship, John Galsworthy. As soon as she learnt of his secret ambition to write, with determination, and in fact against all reason, for his early efforts at writing were very poor indeed, she believed that he would one day become a great writer. When Galsworthy dedicated *The Forsyte Saga* to her, 'without whose encouragement, sympathy, and criticism I could never have become even such a writer as I am', he did so with complete conviction and sincerity. Moreover it was a debt he could never repay; in a sense it was at times almost a bondage of gratitude.

As well as giving him the encouragement and confidence he so much needed, Ada furnished him with a story, her story, that moved him so deeply that whenever he wrote it – and he wrote it many times – it almost carried him beyond himself, he was so deeply moved by the pathos and anguish he saw in her situation, trapped helplessly in her marriage to the odious Major Galsworthy.

Ada was a patient taskmaster; she knew that time only could bring the flowering she expected from her *protégés*. 'Most men aren't so far on as that at 30,' she wrote in a letter of encouragement to Ralph Mottram. 'Look at Conrad, look at Jack Galsworthy, those two whose work I know best. To my mind Conrad has only "arrived" quite recently, *Youth, Falk* . . . Jack G. is a steadier goer though a smaller one – but of course he has been leaping sedately from one method to another in the most surprising way – The book that is just coming out and the one he has just started writing are perhaps really himself [*The Island Pharisees* and *The Man of Property*].'[4]

It was in these circumstances, with Ada spiritually, if not so often physically, by his side, that John Galsworthy set out on the hard task of mastering the art of writing. 'It did not go very fast in the early days. The life social still had its lure for him; he was not very sure of where, as a writer, he was going. He was grimly determined to produce novels, but he was at first hampered and a little depressed by the influence of Conrad, who knew well enough where *he* was going.'[5] Nevertheless he persevered, copying from Ford the idea of a standing desk, using a profusion of coloured pencils, pens and rubbers.

Galsworthy has made no secret of the hard struggle he had to achieve his goal; he was, he tells us, 'writing fiction for five years before I could master even its primary technique'.[6] He studied the works of other authors, and was perhaps too much influenced by what he read; *Jocelyn*, his first novel, had a marked resemblance to some of Conrad's writing (notably *The Outpost of Progress*), and his later style owed a great deal to Turgenev and de Maupassant, whose work he admired enormously. In a letter to a would-be writer, Mr Jones, written 5 June 1920, he advised him to read, in the first place, the Bible, Shakespeare and W. H. Hudson.

Galsworthy's first appearance in print was characteristically hesitant and modest: *From the Four Winds* was published in 1897 under the pseudonym of John Sinjohn (taken from the name of his college friend, St John Hornby). The book was published by Fisher Unwin on a commission basis, an arrangement considered less undignified then than it would be today. Under these terms Galsworthy paid for the printing, while the publisher took a commission on the number of copies sold, thus standing to lose nothing if his new author proved to be a failure. Five hundred copies were printed and, though the book received forty-two notices in various periodicals, the small edition was not sold out. Galsworthy never permitted the book to be reprinted; he was ashamed of it and told Ralph Mottram to burn his copy. But, as he himself recognized, *From the Four Winds* was a landmark in his career as a writer.

> For nearly two years that tale and its successors exhausted my literary afflatus, and my experience was not unlike that of the experimenting aviators of a decade back [he is writing in 1932], who were always trying to leave the ground and always coming back to the ground
> / with the greater regret. And yet, my conscience not having yet been born – I was more proud of the vile little body which bound those nine tales under the title *From the Four Winds* than I was of any of its successors. In 1920, possessed by the desire to prevent anyone else from reading that dreadful little book, I wrote to the publisher. He had twenty copies left.[7]

The stories contained in this volume are almost unreadable and give little hint of the work that is to come. As Galsworthy freely admits, they owe much to Kipling and something to Bret Harte. They are, in the main, traveller's tales, based no doubt on the journeys he had made a few years earlier. Of some interest is the story called 'The Doldrums', which describes an incident that occurred on board the *Torrens* and contains a portrait of Conrad, but the only story that really comes to life is the last in the collection, 'The Demi-Gods'. This is the first piece of writing – the first of a great sequence that stretches throughout his work – describing the pain of his love for Ada, the hopelessness of lovers who are prevented by circumstances from forming a permanent union.

To-morrow was the ending of all life and light, bringing with it for her a separation from the true self, a return behind the triumphant car of a mocking and over-riding fate, to a caged existence, a loathed companionship, a weary, weary beating of the breast against the bars; for him – a legion of mind-devils, torturing, twisting, lying in wait at every turn and corner of life, ever alert and ever cruel, and a dreary craving ache.

To-morrow was the farewell of their love, perhaps till the grave – who knows? their great and burning love, that had given all and taken all, that had cared with an exceeding tenderness for every thought and movement, that was old, yet had not tired, that had known and understood, having no depths to sound, no heights to win; that tree which, planted in the moist, cool earth of comradeship, had grown steadily and grandly till it rejoiced in the sweet foliage of a perfect trust, and the glorious flowers of passion.

It is perhaps an extravagant piece of writing, but this theme of frustrated passion was to be the keynote of Galsworthy's most important writing, the seed from which stemmed much of his philosophy; it is a cry against captivity on the one hand, and possession on the other, that is to recur again and again.

Even before the publication of *From the Four Winds* Galsworthy was at work on his first full-length novel, *Jocelyn*. Like its predecessor this book was also disowned by its author and never again reprinted after its first appearance in 1898. This time, however, Galsworthy refused to publish under the rather unfavourable terms that he had accepted for his first book. On 29 January 1898 he sent the manuscript to Fisher

Unwin's, stating with some firmness the terms he was prepared to accept (in fact it was Conrad who had suggested to him the sort of remuneration he should expect). 'If you decide to take it,' Galsworthy wrote, 'I would suggest – as terms – some such arrangement as the following. Author to receive 5d per copy up to 500 copies; 10d. 500–2000; after that 1/– per copy.'[8] The same day a second letter was sent to Mr Unwin's office, Galsworthy having realized that the manuscript had been sent unsigned. 'It occurs to me that by a most singular oversight, I sent my MSS. to you this morning absolutely unsigned; in fact with no marks of ownership whatever. Would you be so very kind as to see that someone labels it "John Sinjohn" before it goes to the reader's.' Mr Unwin, it seems, was unprepared to take any financial risk on the book, for on 11 February Galsworthy is writing again. 'I am sorry you do not see your way to "venturing" my book. I am disinclined to undertake any of the expense myself.' In fact he did not have to, for a new young publisher, Gerald Duckworth, was prepared to take on the book at his own risk.

The novel *Jocelyn* is in a different class from its predecessor, and there are passages in it as accomplished as any its author ever wrote; in fact it is a book of enormous interest and promise. It is the story of Ada and John, written at a moment when their affair must still have been most painful and poignant. They were still new to the experience of being illicit lovers, only just realizing the extent of their rebellion against the world and the class in which they lived. Ada must often have felt as the heroine Jocelyn did, when she turns against herself in despair after she has allowed herself to be seduced by her lover, Giles Legard.

The story in itself is unconvincing and over-dramatic. The hero, Giles Legard, has married in an unconsidered moment the invalid, Irma; their marriage has dragged on for many years in a state of stagnation and boredom when Giles meets and falls in love with the young girl, Jocelyn Ley. (The roles of Ada and John are reversed, so that it is the husband who is married and trapped, presumably so as to disguise slightly the true identities of the characters.) Giles declares his love and in a moment of passion Jocelyn gives in to her feelings and they become lovers. But the act of love is followed almost at once by feelings of revulsion and despair in Jocelyn, partly because she is friends also with Irma. Irma is aware of her husband's feelings for Jocelyn and takes an overdose of morphine. Giles finds her not dead but in a coma; he sees that she has taken an overdose but leaves her to her fate and goes instead to a previously arranged meeting with Jocelyn. On his return Irma is dead. The lovers feel that they are responsible, directly or indirectly, for Irma's death, and that their love will always be overshadowed by the tragedy. They part, but finding separation intolerable Jocelyn follows Giles, who has left England for a long sea voyage, and the lovers are at last united.

At times the book reads like a romantic novel; but – its biographical interest apart – as a work of fiction it is redeemed by one character, Mrs Travis, modelled on Ada's mother, Mrs Cooper. Mrs Travis is Jocelyn's aunt and travelling companion, and seldom has Galsworthy been more successful in creating a comic character. Mrs Travis is asked her views on art by a young curate: 'Having no views, she was finding it best to agree with everything he said, while her quick eyes took in a large amount of information about the dress and appearance of her neighbours.' Or later: 'Mrs Travis indeed had a high sense of proprieties, but she had a higher sense of comfort; she did not care at all for music or pictures, not much for theatres, so she contented herself and salved her conscience with those entertainments where one ate.' (She is excusing herself for not chaperoning her niece, Jocelyn.) In Mrs Travis there is already the germ of the possessive instinct which was to be of such importance to the Forsytes. Giles is seeing too much of Jocelyn, but 'She [Mrs Travis] always reflected, too, that Giles was a connection of her own by marriage. Mrs Travis possessed that order of mind which looks upon things belonging to themselves as beyond suspicion and reproach. He was a married man, but a connection of her own, immaculate! Nevertheless she resented the dwindling of his bulk; perhaps she considered it indecent; perhaps, in some mysterious way, she regarded it as the removal of her own property. In any case a moody leanness was unpardonable.'

There is a sharpness about much of the writing in this novel, and an acuteness of observation, which make it a remarkable successor to that 'dreadful little book' *From the Four Winds*. It does not deserve the oblivion into which its author cast it; in fact many far less worthy writings were owned by him and allowed to be reprinted again and again.

It may well have been the highly personal nature of the book that made its author glad to see it forgotten, buried under the pseudonym John Sinjohn, but it is this quality that makes it particularly interesting to the biographer. In Jocelyn we see Ada as John first saw her; we also see John as he was at this time. Throughout their lives together the Galsworthys travelled ceaselessly, but it was Ada not John who had this passion for foreign countries: 'Jocelyn hated the grey monotony of English skies. She had a fierce love of the sun, of lands where the colouring hit the eye, where life seemed to throb with a fuller pulse.' And of her character: 'She never stirred a finger to attract admiration or affection, yet without appreciation she drooped as a flower without water,' or 'Jocelyn was so sympathetic a listener, and so devoid of prudery, that insensibly one told her almost everything.' Like Ada and like Irene in *The Man of Property*, Jocelyn is devoted to music and finds her greatest consolation in playing the piano: 'She [Jocelyn] played to herself a good deal, but she found that she missed Giles's grave face looking at her, and a habit which he had, of coming up from behind and touching her on the shoulder, saying, "Play that again".' To the end of his life Galsworthy depended on Ada to 'Play that again', as he wrote his books at his country homes at Manaton and Bury, or in London. It was an essential feature of their lives together.

In *Jocelyn* there is a conflict unresolved; the battle for Ada is not yet won. By the time *The Man of Property* is being written the fight is over; it did not need Bosinney to take Irene from Soames: she was already in spirit if not in fact a free woman. But Jocelyn and Giles are still struggling with their consciences; the book is full of the pain of the conflict that is going on within them. '*His* instinct was to fight for his happiness, to fight for it with pain and trouble – *hers* to fold her hands, and let it drift to her or away.' It was a cruel situation in which fate had placed them, Ada and John, Jocelyn and Giles; two deeply conventional people forced by their love, by their conviction that their love had a right to be fulfilled, somehow to fight their way to a new understanding both of themselves and of the values to which they had been brought up. But it was the making of Galsworthy the writer. 'The evil did not seem to him to lie in the wrong he had done to the woman he loved, nor in the guilty inaction by which he had sought to repair that wrong, it lay further back, in the fibre of his own nature and the infirmity of his will – he felt that he had suffered for it, was always suffering.' Faced with his crisis Galsworthy was forced to explore the depths within himself. It was not a natural activity with him; he was not an introspective person and he despised self-pity. The bulk of his work is concerned with others – the suffering of prisoners, of the underprivileged, of unhappily married wives (not, one should note, husbands.

Giles is unique) and, of course, of animals – but never with his own pain. It is the interest of *Jocelyn* that in this book Galsworthy examines his own suffering, explores it; he is for once the body on the dissecting board. In his subsequent books the whole process of his writing is to work away from himself, from the subjective to the objective: Shelton in *The Island Pharisees* is Galsworthy, but unlike Jocelyn he is no longer writhing with his own agony; he is the observer of pain rather than the sufferer.

Even when Jocelyn finally pursues Giles on his journey to Singapore, it is a philosophy they have arrived at rather than a reality of conviction. As the character Nielsen tells Jocelyn: 'everry man and woman has his place according to the big morrality – so have flies and in spite of everrything they come to it at the last.' They do 'come to it at the last', but still deeply troubled and uncertain.

Jocelyn found little favour with the critics; only the *Saturday Review* was prepared to see any merit in it at all, commenting that it was 'above the common run of fiction' and that its author had 'insight and humour, though lacking any sense of plot'. Conrad, who was always inclined to over-praise his friends' work, wrote in a letter, 'The work is good. *And as work* it *is* inspiring.'[9] Though later in the year he wrote to a Polish relative, 'the novel is not remarkable, but the man is very pleasant and kind.' 'Poor Jack,' as Conrad privately referred to him, because he got so worried about his writing, to which Ford Madox Ford added, with some truth, 'It did not go very fast in the early days.'[10]

Chapter 9

Sinjohn becomes Galsworthy

Two more books, *The Villa Rubein* and *The Man of Devon*, were to be published in the first instance under the pseudonym John Sinjohn, but unlike their predecessors they were later revised and reprinted under Galsworthy's own name.

Writing in 1921 the prefaces for the Collected Manaton Edition of his work that was to be published the following year, Galsworthy sees a definite change in his writing at this point, what we might today term a 'breakthrough'. Not only has he now begun to master the 'primary technique' of fiction writing but, of much greater significance, he sees himself as achieving what he calls 'the union of seer with things seen'.[1]

A writer will often see such a turning point in his writing when it is scarcely, if at all, apparent to his readers. He may feel that a vital corner has been turned, a massive hurdle scaled, while the outsider will only see a small progression, commenting doubtfully that while one battle has been won, another has been lost. So it was with Galsworthy. *The Villa Rubein* was a more professional and more competent piece of work than Galsworthy had yet achieved; it is a charming story delightfully written. Published in 1900, it was more successful than either of its predecessors, and Galsworthy's friends were enthusiastic in their praise. Ford Madox Ford commented that it had the essential quality of 'distinction'. But it lacks the fierceness of feeling that had first shown itself in *Jocelyn*, and that was to be an important element in Galsworthy's best writing. 'There is not enough vinegar in the salad. You are too kind, too deferential to your characters; you haven't enough contempt, enough of the *saeva indignatio*,' Ford Madox Ford wrote to him in a long letter. 'Put more shadow into it; there is more shadow. One's fellow-creatures are despicable as well as pathetic; one is oneself, but that doesn't come into the story.'[2]

The Villa Rubein is based on the story of Galsworthy's sister Lilian and her marriage to the painter, Georg Sauter. Following the intensely

66

personal writing of *Jocelyn* it must have been a relief for Galsworthy to turn his sights upon lives other than his own, upon a drama in which he was not a principal. It enabled him, moreover, to achieve the objectivity that he notes in his preface of 1921. To quote once again from this preface: 'Seer and thing seen, inextricably involved one with the other, form the texture of any masterpiece; and I, at least, demand therefrom a distinct impression of temperament. I never saw, in the flesh, either De Maupassant or Tchekov . . . but their work leaves on me a strangely potent sense of personality. Such subtle intermingling of seer with thing seen is the outcome only of long and intricate brooding . . .'[3] In *Jocelyn* we have a vivid picture of the 'seer', and in *The Villa Rubein* an account of 'things seen', but it is not until *The Man of Property* that Galsworthy achieves the marriage of the two, approaches the perfect balance that he describes.

Georg Sauter, upon whom the painter Harz in *The Villa Rubein* was undoubtedly modelled, was, like his fictional counterpart, born in the Bavarian Alps of a working-class family. 'I was born amongst the mountains,' Harz tells the young girl, Christian (who can legitimately be seen as Lilian Galsworthy), 'I looked after the cows, and slept in the hay-cocks, and cut the trees in winter. They used to call me a "black-sheep", a "loafer" in my village.' Harz, like Georg Sauter, is puzzled by the English middle-class family which he has become involved with. 'You English are so funny. You mustn't do this here, you mustn't do that there, it's like sitting in a field of nettles.' And then in desperation he exclaims to Christian: 'It's a crime not to have been born a gentleman.' It was the beginning of Galsworthy's attack on the establishment, on what he was later to call Forsytism, the hypocrisy and false values of the English middle classes. The story of *The Villa Rubein* follows very closely that of Lilian and Georg, and, after considerable opposition from her family, Christian too is united with her lover, Harz.

It is in his next collection of stories, published under the title *The Man of Devon* in September 1901, that Galsworthy claims to have really found the satirical vein within himself. 'I owe Swithin much, for he first released the satirist in me, and is moreover, the only one of my characters whom I killed before I gave him life, for it is in the "Man of Property" that Swithin Forsyte more memorably lives.'[4]

Galsworthy's friend and biographer, R. H. Mottram, sees this story, 'The Salvation of Swithin Forsyte', as the real turning point in its author's career, and one of the most biographically significant that he ever wrote. I doubt if many modern readers would share this view; they would perhaps see Swithin Forsyte's greatest merit in his refusal to die, in his insistence on remaining instead lurking somewhere in his creator's mind, a fantasy of the future, a premonition of the great genealogy of Forsytes that was to come.

The Swithin Forsyte of the short story *does* die, but as he lies on his death bed his mind wanders into the past and relives an incident that is utterly uncharacteristic of him, or anything else in his life. At that moment, had he not run away from the experience, the whole course of his life would have been different from what it was, he himself would have become a different person. As a young man travelling in Salzburg, he comes across a strange group of Hungarian exiles in a *bierhalle*, becomes involved in their quarrels, and falls passionately in love with the daughter of one of them, a young girl called Rozsi. He is tempted to marry her, but convention and prudence deter him. 'They meant him to marry her! And the horrid idea was strengthened by his own middle-class reverence for marriage . . . he was afraid of the other way – too primitive.' 'He set to thinking what such a marriage meant. In the first place it meant ridicule, in the second place ridicule, in the third place ridicule. She would eat chicken bones with her fingers . . .'

The choice is all too clear, to take this beautiful vision, to make it his own, this chance that has come to him, that will redeem his life from its dreary course, or to flee from it. He chooses the latter. But as he dies he is revisited by the ghost of Rozsi, who reproaches him for his cowardice.

'I could show you things,' she says.
'Where are you?' gasped Swithin; 'What's the matter? I'm lost.'
. . . Suddenly aloud in his sleep, Swithin muttered, 'I've missed something.'
Again fingers touched his brow; again Rozsi's eyes were looking at him from the wall. 'What is it?' he asked, 'Can't I get out of here and come with you? I'm choking.' 'What is it,' he thought; 'what have I lost?' And slowly his mind began to travel over his investments . . . What is it? Things he had never seen, was never meant to see – sacrifice, chivalry, love, fidelity, beauty and strange adventure – things remote, that you couldn't see with your eyes – had they come to haunt him?[5]

Galsworthy later revised this story and cut out most of Swithin's final dream, to the great loss of the story. When it was reissued in 1909 with *The Villa Rubein*, a very different version appeared entitled now 'Salvation of a Forsyte'.

It is an allegorical tale, though the characters bear no sort of resemblance to Ada and John. Yet Ada was John's Rozsi; she was the chance which fortune sent him, the chance to break away from convention and to make this vision of beauty and all that it brought with it his own – in his case the world of imagination and writing. But both Swithin and John made the mistake of assuming that life contains only one such moment, failing to see that the gift of living lies in the ability to remain ever open and receptive to all the experiences that may come.

This story is perhaps the first example of what Galsworthy came to refer to as his 'negative method' of writing: in telling the story of Swithin Forsyte and his terrible deathbed realization that his life, now so nearly over, has in fact never been lived, Galsworthy is telling us the opposite of his own story. He did take his chance, his Ada, and from the struggles of *Jocelyn* we know that there were moments when, like Swithin, he had felt like jumping into his carriage and 'Flying back along the road faster than he had come, with pale face and eyes blank'.

Conrad had much to do with the publication of *The Man of Devon*. 'I've written to Blackwood,' he wrote, 'mainly for the purpose of insinuating amongst other matters that a quick decision as to your story would be welcome.' His negotiations were successful and the book was published by Blackwood in September 1901. Upon its publication Conrad wrote a most interesting letter to Galsworthy; the letter is dated 11 November 1901.

There is a certain caution of touch which will militate against popularity. After all, to please the public (if one isn't sugary imbecile or an inflated fraud) one must handle one's subject intimately. Mere intimacy with the subject won't do. And conviction is found (for others, not for the author) only in certain contradictions and irrelevancies to the general conception of character (or characters) and of the subject. Say what you like the man lives in his eccentricities (so called) alone. They give a vigour to his personality which mere consistency can never do. One must explore deep and believe the incredible to find the few particles of truth floating in an ocean of insignificance. And before all one must divest oneself of every particle of respect for one's characters. You are really most profound and attain the greatest art in handling the people you do not respect. For instance the minor character in V.R. And in this volume I am bound to recognize that Forysthe [*sic*] is the best. I recognize this with a certain reluctance because indubitably there is more beauty (and more felicity of style too) in the M of D.

Written at this early date this piece of criticism is astonishingly perceptive. Conrad points to a danger that is already apparent in Galsworthy's writing, that of shying away from what was most personal, 'a certain caution of touch'. Where Conrad was wrong, of course, was in suggesting that this element in his friend's writing would militate against popularity. Galsworthy was to know a success in his lifetime that none of his English contemporaries were to approach, though after his death it was this very impersonality that was to doom his work for many years to almost complete obscurity.

It is interesting, too, that Conrad should have praised his handling of the 'people you do not respect'; the negative method was already beginning to work, making a convincing case for Swithin, as it was, to a far greater extent, to make for Soames a few years later.

As Conrad says, 'The Man of Devon', the title story of the book, is a far more beautiful and poetic piece of writing than 'The Salvation of Swithin Forsyte'; it is a strange, almost whimsical story written in the first person as a series of letters. The heroine, Pasiance, is an extraordinary character; she has a wild savageness that is reminiscent of Emily Brontë's Cathy Earnshaw. Like Cathy, she is a child of her particular countryside; she knows nothing of the life of the town or the civilized world. In fact in this story Galsworthy sees his beloved Devon rather as the Brontës saw Yorkshire, or Hardy, Dorset; the countryside becomes another character in the story, a force that determines the lives of the people who live in it. Thus it contains within itself elements of tragedy that may ultimately destroy its own, as in the end it does Pasiance, who throws herself over the cliff because she believes her lover, Zachary Pearse, has deserted her:

Fancy took me to the cliff where she had fallen. I found the point of rock where the cascade of ivy flows down the cliff; the ledge on which she had climbed was a little to my right – a mad place. It showed plainly what wild emotions must have been driving her!

Behind was a half-cut cornfield with a fringe of poppies, and swarms of harvest insects creeping and flying; in the uncut corn a landrail kept up a continual charring. The sky was blue to the very horizon, and the sea wonderful, under that black wild cliff stained here and there with red. There are no brassy, east-coast skies here; but always sleepy, soft-shaped clouds, full of subtle stir and change. Passages of Zachary Pearse's letter kept rising to my lips. After all he's the man that his native place, and life, and blood have made him.

With the possible exception of the story 'The Apple Tree' and a few very minor pieces, 'The Man of Devon' is unlike anything else that Galsworthy wrote; there is no element of satire here, no wish to reform or criticize; it is a tale of simple but passionate people set in the Devonshire countryside. Galsworthy is experimenting at this stage, seeking out his true métier, and it is interesting that two stories as different as 'The Man of Devon' and 'The Salvation of Swithin Forsyte' should appear in the same volume. But having found the satirist in himself, he is not easily going to reject his new weapon. Pasiance is the more beautiful character, but Swithin is the more powerful; the choice is made and Swithin Forsyte, in more than name, is to be the first child of Galsworthy's pen.

Chapter 10

London and Edward Garnett

By the time *The Man of Devon* was published John Galsworthy was thirty-four years old. Four books had now appeared under the pseudonym of John Sinjohn, and had earned for their author a certain amount of critical esteem. He was already working on two others, *The Island Pharisees* and *A Man of Property*, works that were to be of great significance in his development as a writer. The time had come to abandon the anonymity of his *nom de plume* and to announce himself to the world as John Galsworthy.

This is also a suitable moment to pause and consider in some detail the way of life of this man who had now so nearly reached the point of 'arrival' in the literary world, the moment of transition which must come to all writers who succeed in worldly terms. One day he is one amongst many, a plant in a field of other plants, and the next he has burst forth, a flowering tree, identifiable to all, famous.

Galsworthy and Ada had now been lovers for almost exactly six years. In 1902 Ada took the daring step of setting up on her own: 'there remains only the Major to breathe forth threatenings and slaughter, which nobody else has seemed at all inclined to do,' she reported to Mottram in July. It was only on their holidays abroad, under carefully arranged 'chaperonage', that the couple could associate freely. These circumstances, as well as Ada's natural liking for foreign travel, may well have set the pattern for the constant travelling that was to form so large a part of their lives together. Ada was fortunate in her companion's profession; as she wrote in her travel book *Over the Hills and Far Away*, a writer 'need never, unless so minded, be separated from his profession. A stiff-backed block of sheets of paper, a pen, a travelling inkstand (for the writer under observation did not thrive on fountain pens: there was something of ritual in the thoughtful, leisurely dipping of pen into ink, something of rhythm, of punctuation, unconscious as breathing, measured, necessary) and all the "plant" was complete.'

For whatever reason, Galsworthy came to see his life as an essentially itinerant one, and himself as having no settled abode. 'I am an erratic beggar,' he wrote to his friend St John Hornby in October 1897, 'never quite knowing my own movements a month in advance, and with a great idea, as you know, that the charm of life lies in motion. You should have pitched upon somebody [for the purpose of filling the post of trustee to his friend's marriage settlement] in a fixed groove with a business or something of that sort to keep him in a fixed place ... I thought it right to tell you that I am not a fixed constellation.'

It is difficult to pin down either place or time for the journeys that the Galsworthys made during these years; Marrot's biography, written with Ada's co-operation, says little about their doings between 1895 and 1905, and Ada has herself cut the pages covering that period from her diary. It seems almost as if in later years she wished to forget that this time of unlegalized love had ever existed; at least it was not to form part of the official life of John Galsworthy.

It is impossible for us to share her view. These years were among the most creative and the most promising of Galsworthy's writing life; fame, marriage and respectability were in the end to be the poisoners of his talent.

Over the Hills remains maddeningly and, I believe, deliberately vague about dates, but it seems probable that this carefree description refers to this period.

In those far-away days we were good walkers; our usual scheme was to fix a base at some lovely spot – Cortina, say – or Landro – and make long whole-day rounds, starting before sunrise and finishing at dark. Sharply cold it was at the start, but unless we were half-frozen for the first quarter of an hour we knew the weather was not right or that we had come out over-clothed. Having taken our coffee and roll in the dim dawn and got going, we were ready by about seven o'clock for a second light breakfast; and so it was throughout the day – light meals only, at two or three hour intervals. We found this plan far more repaying and less fatiguing than the heavy ortho-dox midday meal and the heavy rest after it.

Then there were the 'rest days' when they did not walk, but sat out on 'the heavy wooden balconies where we used to take our coffee, rolls and honey, sitting out in the fresh crisp morning sunlight on rest days; for rest days place themselves very properly among the strenuous

73

days of tramping, rest days, and a little writing for a change.'

They were indeed great walkers; Ada records that their record was no less than '31 miles, and that without undue tiredness, the mountain air being what it is'. This, and many of their early holidays, were in the Dolomites, a favourite part of the world for the Galsworthys.

By the spring of 1902 Ada was living on her own, and when in London she and John, though formally apart, lived geographically near to each other, Ada at Campden House Chambers, John at 16a Aubrey Walk, Campden Hill. Close also were Georg and Lilian Sauter in Holland Park Avenue. The three dwellings were within a few minutes' walk of each other. Lilian Sauter, as we know, sympathized with her brother's liaison with Ada, and was also devoted to her future sister-in-law, and her household at this time must have formed the focal point and nucleus of the small group. Ralph Mottram, visiting Ada and Jack for the first time in 1904, is actually accommodated at the Sauters' house; he describes the unusual but pleasant atmosphere of the household.

> The door was opened, as all such doors then were, by a white capped and aproned maid, who took me up to what seemed a huge and probably was an extra-large-size studio, with all the impedimenta – easels, curtains, frames and paints, pushed against the walls or stacked in a gallery to make room, in a more domestic and 'homey' atmosphere than is perhaps common in such places, for a large and well-stocked tea-table, the cups, plates, and hot-water dish upon which were dominated by a Russian samovar, covered by a special straw woven cosy. It was presided over by Mrs. Lilian Sauter . . . She was supported, on one side by Jack and Ada, and on her other by her husband . . . At their feet, half-concealed in his mother's robes or a rug, was the jolliest and least ordinary of little boys. He was Rudo, then seven years old.[1]

Ralph Mottram at this time was a young man of only twenty-one, but he had known Ada all his life as his father had been trustee and guardian of her affairs until 1900. When she announced her intention of leaving her husband, Major Galsworthy, old Mr Mottram, disapproving and distressed by her intention, resigned his position as trustee. She had then requested that her cousin, John Galsworthy, should be appointed her trustee, and it was on his coming to Norwich about her affairs in 1904 that Mottram first met Galsworthy. Mottram's friendship with both Ada and John continued until the end of their lives, but as a young man the couple took him up, befriended him and encouraged his literary ambitions. This first visit to London in October 1904 must have been an extremely exciting event for the gauche young man from Norwich.

During this particular visit Mottram visits and describes the other two dwellings in the complex, the 'bachelor' apartments of Jack and Ada, both entirely characteristic of their owners. 'Ada's flat, whose grey walls and dainty ornaments subsequently made the background for Anonyma's dwelling in his novel *The Patrician*.' 'On yet another of these days,' Mottram continues, 'we lunched in the studio at Aubrey Walk, the stableman's wife providing cutlets and apple tart, and Jack the excellent hock. I was allowed to see the camp-bed on which he slept, under rugs made from the skins of animals he had shot on his earlier travels. There was also in a corner of the studio, an object quite strange to my country mind, which was explained to be one of the new patent Turkish bath cabinets, for he was already then beginning to feel the rheumatism which was one of the ills of his later years.'[2]

The Galsworthys gave their young visitor and protégé a taste of their London cultural life; it would be, they hoped, both enjoyable and educational. Jack took him to the National Gallery 'for my proper instruction'; they took him to the theatre, but the play, *Merely May Ann* by Zangwill, was second-rate, and the performance disappointing; they took him to the Queen's Hall, where they heard the then new overture '1812' by Tchaikovsky; he visited the studio of a sculptor called Swan. But what must have been most exciting of all to the aspiring young writer was the Literary Lunch at the Mont Blanc restaurant. In his letter of invitation Galsworthy had mentioned this event. 'I can take you to a certain lowly restaurant where Garnett, at all events, and possibly Hudson and Belloc may be met with!' The account of this lunch is so interesting it is worth quoting in full:

a long table was set, in true continental style, with piles of plates and carafes of rough red wine, on a coarse table-cloth. Here sat, at the head, Edward Garnett, something clerical in his garb belied by the fact that he was eating with his fork, holding a book which he was presumably scanning for review in the other hand, and controlling conversation with a full mouth. On his left was Hilaire Belloc, bowler-hatted like myself, talking like a machine-gun between draughts of wine, Thomas Seccombe, and Jack being opposite Hudson, if present, made no impression . . .

Jack, monocle in place, ate sparingly and choicely. I have now a suspicion that he paid for several of the lunches.[3]

By this time it is clear that Galsworthy had already become very much part of the London literary scene. This he owed largely to the influence and interest of one man, Edward Garnett. Garnett is a fascinating and enigmatical figure in the world of writing at this period; he is enormously important, more influential than any one person, and yet wrote nothing of significance himself. He can be seen as the central figure in the group of writers who were beginning to make their names in the early years of the present century: Joseph Conrad, Ford Madox Ford, Arnold Bennett and W. H. Hudson, to name but a few.

Born in 1868, Edward was the son of Richard Garnett the critic and biographer. His wife, Constance, was the translator of Dostoevsky and other Russian authors, who did so much to make Russian literature known in the English-speaking world. David Garnett has seen in both his father and grandfather, Edward and Richard, an 'unworldliness' which made them unwilling to push their own work, but able to find fulfilment in bringing to fruition the talent of others. 'Edward's occupation was the discovery of talent in unknown writers. But when one of his discoveries achieved success Edward sometimes lost interest in his work. He definitely preferred the ugly duckling to the swan . . . His own mission in life was to discover the genius and to fight for his recognition.'[4]

But it was in London, at the Tuesday luncheons at the Mont Blanc restaurant, that Edward Garnett truly held court with his literary protégés. Here 'the elect of the city's intelligentsia lunched and discussed with grave sobriety the social problems of the day . . . under the presidency of Mr. Edward Garnett, who has for so long been London's literary – if Nonconformist – Pope . . .' Ford Madox Ford wrote to his agent Pinker.[5]

John was at this time already a frequent visitor at the home of Edward and Constance Garnett, the Cearne (nicknamed by Edward 'Dostoevsky Corner'). He had long admired Constance's translations of Turgenev and had corresponded with her about his work, but according to Edward Garnett it was Conrad who first brought Galsworthy to lunch at the Cearne. This house has a strange literary history; the Garnetts, inheriting money from Constance's father, determined to build for themselves a remote country house, but near enough to London for Edward to travel up for his work. They chose the area of Limpsfield Chart in Kent, then a beautiful and unspoilt place, because their friends, the Sydney Oliviers, had just settled there. A completely isolated field surrounded by woodland appealed to them both, and here they built the Cearne to their own design. Small and L-shaped, with enormously thick walls and gigantic stone fireplaces, it provided only very small rooms, and the final building must have made an awkward, unmanageable house. However it suited the Garnetts: it was isolated from the local community; here they could work and entertain their friends, and it became from time to time almost a literary ghetto. At one time Ford Madox Ford and his wife Elsie lived in Gracie's Cottage nearby; Ford, going through his 'farming period', strutted about in a 'smock frock and gaiters' and kept ducks.[6] But he also felt it important that he should live near his mentor, and the 'centre of things'.

In such an environment Galsworthy, with his well-bred manners and well-groomed exterior, must have seemed something of a fish out of water. He must have suspected that Garnett thought him, as an author, unusual, for Garnett himself describes how, as they parted after their first lunch together, 'Galsworthy remarked, with a gleam in his eye, "I'm not such a fool as I seem".'[7] To the young David Garnett, Galsworthy was not an unglamorous figure either: he was impressed by his tales of stalking deer with a Red Indian guide, and secretly named him Running Elk. He was also impressed by the calm way in which, on his first visit to the Cearne, Galsworthy dealt with a cat in a wild fury because her kittens had attracted the attentions of the Garnetts' dog; he carried the maddened cat away as if it had been 'gently purring for all the emotional response it evoked from him'. He continues with another revolting story of how the same dog Puppsie dug up and brought into the house a bullock's head, stinking and covered with maggots; he 'did not turn a hair though the stench would have overpowered most people. He calmly fetched a shovel and a wheelbarrow, conveyed the horrible object to the bottom of the garden, dug a large hole, buried it and then returned to wash his hands carefully and dust his knees with a handkerchief scented with a few drops of eau de Cologne.'[8]

Small incidents, but they tell one much about Galsworthy, his calm imperturbability under almost any circumstances, and yet his excessive personal fastidiousness. It also tells one why people so utterly different in character and temperament from himself as Conrad, Ford or Garnett loved and admired him for these very differences.

Garnett's relations with his authors were seldom completely happy. 'A friend to me my enemy is,' Ford wrote to Stanley Unwin, voicing the feeling that his other writers certainly at times shared. Galsworthy's association with Garnett was no exception, and a most uncharacteristic outburst in a letter written to Garnett about his novel, *The Patrician*, in September 1910, ten years after their first meeting, reveals that Galsworthy never felt that Garnett had fully got over his first unfavourable reaction to his writing. (When a reader for the publisher, Fisher Unwin, Garnett had unofficially seen the manuscript of *Jocelyn*.)

> I have always suffered a little from a sense of injustice at your hands – ever since I read an extract from your report on *Jocelyn* (which should never have been sent to me) to the effect that I should never be an artist but always look at life as from the windows of a Club. Well, book by book, I've always a little felt, that you *unconsciously* grudge having to recede from that position. That, with your strong, and in those days, still more set belief in your own insight (which is very great), you had summed me up and could not be wrong. I have always felt that I am deeper, more fluid, perhaps broader than you think. Being dumb, I've never said so – but perhaps you'll forgive me once in these ten years (and more) saying out my feeling. In fact I've always felt that I was contending with a *parti-pris*, perpetually confirmed in you, whenever we are together, by my slowness of tongue and manner. You say 'this book is not you', but this seems to suggest that you have fixed me as something special, definite, narrow. This is what I always feel in you. 'Jack is so-and-so, et voila tout!' It is the habit, I suppose of the critical mind which has to form its judgement on definite things, to deny the possibility of change or growth until that change or growth has utterly fulfilled itself.[9]

The letter says much of the character of the two men, and it is to the credit of both that two such different people could in the main work so profitably and harmoniously together.

Nevertheless the sting of Garnett's unfortunate comment on *Jocelyn* was something that Galsworthy never completely got out of his system. The last thing he wrote, the draft speech which was to be delivered at the awarding of the Nobel Prize, contains a long justification of himself. 'The letter in which he [Unwin] sheltered himself from having further dealings with me contained a quotation from his reader's report: "The author is essentially a Club man." I took that hard . . .' And he goes on at length to describe what a club did mean to him, and how little: 'a place where I could hang up my hat, weigh myself, sink into some chair with a book, and believe in critics.'

On Galsworthy's side at least the relationship with Garnett continued to be a highly nervous one. In February 1902 he sent Garnett a first draft of *The Island Pharisees* (originally titled *The Pagan*). 'I am not sure that I am doing wisely in sending you the M.S. so early [but] will do it all the same, and trust to you not to crush it altogether until I have finished it.'[10] The extremely delicate relationship between author and critic was getting into its stride: Galsworthy felt the need to expose himself to Garnett's criticism, and at the same time resented the criticism when it came. He packs off the parcel of newly written manuscript, the ink still wet, the characters still too close to their creator's mind to bear much adverse comment; it is because it is so new, so vital to himself, that he must put it before another's eye, especially one so experienced, so highly thought of, as Edward Garnett's.

It was a delicate relationship but one that established a certain intimacy more quickly than the normal paths of friendship. 'At present, quite independently of all criticism, let me simply say that your MS. [*The Pagan*] makes one like you as a *man*; and that an MS. may have great value to a writer and to a reader together, as tending to remove both distance, diffidence and misunderstanding.'[11]

Later one may legitimately raise the question as to how beneficial Garnett's influence on Galsworthy was; there were times, particularly during the final writing of *The Man of Property*, when Galsworthy found his friend's criticism disturbing and destructive. But during the early years of their association there can be little doubt that Garnett's support and help did a great deal for Galsworthy; here was someone highly influential who could advise and guide him on the marketing of his work, not only over the publishers who would consider his novels, but magazines and periodicals who would, on Garnett's recommendation, give a sympathetic reading to his shorter articles and poems. In April 1901 he suggests that the *Speaker* or the *Manchester Guardian* might accept two poems, 'Courage' and 'Errantry', and on 14 June Garnett wrote, '*The Speaker* Editor writes to me that he will print the verses, but he is still "full up" – later.' His letter of 20 May 1903 is full of advice on the placing of *The Pharisees*, as *The Island Pharisees* is called at this stage. 'It is good criticism of life, and brilliantly written. I have repeated this to Duckworth yesterday; and have told him I advised you to try people like Heinemann and Methuen, and come back to him later, on your half-profit system – if necessary.'

But whatever the disadvantages of Garnett as adviser and mentor, Galsworthy and his circle seem to have regarded friendship with him as an inevitable adjunct to a serious literary career. 'Those of us who want to do good work generally come to him sooner or later, why not sooner?' Galsworthy wrote to Mottram in 1904.

Chapter 11

Conrad and Ford Madox Ford

What emerges from this early correspondence with Edward Garnett is that Galsworthy had by now become a person who knew his own mind; he knew where he was going and what he wanted to do. He needed Garnett's professional assistance in achieving his ambitions, but he did not need Garnett to tell him what those ambitions were; the work he had already published had proved beyond question that he had it in him to be a writer, perhaps even a great writer. He had discovered his talent as a satirist, and satire was exactly the weapon he needed; his writing would be a mirror in which society could see itself for what it was, see its selfishness, its hollowness, its false values, and its hypocrisy.

He had by now come to terms with his own problems; he was no longer the inward-looking, despairing Giles Legard of *Jocelyn*, but he was still an outsider. His affair with Ada ensured that he would not be received or regarded as respectable by most of his own class: Mottram describes how, when Galsworthy took him to lunch at his club, the Junior Carlton, he was most pointedly cut by a fellow member.[1] Later he felt obliged to resign from his clubs and companies. But as an outsider he could the more easily join cause with other outsiders, the poor and the underprivileged, the prisoners, the outcasts of society. These were the things he was going to write about, these were the pre-occupations of Richard Shelton, hero of *The Island Pharisees* and the ultimate justification for his attack on Forsytism, the creed of the privileged, the self-satisfied, the elect of society.

But ironically Ada, the cause of his ostracism, the most potent single factor in Galsworthy's crusade against society, was in the end to lead him back into society, to build him up from the struggling 'angry young man' of 1905 to the establishment figure of the 1920s. Could anyone put it more significantly than Mottram, when he wrote, without apparent resentment, that when Galsworthy had become 'one of the imposing figures of the world, Ada gently changed it [his name] to "J.G.", reserving "Jack" and occasionally "John" for her private and personal use'.[2]

But though ostracized by some circles, perhaps even because of it, this period was the one in which Galsworthy mixed most with other writers, making many close friendships. In the later years, friends tended to become acquaintances, and intimate friends were few outside the family circle, though he and Ada were to meet socially an enormous number of people; Ada lists them in her diary, John complains that his arm aches from the hands he has had to shake.

As well as the development of his friendship with Edward and Constance Garnett, and his visits to their home, Galsworthy was also a frequent visitor at the constantly changing homes of Conrad and his wife Jessie: 'I used to stay with him [Conrad] a good deal from 1895–1905; first at Stanford in Essex, and then at Stanford in Kent. He was indefatigably good to me while my own puppy's eyes were opening to literature.' Then later at the Pent, near Aldington in Kent, 'a friendly dwelling where you had to mind your head in connection with beams; and from whose windows you watched ducks and cats and lambs in the meadows beyond'.[3]

Joseph Conrad had by this time abandoned the sea, and was trying with enormous difficulty to support himself and Jessie by his writing. Jessie was a homely, domestic person, but no sort of intellectual companion for her husband; thus he depended almost entirely on his friends for encouragement and sympathy with his work. 'I was thankful when one of those most intimate friends, John Galsworthy, Edward Garnett or E. L. Sanderson could be induced to pay us a visit, for a long weekend. The effect of their sympathetic and sustaining presence would lubricate the mental machinery, so to speak, and a good advance would be made,' Jessie wrote after his death.[4] Conrad, moreover, was a writer who needed encouragement, who easily despaired of his work, becoming depressed and unsure of himself: 'Everything, every achievement seems so hopelessly, hopelessly far away, as it were beyond one's own region of time, the tiny minute ring within which one is trying to bustle about,' he wrote in a letter to Galsworthy. 'You have no idea how your interest in me *keeps me up*. I am unutterably weary of thinking and writing, of seeing, of feeling and of living.'[5]

The friendship between the two writers was to remain deeply affectionate throughout their lives, but it was during the ten years before Galsworthy's marriage that they saw most of each other and corresponded almost weekly, though unfortunately Galsworthy's side of the correspondence has been lost. Surprisingly Galsworthy never told Conrad of his own literary aspirations until the thing was a *fait accompli* and *From the Four Winds* was already in print. 'The sly dog never told me he wrote,' Conrad wrote to Unwin in March 1897. 'He is a first-rate fellow, clever, has seen the world.' Presumably he was not enormously impressed by his friend's first effort, for on reading *The Man of Devon* he wrote to Galsworthy: 'That the man who has written once the *Four Winds* has written now the *M of D* volume is a source of infinite gratification to me. It vindicates my insight, my opinion, my judgement – and it satisfies my affection for you in whom I believed and am believing.'[6]

Ada, too, entered into the friendship, took a keen interest in Conrad's writing, and later invoked his help with her translations from the stories of de Maupassant entitled *Yvette*. 'I am having great conclaves with J. Conrad lately, he is helping me with some translation from the French: . . . it seems quite a relaxation to him, and he can't do his own original writing all day long.'[7] 'Ada of course is an angel,' Conrad told Galsworthy.[8]

The friendship between the two households was pleasantly informal: 'Borys [Conrad's small son] wants to know whether you are related to Jack the Giant Killer – otherwise he is well.'[9] And in 1906 the Conrads have borrowed the Galsworthy's London house: 'I don't know that I am writing much in the little wooden house [out in the garden] but I smoke there religiously for three and a half hours every morning with a sheet of paper before and an American fountain pen in my hand. What more could be expected from a conscientious author I can't imagine.'[10] But above all Conrad found Galsworthy's steady character, enormous personal integrity and generosity a tremendous support to his own more mercurial character. When he was not elated he was given to despair, and indeed he had cause: his health was bad, his work progressed always with great difficulty, he was constantly financially worried. His letters are full of his distresses: 'I am not very happy finding a great difficulty in writing. I am either getting stale or becoming an idiot.'[11] 'What a help in life your personality is to my shadow.'[12]

Galsworthy must often have been aware of the great difference in character and background that existed between him and the writers with whom he was now becoming intimate. He had been brought up as an English gentleman; he had learnt to be restrained and moderate in his behaviour, and above all reserved and careful never to give way to his feelings. He had also, what his new friends had not, financial security; he had the means to lead an ordered life, to maintain a comfortable home, and to travel when he wished. Above all he could pick his terms with his publishers, or indeed, as in the case of the *Four Winds*, pay for the publication himself. It could be argued that such security was at times a disadvantage; without the tensions and financial worries that dogged the lives of Conrad or Ford, sometimes perhaps life was too easy and too calm. An artist often flourishes in adversity, and his talent withers when there is nothing for him to kick against. But during these years Galsworthy had his troubles, his secret life with Ada, and from them his best work was to grow.

Through Conrad Galsworthy met the highly eccentric Ford Madox Ford, who was at this time living at the Pent near Aldington. (Conrad took over the tenancy in September 1898, and Ford and his wife moved into a cottage in the village.) 'Hueffer [Ford] fell in love with *The Four Winds*,' Conrad wrote to Galsworthy,[13] and after this Ford followed his work with interest. Of 'The Salvation of Swithin Forsyte' he wrote, 'it is far and away the best thing you have done'.[14] It was at the Pent, while visiting Conrad, that Galsworthy first met Ford, as Ford describes in his memoirs:

I was prepared for something remarkable by Conrad's really radiant expression when he said: 'Jack wants to know if he may come down.'

I was driving a wagonette with a pretty good mare. He [Galsworthy] swung his grips over the side of the cart and would not get in because, he said, he wanted some exercise ...

I touched up the mare. She was a pretty good goer, aged, but with a strain of Wilfred Blunt's Arab blood. I did not expect to see that fellow again until a quarter of an hour after I got to the house ... But there he was, still beside the box-seat, trotting along with the utmost equanimity. And, as if we had been strolling down Piccadilly he continued conversing ... about the land of the Pent, which is a clayey loam in the bottoms till it runs into the chalk of the Downs; and about how the young partridges were coming on; and about Selby Lowndes, the redoubtable Master of the East Kent Hounds, who had once had a trencherfed pack in the Cleveland. Englishmen have to know all these things or they are not 'sound'. So he trotted the mile and a quarter to the Pent. I felt like Maupassant when the head of Swinburne rose out of the Mediterranean beside his canoe and the poet swam to shore beside him, conversing joyously of Anacreon.[15]

This anecdote reminds one that Galsworthy was, in a quite different way, as much an oddity to his new friends as they were to him.

In London (Ford returned there in 1903) there was a pleasant casualness about these semi-bachelor days. Galsworthy entertained his friends to breakfast: 'Tomorrow I *breakfast* with Galsworthy (fancy my early rising),' Ford wrote to Elsie in February 1903, and later, describing Aubrey Walk: 'the doors and windows [were] always open, the sunlight streaming in on the hissing silver tea-kettle, the bubbling silver entree dishes, the red tiles of the floor, the bright rugs, the bright screens. And we would talk until it was time for me to go back along the waterworks wall and take up the interminable job of writing.'[16] Presumably the visits were returned, for when Ford left London in April the following year Galsworthy wrote: 'I shall miss you very much – it was so nice to feel one could "drop in".'[17]

Camden Hill must have had something of the atmosphere of an artistic community during those years; reference to a map of the area will show how close the houses of this small circle were to each other. We have already seen how Ada's flat and the Sauters' house were within minutes' walk of Galsworthy's bachelor home in Aubrey Walk; Ford was even closer – as he said just across the reservoir in Airlie Gardens – and still not far away the Conrads established themselves briefly at 17 Gordon Place; that is, when they were not actually living in their friends' houses – Ford complains of Conrad using his study to write *Nostromo*, a book which they at times almost collaborated on.

Later Ford settled at 84 Holland Park Avenue, which also became the headquarters of the *English Review*. Then again South Lodge, the home of the ill-fated Violet Hunt, was at 80 Campden Hill Road. It is incidentally interesting to note that it was at a dinner party at the Galsworthys' on 21 March 1907 that Violet Hunt and Ford Madox Ford met for the first time since childhood, a meeting that was to be the starting point of one of the most fantastic romances in literary history.[18]

Chapter 12

The Island Pharisees

This then was the background against which Galsworthy settled down to his years of most challenging, and ultimately most successful, writing. Among his fellow writers and critics he had established himself as a writer of considerable promise, but he still had to write a book which would attract the attention of a wider public, and so far he had made no money out of writing. 'For nine years, indeed for eleven years, I made not one penny out of what I, but practically no others, counted as my profession. Mine indeed was a deep dark youth, an apprenticeship cheered on by some driving quality within me, and by the belief that I would some day be a real writer.'[1]

It is strange that at this moment Galsworthy chose to work on not one book but two, for during the years 1901 to 1905 he was engaged on both *The Island Pharisees* and *The Man of Property*; according to his account both books took him three years to write, and the former was written three times before he, or possibly Edward Garnett, was satisfied. 'I cannot recollect writing the first words of the *Island Pharisees* – but it would be about August 1901.'[2] The first draft must have made reasonable headway, for in February he is submitting it to Garnett with some nervousness as to his reaction. In the first instance the novel was titled *The Pagan*, and it seems that it was in this version that Garnett found much to criticize. Galsworthy and Garnett were at this period dining together regularly – 'every month' Garnett tells us – and it must have been at these meetings that the vexed question of the new novel was thrashed out, for the correspondence between the two says nothing of it.

> Now came my tug of war. I began a book which in the end became *The Island Pharisees*. The first draft was called *A Pagan*, and was a string of episodes recounted by Ferrand in the first person. When it was nearly finished I showed it to Edward Garnett. 'No, my dear fellow,' he said, 'it's all very well, but you shouldn't have done that fellow subjectively. You can't possibly know the real inside of a

vagabond like that; you ought to give him to us objectively, through a personality like your own.' I gnashed my teeth, set them, conceived Shelton, and rewrote the book. I made a half-baked job of it. 'Better,' said Edward Garnett, 'but do it again!' I re-gnashed my teeth, re-set them, and wrote it a third time. So in 1904 it was published – first of my books under my own name. Perhaps I made fifty pounds out of it: but this thrice-written book wasn't 'written'! It underwent a thorough Spring-cleaning before it assumed its final form in 1908.[3]

It was a book that Galsworthy couldn't leave alone: the 'Spring-cleaning' of 1908 was an unnecessary, pernickity affair; it was the work of an older man trying to rethink and to modify the work of his younger self. For The Island Pharisees, even though Galsworthy was thirty-four when he began it, is a young man's book.

Just as Jocelyn is the most personal account that he ever wrote of his feelings towards Ada, and the emotional trauma he experienced in loving a married woman, so Richard Shelton, the hero of The Island Pharisees, is Galsworthy in his most unguarded and explosive mood against society. Shelton is a young man, who, like his author a few years earlier, is uncertain what to do with his life, having abandoned his career at the Bar. To quote the 1904 edition, which is nearly always more vivid than its successor, he found that 'being in love was in itself a pursuit occupying more than all his time . . . To have nothing to do is unworthy of a man – he knew that. The odd thing was that he had never felt as if he had nothing to do.'

Shelton is a naïve character, constantly surprised by the reactions of the people he meets, and most of all by those of his fiancée, Antonia. He observes the somewhat sterile marriages of his acquaintances with horror: 'It was like knocking at a never-opened door, looking at a circle – couple after couple all the same. No heads, toes, angles of their souls stuck out anywhere. In the sea of their environments they were drowned . . .' He rushes back to his room to pour out his feelings to Antonia in a letter: 'There's something about human nature that is awfully repulsive, and the healthier people are, the more repulsive they seem to be . . .' He is confident that she will share his views, and is dashed when her reply comes back: 'I don't think I understand what you mean . . . one must be healthy to be perfect, mustn't one? I don't like unhealthy people. I had to play on that wretched piano after reading your letter; it made me feel unhappy.' Increasingly this becomes the pattern of their relationship. Shelton longs for an intimacy that she is incapable of: 'I must be everything to you. Do you think I shall?' Like her mother, Mrs Dennant, Antonia feels that Shelton has 'been thinkin'' too much lately', and this makes her unhappy.

But parallel to this main theme of Shelton and Antonia is the development of a very different friendship, that between Shelton and the impoverished Frenchman, Ferrand. Ferrand occurs again and again in Galsworthy's writings, in the short stories, and particularly in his play *The Pigeon*; he is almost a symbolic figure, the outcast, he speaks for the underprivileged, the have-nots. He is based on a real character, 'who died in some "sacred institution" many years ago of a consumption brought on by the conditions of his wandering life. If not "a beloved", he was a true vagabond, and I first met him in the Champs Elysees.'[4]

In the Nobel Speech Galsworthy is even more explicit about the significance of Ferrand to him. Having described their meeting in Paris he goes on to say:

> there developed between us something of that conflict between man's natural comfortable laziness, and his better, or shall I say, more ragged self. The world of failures, of the rolling stones, the underworld became disclosed to me. I have often been told that I feel for my characters more than they feel for themselves. I daresay that is true, but when I look at the faces of those who make up this world of ours – this world that knows where its breakfast is coming from so well that it has reached a comfortable acquiescence in the lack of breakfast for others, when I look at those faces, I still find it difficult to assume that well-fed philosophy which feeds and says: 'The poor are always with us.'
>
> I have some of Clermont's letters now, yellowed and worn. 'Verily I say unto you it is harder for one of the black-coated fraternity to enter the world of the disinherited than for a camel to pass through the eye of a needle.' It has been too hard for me. But from that chance meeting among the sparrows in the Champs-Elysees sprang my fifth book.

Ferrand speaks for Galsworthy – in a sense he is Galsworthy, his outraged cry of pain against the injustices and inequalities of society – and

the concept of the book is the conflict between the two sides of Galsworthy, the conventionally brought up Shelton who is attracted by
Antonia, and the outcast Ferrand.

The climax of the story is reached when Ferrand is introduced into
the highly formal household of Antonia's parents, Holm Oaks, and
seeing the two together Shelton is forced to realize that Antonia will
never be able to understand much of his character.

> There was tragedy in the way she watched Ferrand, and in the way
> Shelton watched her. If he had been told that he was watching her,
> he would have denied it in good faith; but he was bound to watch
> her, to find out with what eyes she viewed this visitor who em-
> bodied all the rebellious under-side of life, all that was absent in
> herself.*

But at last the third writing was complete and Galsworthy and Garnett
were satisfied: 'I should like to say however . . . how very strong and
good I think the *Pharisees* is, how very original I feel it to be, and how
in writing it, you have achieved something that remains there, to last
and be looked back on with a real and modest pride.'[5] To which
Galsworthy replied: 'I have seldom had a letter that gave me more
pleasure than yours.'[6]

There still remained the task of finding a publisher. In August 1902
Conrad had enthusiastically offered what was probably the second
version to Hallam Murray, but in October he had to write to his
friend: 'Dearest Jack, – they are beasts. I've just received a note from
H.M. declining with many complimentary expressions. I am sending
you the MS. by this same post registered. After all we must expect this
sort of thing. No work is judged on its artistic merits: and there's no
doubt that the book must rub many susceptibilities the wrong way.'[7]

But even the third version did not easily find a publisher. Galsworthy
first offered it without success to Constable, and finally Conrad inter-
vened once again and recommended the book to Sydney Pawling at
Heinemann. On 2 October he was able to write the good news of its
favourable reception. 'I was delighted to find him [Pawling] extremely well-disposed towards the book. Heinemann himself, I understand, was doubtful, not of the value but of the expediency. However

* 1904 edition. 1908 edition: 'She watched Ferrand, and Shelton watched
her.'

89

that's his normal attitude towards every new work and in your case is no obstacle to publication by them.'

All went well with the negotiations and a contract was signed with Heinemann, which included an agreement that Galsworthy should give them the first option on his next book, which was to be *The Man of Property*. Conrad wrote to congratulate him: 'I think that the terms arranged with P. are fair. The royalties are decent: but the best feature is the limit of time. That is really a master-stroke on which I congratulate you. It may save no end of worry in the future – that *certain* future which you *are* to have.'[8]

So, one might have supposed, the book was done with: three times revised, satisfactory terms agreed with a good publisher, the warm approval of his friends won. The book appeared on 28 January 1904, under its final title: '*The Island Pharisees* by John Galsworthy (John Sinjohn) Author of a "Man of Devon", "Villa Rubein" etc.' The criticisms received by the book were mixed; out of forty-three reviews ten were definitely enthusiastic, and eight equally definitely against it, finding fault with its moralizing tone: Galsworthy was already in danger of sacrificing art to his message.

Galsworthy's first five books appeared in small editions (the first English edition of *The Island Pharisees* was only fifteen hundred copies, of which 750 sets of sheets went to America with Putnam's imprint), and it was not until the success of *The Man of Property* that there was any demand for a re-issue of his early works. It was then, presumably, that Galsworthy was faced with the question as to how much of his early work he wanted to preserve for posterity, and in what form? *From the Four Winds* and *Jocelyn* were rejected: the former is a very bad book and deserved oblivion; *Jocelyn*, on the other hand, now appeared too personal to find favour with its author, now ten years older, a married man and already something of a public figure. 'It [*Jocelyn*] was, however, a bad novel; it was not what is called "written". The technique limped; the characters had stringhalt; and the clothing sentences were redundant or deficient' (*Glimpses and Reflections*, p. 154). *The Villa Rubein* and *The Man of Devon* were revised and reprinted together in 1909.

The Island Pharisees, the first to reappear, presented the greatest problem to Galsworthy: he undoubtedly regarded it as his first important work, it had taken him three years to write, and it included much of his personal philosophy, but by 1908 its writing seemed to him

almost offensively outspoken and immature. His reputation had by
that time been made by two novels, *The Man of Property* and *The
Country House*, and the play *The Silver Box*. What was he going to do
with this loud-mouthed child of his? Was it to die in silence like
Jocelyn or would he let it live, a shadow of its former self, speaking in
muffled tones? He decided on the latter course; red pencil in hand, he
set to work to 'spring clean' his *enfant terrible*.

The red pencil did its work with great thoroughness; like a bulldozer
it charged through the pages. Sometimes its alterations are purely
fidgety, words being replaced by synonyms, either pointless, or producing a weaker and less striking effect than the original word:
'exemplary' becomes 'perfect', 'fundamental respectability' becomes
'fundamental domesticity' (the term is used derisively and the revision
is less sweeping than the earlier phrase), or simply 'sofa' becomes 'chair'!
But more unfortunate are the erasings of descriptive passages leaving
perhaps one word, which by itself fails to convey the author's original
idea: thus 'his uncle's face had a look of crucifixion' is surely meaning-
less, but the original version – 'his uncle's face had a kind of crucified
look, as if feelings had worn their way to the surface, like the points of
nails through the inner sole of a boot' – a lively and interesting piece of
writing. The book suffers again and again from this sort of treatment,
and the overall effect is to make the second version much duller than
its predecessor.

But Galsworthy's intention was perhaps to take some of the bite out
of the book. He is an older man rebuking the impetuousness of youth;
he has become himself more worldly; he has begun to see the tactical
advantages of prudence and restraint. Shelton in 1908 is less hot-
blooded than he was in 1904: tantalized by the attractions of Antonia,
in 1904 'he was silent with straining eyes and twitching hands and
fierce longing'; now 'he was silent with a beating heart'. Shelton is also
more tactful in his reflections about society: 'What business has our
class to turn up its nose at the rest of the world?' he thought in 1904.
In the later version: 'What business has our class to patronize?' One
last alteration is worth noting: in the earlier version a character is
described as having been made by the death of his father 'a man of
property'; in 1908 this is revised to 'a man of means'. By the later date
the former phrase had taken on a far wider meaning for
Galsworthy.

I have felt it worth while to go into this revision in some detail because it reveals so clearly the enormous changes that were taking place in Galsworthy's life and outlook. It is true that only a period of four years is in question, but as we shall see in the next chapters they were four years of tremendous activity and significance.

Chapter 13
The Man of Property I

The Man of Property took Galsworthy three years to write, but even so it was less troublesome to its author than *The Island Pharisees*; for much of the time he was at work on both books concurrently, as if for relief he turned from the awkward Shelton to the far more easy-going Forsytes. *The Man of Property* was a natural book for Galsworthy, and the great clan of Forsytes natural people for him to write about; they were a class of people he knew intimately from the inside, they were his own aunts and uncles.

In a sense *The Island Pharisees* was a liberating book, for many of Galsworthy's personal angers had found expression in the mouth of Richard Shelton. He was angry about the position of women in society, he clearly saw that they were always treated as inferior to men, whether they were wealthy women being given in marriage with settlements that curtailed their freedom to remarry even after the death of their partner, or poor women soliciting the attentions of men in the street, men who demanded their sexual favours and then punished them for giving them. 'We get the benefit without soiling even the hem of our reputation – the women are the only ones that suffer. And why shouldn't they – inferior things?' Shelton ruminates angrily in his club. Shelton, as Galsworthy himself had done, visits Dartmoor Prison and is shocked at the conditions in which the prisoners live; like Galsworthy too he has wandered in the unsavoury areas of London and seen for himself the appalling living conditions of the poor. (Galsworthy was of course directly using his experiences when as a young man in London he had had a 'fondness for wandering about at night in the poorer districts'; he had also seen inside working-class homes when collecting rents from his father's properties.) But most of all Galsworthy was appalled by the indifference of his own class, by their easy acceptance of the wide disparity between their own comfortable circumstances and those of the Ferrands of the world.

Shelton is too angry to be a very satisfactory character; he never relaxes, never stops moralizing. As in a boiling kettle the pressures had built up; there was too much that Galsworthy had to say, and Shelton, overburdened by his author's conscience, had to say them. But the book once written left Galsworthy a freer man and in a mood that was calmer and more dispassionate he was able to create his true world, the world of the Forsyte Saga.

The first mention of the new book is a reference to it in a letter from Conrad dated June 1903:

> I am excited by the news of the novel you are hatching. It is good news; for you are a man of purpose and know what you want to do. But what is it that you exactly want to do? That is – for me – the question. The name of the people suggests the moral shape of the thing; yet I would like to know – to know absolutely – to know as much as you know (or think you know) of what is going to happen to the doomed crew of Forsythes [*sic*].

From the beginning Galsworthy realized he had struck gold; the writing came easily and he knew with complete certainty that the book he was writing was more than good, that it was, possibly, a work of genius; after so many years of hard work, after so many false starts, he had found a subject and a mode of writing exactly suited to his pen. The first comments from Garnett showed that this was his first reaction to the book: 'Chapter I is splendid, perfect in phrasing and conception – and really deep,' he wrote on 12 June 1904; and in his postscript to the letter he says: 'Those Jameses and Soameses, etc you have really *got* in the most uncanny fashion.'

It was at this time that editor and author set off together for a walking tour in South Wales, and in this same letter Garnett confirms the rendezvous that they had planned: 'Right. Cardiff station for the train at 5.45 – or Abergavenny *Station* at 6.55, Saturday next.'

It is not difficult to imagine the two writers, both in their mid thirties, in fact almost the same age, trudging across the country, their rucksacks on their backs. They were both at a stage when life seemed to have everything to offer: the disappointments and the failures had not yet begun to bite; the horrors of the First World War were ten years ahead; they could still believe in the value of their own work and in the civilization in which they lived. Many years later Galsworthy recalls his 'memories of our many discussions in those old days, and of cosy dinners with Compassionate Waiters brandishing the Voslauer

Goldeck above our table; and of our long walk in Wales, and the morning we went up the Carmarthen Van in dense fog and talked of *The Man of Property* (then on the stocks) on the way down.'[1] Garnett has a slightly different version of the foggy excursion: 'It was a foolhardy thing to do, since we groped our way up the mountain to the two lakes, which are hemmed in by cliffs; and I insisted on swimming in the first, while Galsworthy stood, a dim figure on the shore, fuming watch in hand, waiting for me. However fate was kind; just before we had reached the second lake a great wind arose and tore the mist away, giving us a surpassing view of the country beneath to the south.'[2]

It was on this walking tour that another event occurred that was to have far-reaching consequences for Galsworthy; this was the discovery of Manaton, a little hamlet in Devon situated between Moretonhampstead and Bovey Tracey.* Manaton was to mean more to Galsworthy than any other one place; here, in the farmhouse, Wingstone, he was to spend some of his happiest years, for in 1908 he and Ada became permanent tenants of the farmhouse, and it was to be their main country home until 1924. Of course, on account of Ada's restless passion for travelling, their visits there were sporadic; throughout the years, with the exception of the war period, their lives were a pattern of ceaseless coming and going, of endless packing and unpacking, and one can only wonder at the resolution that enabled John to write anything at all. But for John, Manaton had everything he desired; his love of nature, of wild life and open spaces, his need for solitude, to get away from the hurly-burly of the town, all these things it satisfied. His story 'Buttercup Night' describes his first coming to Manaton, his immediate recognition that this indeed was his spiritual home:

> Why is it, that in some places one has such a feeling of life being, not merely a long picture-show for human eyes, but a single breathing, glowing, growing thing, of which we are no more important a part than the swallows and magpies, the foals and sheep in the meadows, the sycamores and ash trees and flowers in the fields, the rocks and little bright streams, or even than the long fleecy clouds and their soft-shouting drivers, the winds?

* A private note of Ada's suggests that she and John in fact visited Wingstone in Easter 1903 and 1904; in this case when she told Marrot that John's visit there in the summer of 1904 was his first she was probably still trying to 'forget' some of the details of their early association.

True we register these parts of being, and they – so far as we know – do not register us; yet it is impossible to feel, in such places as I speak of, the busy, dry, complacent sense of being all that matters, which in general we humans have so strongly.

In these rare spots, which are always in the remote country, untouched by the advantages of civilization, one is conscious of an enwrapping web or mist of spirit – is it, perhaps, the glamorous and wistful wraith of all the vanished shapes once dwelling there in such close comradeship?

It was Sunday of an early June when I first came on one such, far down in the West Country. I had walked with my knapsack twenty miles, and there being no room at the tiny inn of the very little village, they directed me to a wicket gate, through which, by a path leading down a field, I would come to a farmhouse, where I might find lodging. The moment I got into that field I felt within me a special contentment, and sat down on a rock to let the feeling grow.

Leaving the rock at last, I went towards the house. It was long and low and rather sad, standing in a garden all mossy grass and buttercups, with a few rhododendrons and flowery shrubs below a row of fine old Irish yews.

Galsworthy must have returned from his walking tour full of ideas and encouragement, for he and Garnett had discussed his book exhaustively; surely now he would have a long and uninterrupted period of writing and the work would soon be finished. But, as so often happens, events occur that are beyond our control, which can completely alter the course of our lives. On 8 December 1904 Galsworthy's father died at the age of eighty-seven after a long and harrowing illness. 'When you consider that two and a half years ago he was given a few weeks of life, by all the doctors who attended him, you will understand something of the indomitable nature of his mind, and the horror to us of his running fight with death. I am left with a feeling of amazed resentment with the inscrutable brutality of Nature,' Galsworthy wrote to his friend St John Hornby.[3] And the illness was not the only distressing circumstance of the last years of his father's life; the year before his death his mother, Blanche, had left her husband, accusing him of an attachment to his grandchildren's governess.

For his son this death must have led to the most conflicting emotions, but undoubtedly, whatever his sorrow at losing a father, his over-riding feeling must have been one of release. At last he was free to take the necessary legal steps that would make his marriage to Ada possible. Ten years ago they had decided that to make their liaison public would be too painful to John's father, but he was then seventy-seven years old; how could they have guessed that the period of waiting would be so long, or indeed ever have imagined how traumatic such an experience would be? To Ada, especially, the wounds to her personal esteem were ones from which she would never completely recover; it made their relationship uncomfortably delicate. John's nature was to spoil and pamper the person he loved, and there seemed to be no end to the spoiling and pampering that was required: Ada had to be taken here, there and everywhere for her health; she had to be protected from anything that was difficult or unpleasant; like a child she had to be petted, given into over everything; even games had to be contrived so that she should emerge the winner. It was as if nothing would ever make up for what she felt she had endured during those years of waiting. Tragically unaware of what she was doing, she demanded more and more of John, until in the end the sacrifice was complete, and the writer, who in the first place had been given life by her encouragement and belief, perished in the ever-narrowing confines of their marriage.

Chapter 14
Freedom at Last

John and Ada lost no time: publicly they went together to Manaton for Christmas, that place that was already 'special' for them, and, as they hoped would happen, Major Galsworthy, no longer able to entertain any delusions about Ada's fidelity, instituted divorce proceedings against them. To escape the publicity and embarrassment of the months that must intervene before Ada's divorce could be made absolute and they were free to marry, the couple decided to go abroad.

Before leaving England there must have been much to do: now that the time for secrecy was over, close friends at last had to be told of the true state of affairs between John and Ada; he had to resign from clubs and directorships. Though Galsworthy felt so strongly that the course that he and Ada were taking was under the circumstances a perfectly proper one, though he had already argued the case of the unhappily married woman in his writings, he nevertheless felt that his closest friends had the right to condemn, and possibly disown, him for what he was doing; he had no doubt that, as society was, he had forfeited the right to be accepted as a responsible and respectable member. 'My dear Horn,' he wrote to St John Hornby on 8 January,

> I write to resign my trusteeship in your marriage settlement. It is not as you may imagine because of the labour it has given me; I wish all my trusteeships were of its painless and pleasant character; but because I am about to become an unfit person to undertake its blameless duties. In other words I am leaving England with someone, between whom and myself there has long been a devoted attachment. When the undefended proceedings are over, and the due time comes we shall (the fates willing) be married and return to England.
>
> I don't feel like enlarging upon the situation, except to say that her marriage was dreadfully miserable from the first; that I did not come on the scene till there was separation in all but the merest form; that

what blame attaches, attaches to me, but that I do not feel it, and shall never admit or believe that either of us could have acted differently. Her husband is my first cousin, which will explain the fact that during my Father's life we could not face the pain to *him* of an esclandre.

We are absolutely devoted to each other, we do not expect to be swallowed by the world, and we do not want to be; those who know us best have so far found no difficulty. I've given up Companies, Clubs etc and shall at last have time and a mind at ease for writing.

To Ralph Mottram, who knew them both and must have had a fairly good idea of the situation already, he wrote in a similar, though less apologetic, vein:

I'm going abroad for six or seven months, in fact till Ada and I can be married. The hydra-headed monster of waiting will be slain, I trust this month, by what are called 'proceedings' against us in the so-called Courts of Justice.

When we return, if you still look upon us as sufficiently respectable, I trust you will come and visit the little house I have taken. In the meantime, my dear boy, I leave behind with you the warmest sympathy, and I urge you to go on [with his own writing] and not be cast down.

. . . This is a curious and fascinating time, for thank God – Ada is not exactly what you would call an ordinary woman, neither has our devotion been through the fire for nothing. It is most interesting to watch how people take it. On the whole it strengthens one's belief in human nature.[1]

By the terms of his father's will Galsworthy had a far greater financial independence than before; he would have no difficulty in supporting himself and Ada in the wandering life he envisaged for them at the same time as maintaining at first one, and later two, houses in England. It was to be a costly way of life, and as yet he was earning nothing from his writing. John Galsworthy senior had remade his will in 1903 when his wife left him, and while reducing her legacy he had greatly increased the legacies to his children: John received £2,500 free of duty, and his income was increased from £400 to £700 a year; moreover, in seven years' time the remainder of his father's estate was to be divided equally among the children, the sons to inherit absolutely, the daughters' shares to be held in trust for them and their children.

The Galsworthys first set out for Italy, and by 1 February John could write to Edward Garnett that their address for the next fortnight would be the Grand Hotel, Levanto, near Spezia. Ada's account of their stay there suggests that it must in fact have been for a longer period:

Being at Levanto on the Italian Riviera for a fairly long stay, we discovered many good walks. Mornings were devoted to writing – Himself putting the finishing touches to *The Man of Property*, and I following after with the typing of the whole novel; afternoons were given to exploring the country. And very pleasant we found it, though I must confess that most of them were reached only by starting out on the same tiresome bit of level suburb and road about a mile and a half in length. This very great bore was somewhat mitigated by the sight of several peasant women standing in their doorways, spinning; the thread growing evenly under their fingers, the spindle dangling. I have reason to remember the Levanto walks, for in my spare moments from typing the novel, I compiled a guide-book . . . North and south along the coast there were enchanting ways, northward especially. We delighted in one cliff topped with splendid pines, the deep blue sea showing between their great irridescent trunks. This high plateau we called 'Greek' for short, knowing very well what we meant though never having visited Greece.[2]

These months must have been some of the happiest for Ada and John: now they were married in all but name, their life together was assured; John was working on what was to be his most successful novel; Ada, as she longed to do, was acting as helpmate and support of a great writer. In 1932 Galsworthy wrote down his memories of the writing of *The Man of Property*, recalling the deep contentment he felt at that time:

The Man of Property was conceived in satiric mood and carried to its close in a larger spirit; it was written here, there, everywhere, the most scattered of my manuscripts, at the time of my life most poignant. Two-thirds of it had taken nearly two years to write; the last third was written in six weeks, with the pale north-Italian sunlight filtering through winter branches on to the pages. I was, indeed, in no hurry for the appearance of that book; I knew it to be the best I had written; and the revision of it, sentence by sentence, gave me more intimate pleasure than I am likely to have again.[3]

He was in no hurry for the book to be published. In his letter to Garnett he is more explicit: 'I don't want the book to come out before October certainly, and probably not before Xmas, not in fact until we are married.'[4]

From Levanto they continued their journey to Amalfi. Here Galsworthy hoped that he could persuade Garnett to join them at the end of March: 'It would be so much more satisfactory if you cast your eye over the MS once more, and it would be so awfully jolly if you could do so in Italy with us, that I want you to spare the inside of a fortnight at least, the last fortnight in March, and come to us at Amalfi. I *of course* providing the wherewithal.'[5] Presumably, as the final discussions on the book were carried on in a lengthy and emotionally fraught correspondence, Garnett did not in fact travel out to Italy. But *The Man of Property* was completed in Amalfi: 'I finished revision yesterday,' he wrote on 20 March to Ralph Mottram. 'The book bulks well over 100,000 words, and is what Belloc would call a more "considerable" work than my others . . .'

The climate was too hot for walking: 'the further south one goes the less natural it seems to indulge in walking, though we did some strolling around Sorrento and Amalfi.' And they visited Conrad and his wife, who were taking a holiday on Capri. 'We stayed a week at Sorrento then nearly a week at Capri where the Conrads are settled. We saw a good deal of them and he saw us off at Naples.'[6]

'I look on you as a sort of Odysseus, bringing home by and by to the Addison Road a strange deep budget of human experiences from mountains, diligences, peasant wives and hotel waiters. You are exceedingly popular and esteemed, I may add, in the memories of your friends,' Garnett wrote to Galsworthy in May,[7] almost as his friend was packing into boxes the finished first draft of *The Man of Property*. The all-important parcel was posted at Naples to his sister Lilian, who was to cable immediately its safe arrival; he would then send the second copy direct to Garnett.

The couple then left Naples and travelled via Florence to Austria, first to the Mendal Pass Hotel, in the Tyrol, and then on at the end of

May to Madonna di Campiglio. All this travelling and the months spent in hotels were made much easier for them by the fact that they already shared the same surname; it was a kind stroke of fate, without which it is unlikely that these long holidays together would ever have taken place, for Ada was not the woman who could have tolerated the constant, if tacit, criticism by strangers. The Tyrol was an area to which the Galsworthys returned again and again; they loved the mountains and the mountain walks, and the hotel, the Mendalhof, was run by a family called Spretter who welcomed their guests as friends.

Madonna di Campiglio Ada did not find so congenial, even though at one spot she heard nightingales 'singing all day long'; the bird, she felt, should keep its song for the night, and she 'would still rather hear a blackbird at his best and loudest'. She complained that the country-side was comparatively tame and orderly, although in a snapshot taken by one of their friends 'a bear was disclosed, looking down at the party from above'.[8]

It was from the Mendal Pass Hotel that Galsworthy, having heard that the first copy of *The Man of Property* had reached his sister safely, sent off the second to Garnett 'registered and insured. It's my only complete copy, and I'm nervous about it, for I should with difficulty find the pluck to tidy up the other copy.' One must assume therefore that Galsworthy was still fiddling with the manuscript and had made considerable alterations since the first copy had been sent off at Naples. He now believed it to be finished, and he asked Garnett to get it '*well* typed with specially careful *Supervision* for which I will pay special rates, also for expedition.' He now had to wait anxiously for the verdict on his great work, and to wait under depressing circumstances, for they had had 'nine days pouring rain out of the last twelve'.[9]

It was on 27 May that the letter came, bringing the all-important verdict on his book. In fact its contents triggered off a first-class row, an almost historic row between editor and author, raising the question as to whether anyone has the right, or indeed the ability, to come between an author and his characters. They are the children of his imagination: can anyone but he know how they should or would behave under certain circumstances? And yet, the very fact that an outsider can heatedly say, as Garnett did, so-and-so (this so-and-so was in fact Bosinney) would never have acted this way, it is not in his character to behave as you have made him behave, is in itself a proof that the book and its people live in their own right, are beings apart from their creator.

Garnett's letter begins with complimenting Galsworthy on the book, but almost at once he embarks on his main theme, that is, that the ending of the book is a disaster. This first ending is that Bosinney, the lover of Irene, is so distressed at finding that her husband, Soames, has forced his love on Irene, that in despair he walks out into the night and throws himself beneath a cab with the *deliberate* intention of ending his life.

> Briefly I regard it as containing splendid stuff, all on a high level, and containing two or three passages *near to genius*. *But*, and I emphasize this in every way, I consider Bosinney's Suicide an *artistic blot* of a very grave order, psychologically false, and seriously shaking the illusion of the whole story.[10]

He then goes on to list no less than eight reasons why he regards Bosinney's suicide as being completely out of character and 'incredible'.

Much of Garnett's argument turned on one point, Galsworthy's lack of understanding of those less well off than himself. 'Any man,' he wrote, 'who has fought his way, and lived on bread and cheese, is semi-proof against such "financial ruin", until family cares and age weaken him.' To Galsworthy this must have had overtones of that earlier, painful accusation: did Garnett still think he saw the world only through the windows of his club? Was he never to be able successfully to put himself in the position of those quite differently placed in life from himself? And Garnett has to make his point yet again, rubbing more salt into the already deep wound; he ends his letter with a final note: 'You have imported the attitude to life of the man-who-has-always-had-a-bank-balance into the soul of a man-who-despises-a-bank-balance, and mixed up the two.'[11]

The answer – or rather answers, for Galsworthy wrote three letters in rapid succession – came immediately. 'I got your letter just now after a nine-hour drive up here, and I daresay I am answering it too soon, but I can't help it because when you are unhappy you want to work it off. I am unhappy because this looks like being the first real split in art between us.'[12] It is easy to see that Garnett did not see what was of paramount importance to Galsworthy. Galsworthy felt that in failing to make Bosinney's motive clear he had failed in his task as a novelist; Garnett felt the inevitable conclusion of the book would be the two lovers eloping, taking with them '£50 and *her* jewels! say £30 worth!'[13] Such an ending would have been abhorrent to Galsworthy. Irene, and her prototype Ada, were proud women who would have scorned the idea of taking anything from their detested husbands; they were also, as Galsworthy emphasizes, passive. What was difficult for Garnett, or indeed any reader of Galsworthy, to appreciate, was the absolute horror with which Galsworthy viewed the situation of a woman who is forced into the sexual act with a man she does not love, and the despairing (even suicidal) effect such an event would have on a man who loved her as Bosinney did Irene; a 'great mental shock', Galsworthy calls it, 'perhaps the greatest mental shock a man terribly in love can have'.[14] An almost exactly comparable event occurs in his last novel, *Over the River*, when Clare is unwillingly bedded by Jerry Corven, the husband she has left, an event that throws her would-be lover, Tony Croom, into the deepest despair. One can only deduce that Galsworthy had had similar experiences in his own life with Ada, and that while she was still living with her first husband she must have stirred the imagination of her over-sensitive young lover with harrowing tales of her marital life.

These were the details that disturbed Galsworthy in his friend's criticism, but more than this he was concerned that Garnett should have misunderstood his ultimate motives. The end, as he had conceived it, leaving the lovers parted forever, was, he argued, the more complete defeat of 'Forsytism'. Forsytism, the philosophy of property and ownership, was, as we shall see later in greater detail, the specific target which he now set out to attack, and he felt that it was more completely defeated by leaving the apparent victory with Soames, showing what '*an empty Shell*' property is.[15]

The letters that Galsworthy wrote to Garnett from the Tyrol during the first fortnight in June show him gradually conceding to his friend's judgement as to the end of Bosinney. 'I have been working in advance on Part III and I think I am meeting your point as to B's suicide. I feel that you were very right; as the thing was written the technique was grievously in fault and, after all, in fiction there is no such thing as psychology.'[16] And in his next letter to Mrs Garnett: 'I know you will rejoice to hear that I have thrown up the sponge. Between you, you have made me believe that Bosinney is really alive, and not merely a figure – haunting the book for the purposes of the story.' Later, in the same letter, he explains: 'When I finished the book at Sorrento I was so spun out that I couldn't even write a letter for five or six weeks; and I think the knowledge of this has contributed to the desperation with which I clung at first to Bosinney's suicide.'[17] So compromise is reached: Bosinney falls beneath the wheels of a cab in deep fog, and it is left to the reader to decide whether he died by chance or design. It is strange that Garnett found so much to object to in Bosinney, for though he is not a satisfactorily conceived character, Garnett's son, David, wrote in his biography that his father was in fact the original. But can this be so? Galsworthy in a letter of 2 June makes the comment: 'By the way, though this is perhaps against me, we both think here that the man I originally took the idea of Bosinney from is as likely a man *qua* temperament to commit suicide as we know; but, as I say, that amounts to nothing because men of all temperaments do it.'[18]

This correspondence, the fate of Bosinney, the implications of his character, must have been the subject of endless conversations between John and Ada in their various hotels in the Tyrol, and what they said no doubt formed the basis of the arguments put forward in his letters to Garnett. But at last the book was once again completed with its new ending, and on 13 July Galsworthy could write triumphantly to Garnett:

I've just sent off the MS. from here in *one parcel* (but uninsured), hoping it may reach you quicker than if insured. I've sent it c/o Duckworth. If it doesn't arrive by Wednesday it will be sad. But to send it as registered letters, it appears, would have cost about £3. I can't understand the Postal arrangements in this country, they seem to vary every week. We walked down here carrying the blessed thing in a bag, like a cat we intended to drown. We walked nearly four hours to find a reliable post office, and are just going back.[19]

All went smoothly with the arrangements for publication, and by 26 July Garnett was able to report to Galsworthy that Pawling of Heinemann would '*certainly* accept *The Man of Property* on your terms'. But Garnett still had reservations about the last chapters – 'the workmanship is uninspired and tame' – and he felt that later Galsworthy would need to work over them.[20]

Was it an olive branch that Galsworthy was extending when he wrote a PS to a letter written to Garnett in January the following year? 'P.S. Jan. 6–7 – Dear Edward, I forgot to say would you mind if I dedicated *The Man of Property* to you? Don't hesitate to say so. – Yours Jack.'[21] It was a sturdy olive branch if so, for Galsworthy must have dearly longed to give the book to Ada, his Irene, now in fact his wife.

Chapter 15

The Man of Property II

Galsworthy expressly wished to delay the publication of his new novel until he and Ada were married, and there were still several months to go before they could hope for her divorce to be made absolute. It was a no-man's-land in which they lived, poised rootlessly between the old life and the new, travelling from one hotel to the next: from the Tyrol alone Galsworthy wrote to Garnett from no less than six different hotels. The final dispatch of *The Man of Property*, and its acceptance by Heinemann, may have signalled the moment for a new phase to their journey, for at the end of July Galsworthy is writing to Garnett informing him of their plans: 'We leave here on July 29th, train to Sterzing, walk thence over the Janfen-joch to Merna, and on Aug. 2nd drive thence over the Stelvio to Bormio and Pontresina to the railway, by which we go to Mannheim, take the Rhine there and come right down to Rotterdam; and then take up headquarters at The Hague or Scheveinnjen [sic], and see Holland.'[1]

He also had extensive plans for writing; it was a moment when vistas stretched ahead. In his personal life and in his writing life, there seemed no limit to what he might achieve. 'I write now however to ask your advice on another matter,' he wrote to Garnett.

At the very back of my mind, in the writing of this book (and indeed of *The Island Pharisees*, but put that aside) there has always been the feeling of the utter disharmony of the Christian religion with the English character; the cant and humbug of our professing it as a *national* religion. Not an original idea this, but a broad enough theme to carry any amount of character study. I've got it in my mind now to carry on this idea for at least two more volumes. Just as the theme of the first book is the sense of property, the themes of the next (or rather the national traits dealt with) are (1) the reforming spirit, (2) the fighting spirit – done of course through story and definite character study. The theme of the third book would be the spirit of advertisement, self-glorification, and impossibility of seeing ourselves in the wrong, and it would deal with the Boer war (of course only through character, not in story). I call the second book *Danae* and the third *The Mouth of Brass*. Six years elapse between each book, and I carry young Jolyon through all three as commentator. I have my figures for the second book, but only the idea for the third.

Now what I want to ask you is this.

Is it worth while to put after the title *The Man of Property*, etc., some such addition as this:

National Ethics – I

or Christian Ethics – I

or Tales of a Christian People – I

in other words to foreshadow a series upon that central idea?[2]

We have not Garnett's answer to this letter. Presumably he resisted the pretentious sub-titles, or Galsworthy's sense of proportion told him that to sub-title a series of novels 'Christian Ethics' would not do. In fact *The Man of Property* can be seen as the first in two entirely different series: it is the first of the social novels, followed by *The Country House* and then by *Fraternity* and *The Patrician*. But the Forsyte family would not die; they were too close to Galsworthy and refused to be dismissed in a single volume dealing with the subject of property. It was with relief, after the troubled early years of the 1914–18 war, and in a more tranquil mood than he had experienced for a considerable time – 'On the whole I think the most tolerable time since the war started,' he wrote on 27 March 1917 – that he picked up his pen to write 'The Indian Summer of a Forsyte', a story which brought the whole clan back to life, to live successfully on for another five volumes.

But all this lay in the future, and for the moment the Galsworthys journeyed on, on what must have seemed at times like a lengthy pre-marriage honeymoon, waiting until the proceedings of the law would declare Ada a free woman. Despite the constant travelling Galsworthy did manage to start work on his next novel. 'I've begun a new novel, and feel like a puppy learning to swim. That early stage until your characters have set is so lacking in conviction, that it's a wonder one ever does anything at all,' he wrote to Ralph Mottram at the end of July from the Hapsburger Hof, Meran.[3] The novel was of course the first draft of *The Country House*.

Early in September the Galsworthys returned to England; the time when Ada's divorce could be made absolute was now very near. Needless to say the wedding, a mere regularization of the existing state of affairs, was to be completely private. On 23 September, the first day of her freedom, they were married. 'The deed is done,' Ada wrote to Mrs Mottram in Norwich. 'Yesterday at 10.30 a.m. we were very simply married before the Registrar of St. George's, Hanover Square, and at 11.15 making our way towards Addison Road with 14 boxes and bundles . . . and tomorrow settle in at the little house which is still decidedly chaotic but inhabitable . . .'[4]

In fact they spent the first weekend of their 'married' life at Littlehampton, a place they were often to retreat to in times of stress, for it is from there that John wrote an exuberant note to Ralph Mottram: 'Fini-fini as the French Girl said as she jumped on the bed after saying her prayers. We go home on Monday to 14 Addison Road.'[5]

What was married life for the Galsworthys really going to be like? After ten years of his half-life with Ada, and eight months constantly in her company in foreign hotels, John must have had some idea of the difficulties and even limitations of the woman with whom he was to spend his life. Her health was certainly not good, though in the light of her comparatively healthy widowhood of some twenty-three years it would seem that John's constant attentiveness and the endless holidays abroad did nothing to improve it; her complete dedication to him and his work, though in many ways a wonderful thing, must at times have been claustrophobic. Above all, she had not the vision of John, nor the generosity to let his spirit rove where hers could not follow. The dog on the lead was too big for her, but in the end it was the dog who had to diminish in size.

But whatever his private fears may have been, John was not the man to show them. Their devotion had not been 'through fire' for nothing; from their ordeal was born a union that nothing would ever sever. Moreover, now, at this very moment, was coming to fruition the true child of their partnership, their story, a novel that was a real *tour de force*, *The Man of Property*, and the first months of marriage were devoted to finalizing its passage into the world.

Life began for Ada on 23 September 1905, or at least what went before she wished to relegate to fiction.* With scissors she cut away

* This 'combined' diary was probably a précis of diaries kept by herself and John, the originals then being destroyed. Originally it went back to 1896, but the earlier pages were removed at a subsequent date, and it is just possible to make out the dates.

the earlier pages of her diary, and the first official entry begins: 'Winter of 1905–1906 spent at Bold Head, Devon, correcting proofs of the novel *The Man of Property*, and began to write 1st play, *The Silver Box*. Becoming more and more dissatisfied with the beginning of *The Country House*, which had then not even its subsequent title.'[6]

But apart from the proofs of *The Man of Property* Galsworthy had the far more difficult problem of dealing with the personal implications of his new book, and the reactions of his family to finding themselves so recognizably portrayed. On his return to England in September he received a letter from his sister Lilian, explaining the alarm that she and her sister felt on reading the book. Apart from recognizing many of the portraits, she was amazed by the openness with which her brother was now telling the story of Ada's unhappy marriage. These matters were so personal, so intimate; if they had to be made known to the world, should it not be under the disguise of a pseudonym? Her letter no longer exists; it is from his reply that one can deduce the contents of hers:

The first thing that strikes me on a whole review of the letter is that it is the cry of one temperament to a very different one. I have long known that in essence of outlook we are very unlike. We have much of the same sympathy, much of the same width, but at the very bottom there is a difference. You have not the vein of realism, cynicism, satiricism, impersonalism, call it what you will, that I have. You are an optimist, an idealist. I am not an optimist, nor a pessimist, and if I have ideals they are not yours.

Then artistically we are not the same in our cravings. To put an example, you would have a contrast so given as to enlist the reader on one side, and against the other. I don't feel like this. I feel more like a sort of chemist, more cold, more dissective, always riding a philosophical idea, and perverting, if you like, my values to fit it. I start out from the thesis that property is not exactly a christian, a decent idea, I perhaps expect people to see this; in any case I deal always negatively, destructively, I can't bear the idea of the beautiful character, it seems to me so obvious, commonplace and disgusting, above all eminently unphilosophical. This may be, probably is, a defect, but it *is*, and can't be got over. I cannot take the human being so seriously. There are things I like, there are things I love in people, but if I start out to treat them be sure I shall do more than justice to their darker side. This is my genre. I can't alter it. I daresay it grieves you.

. . . And first as to the personal question. Do you really think it matters? Apart from yourself, Mab and Mother (who perhaps had better not read the book) who really knows enough or takes enough interest in us to make it more than a two days wonder that I should choose such a subject? Who knows enough even to connect A with I, especially as I have changed her hair to gold?

. . . This book is undoubtedly my best so far, very undoubtedly, which brings me to the real difficulty of your letter.

Practically you say: Don't publish. At all events for years. You speak, if I may say so, dear girl, cheerfully upon a very delicate subject.

The alternative to not publishing now is publishing never. The book in two months (practically now) will be dead in my mind, never to come to life again. It has been slowly dying since May. Another book is begun. I merely compare the other books I have written. None of these could I look at again for the purpose of alteration; the plants have died for want of ordinary everyday watering. So with this. I can never alter it.

This clears the ground.

The question is, do you and Mab feel strongly enough that the book is sacrilege to consign it to the flames? I can't publish it anonymously, because that would mean publishing the present book and the one after also anonymously – 'Young Jolyon' and others running through all.[7]

This is only a small portion of the long letter he wrote to his sister in defence of his novel; no one, he argues, outside the 'family cradle' will recognize the portraits in the book, and it is only because she is 'criticizing with the family eye, feeling with the family pulse' that she feels as she does about it.

How far Lilian was converted by her brother's arguments we cannot know, but the book appeared, unaltered from the manuscript that she read, and under the author's own name, on 23 March 1906.

Galsworthy's younger sister, Mabel Reynolds, in her *Memories* of her brother, is very firm on the matter of identifying the characters of the Forsyte Saga with her family:

to my mind, apart from the one acknowledged instance of Old Jolyon, too much has been made of the supposed likeness to real persons of the 'Forsyte' family in general. My brother did indeed observe and adapt many typical characteristics and idiosyncrasies of his relations, but in every case the individual underwent such drastic alteration at his hands that to label any one person in the 'Saga' as definitely 'taken' from any one relative in real life is to give a false impression.[8]

But by the time Mabel wrote her book thirty years had passed since she and her sister first read the typescript of *The Man of Property*: time had healed many of the wounds, her parents had long since been dead, and John at the time of his death, two years before she wrote, had lost almost all resemblance to the 'angry young man' who first wrote of the Forsytes. John Galsworthy, O.M., had become respectable and establishment; there is no anger in his last books, no cruel, biting portraits, but compromise and some sadness. Galsworthy had learnt, as others had done before him, that society may see itself in a mirror, may see its injustices and follies derided, but will merely shrug its shoulders and carry on as before.

The Man of Property was a success; it was the first torch in the darkness. *The Island Pharisees* had proclaimed its message but it had failed as a work of art. The Forsytes, on the other hand, were real people; they lived and walked in their world; they carried conviction. But at the same time they were allegorical; like the characters of John Bunyan or Dickens, they were people of darkness and light.

As Galsworthy said so often, his was essentially the 'negative method'; he reiterated this in his letter to Lilian: 'I deal always negatively, destructively, I can't bear the idea of the beautiful character.'[9] So it is that Soames, the 'Man of Property', towers above all others in the book. His acquisitiveness, his possessiveness, are shown in their full horror, and yet he has pathos; we share his agony as he rattles the handle of Irene's bedroom door. 'His hunger could only be appeased by his wife, inexorable and frightened, behind these shut doors. No other woman could help him.' By comparison young Jolyon, the good man, is a pale character. He was envisaged at this stage as a 'commentator' running through the trilogy which Galsworthy suggested in his letter to Garnett, and this indeed is his role in this first book of the sequence.

The true 'hero' of *The Man of Property* is a composite one; it is the family itself, the clan of Forsytes, a great octopus-like creature of which every member is part of the whole, each tentacle bearing the same characteristics and sharing the same blood: even the good Jolyon, cousin to Soames, has Forsytean characteristics of 'possession', which he despises in himself, and Fleur, a child of the third generation, is prepared to sacrifice all on the altar of possession.

The book opens magnificently with the family gathering at Old Jolyon's to celebrate the engagement of June, Jolyon's daughter by his first marriage, to the architect Bossiney, the scene in which Galsworthy firmly places his family in the foreground, establishing its importance to his theme. Moreover, the family stretches back through generations of dead Forsytes, Devonshire yeomen, and lastly the father of the present generation, 'Superior Dosset', who came to London to found the family fortunes, and it stretches forward through their wealth and property.

> Those privileged to be present at a family festival of the Forsytes have seen that charming and instructive sight – an upper middle-class family in full plumage . . . He has been admitted to a vision of the dim roads of social progress, has understood something of patriarchial life, of the swarmings of savage hordes, of the rise and fall of nations. He is like one who, having watched a tree grow from its planting – a paragon of tenacity, insulation, and success, amidst the deaths of a hundred other plants less fibrous, sappy, and persistent – one day will see it flourishing with bland, full foliage, in an almost repugnant prosperity, at the summit of its efflorescence.
>
> On June 15, late in the eighties, about four of the afternoon, the observer who chanced to be present at the house of old Jolyon Forsyte in Stanhope Gate, might have seen the highest efflorescence of the Forsytes.

From the general the scene closes in, giving us the exact date and time and place; like a man focusing on a detail in a landscape, Galsworthy admits us into the centre of his family, his principal character. In the foreground there are the immediate protagonists, Irene, Soames and Bosinney, and yet compared to the family their affairs are ephemeral. They are actors on a stage, playing out their brief lives, their loves and hates, but ultimately, stronger than they are, it is the family who will remain when they are silent.

The story of Irene is, of course, the story of Ada; in his letter to

Lilian Galsworthy admits this, though naïvely he professes to believe that she will not be recognizable, except by a few members of the family who know the facts of his affair because 'I have changed her hair to gold'. That Ada herself completely accepted the identification is shown beyond doubt in a letter she wrote many years later to Rudolf and Vi Sauter: 'Rosalie was here yesterday, and brought news of the death of "Soames" (Major Galsworthy). She says that two days before his death the local parson called and wished to ministrate. But the Major said: "No, and tell him the funeral will be at three." Witty to the last.'[10] One must also assume that in retrospect the Major did not seem so boring as he had done during their brief years of marriage.

Briefly *The Man of Property* is the story of Irene's fight to free herself from her unhappy marriage to Soames Forsyte and of Soames's attempt to keep her. He sees her as his possession, a part of his property, and to make her more content he plans and builds the magnificent house at Robin Hill, of which Bosinney is the architect. Bosinney, though betrothed to young Jolyon's daughter, June, falls in love with Irene, captivated by her irresistible charms. The book ends in tragedy: Bosinney, distraught because Soames has forced his unwanted love on Irene, walks out into a deep fog, falls beneath the wheels of a cab and is killed. It was on this point that Garnett so strongly criticized the book, maintaining that no man would take his life for such a reason, and, in the end, whether Bosinney meant to kill himself or not is left deliberately vague.

This is only a brief outline of the main plot of the book, but it is the structure within which Galsworthy set up his case against the philosophy of life he called Forsytism. It is young Jolyon, the 'commentator', who warns Bosinney of the dangers of setting himself against the Forsytes and their property:

'A Forsyte,' replied young Jolyon, 'is not an uncommon animal. There are hundreds among the members of this club. Hundreds out there in the streets; you see them wherever you go!'

'And how do you tell them, may I ask?' said Bosinney.

'By their sense of property. A Forsyte takes a practical – one might say a commonsense – view of things, and a practical view of things is based fundamentally on a sense of property. A Forsyte, you will notice, never gives himself away.'

'I should like,' said young Jolyon, 'to lecture on it; "Properties and quality of a Forsyte. This little animal, disturbed by the ridicule of his own sort, is unaffected in his motions by the laughter of strange creatures (you or I). Hereditarily disposed to myopia, he recognizes only the persons and habitats of his own species, amongst which he passes an existence of competitive tranquillity".'

'You talk of them,' said Bosinney, 'as if they were half England.'

'They are,' repeated young Jolyon, 'half England, and the better half, too, the safe half, the three per cent. half, the half that counts. It's their wealth and security that makes everything possible; makes your art possible, makes literature, science, even religion, possible. Without Forsytes, who believe in none of these things, but turn them all to use, where would we be? My dear sir, the Forsytes are the middlemen, the commercials, the pillars of society, the corner stones of convention; everything that is admirable!'

But Galsworthy could hit harder, more bitterly, than this. There are moments of such vicious satire in the text that one must wonder what circumstances can have led so mild a man to bite so savagely the hand that fed him? The only answer can be those years when he and Ada lived as outcasts from the society of 'respectable' Forsytes – though it must be emphasized that this did not include his immediate family, his sisters and brother, who immediately welcomed Ada as their sister. To take two examples: first, a description of Bosinney's aunt, Mrs Baynes:

This great and good woman, so highly thought of in ecclesiastical circles, was one of the principal priestesses in the temple of Forsytism, keeping alive day and night a sacred flame to the God of Property, whose altar is inscribed with those inspiring words: 'Nothing for nothing, and really remarkably little for sixpence.'

Or young Jolyon's description of Forsytism:

Nothing in the world is more sure to upset a Forsyte than the discovery that something on which he has stipulated to spend a certain sum has cost more. And this is reasonable, for upon the accuracy of his estimates the whole policy of his life is ordered. If he cannot rely on definite values of property, his compass is amiss; he is adrift upon bitter waters without a helm.

It is impossible to do more than give a suggestion of the quality of the book by these few quotations. A novel is essentially a whole and can only be judged by the gradual building up of plot and character. The achievement of the book is amazing – it is so far ahead of *The Island Pharisees* that preceded it, or even of *The Country House* that followed.

It might so easily have been spoiled by its satirical character, or by its 'message', always a dangerous ingredient in a novel, but it has a life of its own, able to carry along its author's earnest desire to instruct and improve the world.

'Book successful . . . excellent reviews,' Galsworthy was able to write to Ralph Mottram in April, with the additional item of news: 'My play is taken at the Court Theatre in the autumn. October, November, December. 8 matinees: evening bill if successful. They are keen about it. It's called the *Silver Box*.'[11] This was indeed success, a success which was noted with some jealousy by his fellow authors. 'Galsworthy is almost more than I the coming man,' Ford Madox Ford wrote to his wife Elsie,[12] and Conrad, in a letter that is mainly full of praise, comments: 'I have also heard that directly on its appearance the book began to be talked about in – journalistic circles! I confess I felt slightly sick at that, till I reflected that the *quality* of your book was too high to be affected by false admirations. And take it from me, my dear Jack, that the *quality* of your work is very high – '[13]

The book was widely reviewed. Marrot notes: 'Out of some forty-odd notices twenty-eight expressed various degrees of enthusiasm, four qualified praise, four hovered over the critical fence without alighting; and a solitary grumbler alone found that "the effect of the book as a whole is somewhat dull and uninteresting".' The most interesting of the notices was that written by Conrad in *The Outlook*: *The Man of Property*, he wrote, 'reveals Mr. Galsworthy's very considerable talent as a writer . . . The foundation of this talent, it seems to me, lies in a remarkable power of ironic insight combined with an extremely keen and faithful eye for all the phenomena on the surface of the life he observes.'[14]

Chapter 16

The Silver Box

The Galsworthys moved into their first home together, 14 Addison Road, immediately after their legal marriage. It was, we are told by Mottram, a very ordinary, almost suburban house as seen from the street, but its small, private garden overlooked Holland Park, so from the rooms it would have seemed almost as if you were living in the country, it was so surrounded by trees and open space. 'Settling into this little house has taken all my energy,' Ada told Mottram. 'It is wonderfully quiet here however, the only sound at the back of the house is the call of pheasants in Holland Park.'[1] Moreover, they were still close to the family dwellings: the Sauters in Holland Park Avenue were near neighbours and John's younger sister, Mabel, now married to Thomas Reynolds, lived at Tor Gardens also just across the park. Ada undoubtedly had the ability to create elegance around her; her drawing-rooms always contained her piano and her music, her collection of delicate china, and 'beautiful pieces of embroidered silk that were always found draping things wherever Ada was'.[2] It was also, Mottram tells us, a very modern house; it contained a bathroom (rare in those days), and linoleum under the carpets to cut down noise, and early morning tea was brought on a tray (also an innovation).[3]

Once again one must remember that there was nothing 'Bohemian' about either of the Galsworthys. John may have derided the Forsytes, but in his own fashion he still lived very much like one; he had no financial problems; bills were paid promptly; meals were served at regular hours by servants who inhabited the basement floor; Ada dressed for dinner and, in the early days of their marriage, John put on 'morning coat and grey trousers'.[4]

Most important of all was the spaniel Chris, whom Ada described as '*the* dog of our life',[5] who slept on the end of John's bed and on the sofas, and who was later to become the subject of *Memories*. The Galsworthys were both devoted to animals; they had no children – according to Rudolf Sauter his uncle would not 'allow' Ada to have children because of her delicate health – and Mottram has said that Chris was almost a 'child' to them. He belonged to that period of their life when they were lovers but still unmarried; when he died Ada was heartbroken. But were they 'sentimental' in their attitude towards animals? John, I would say, definitely was not; it is not sentimentality that enables a man to stand for hours watching animals slaughtered in the most cruel fashion in order that he may write a paper to bring about the more humane slaughtering of animals.

It might be expected that after the long years of wandering from one foreign hotel to another the Galsworthys would have been only too ready to settle down in their new home. By October Ada was beginning to get the place straight, but she was also feeling troubled by the London climate. 'I rush the little house along,' she wrote to Ralph Mottram. 'No really, we are getting tidy. Jack has got a terrible cold, so we gave up our country week-end. Norwich is not quite so black a hole as London during the winter – I don't even enjoy the rust-coloured fog with a copper sun that we had this morning – no, I put up a handkerchief to keep the condemned tickle out of my lungs.'[6] So it was probably Ada's health that decided them once again to move back to hotel life, this time to the Bolt Head Hotel, at Salcombe, Devon.

It was here that they spent the winter of 1905–6, among other things correcting the proofs of *The Man of Property*, and here also that Galsworthy wrote his first play, *The Silver Box* (first titled *The Cigarette Box*). Galsworthy did however find time to take an interest in the political situation: 'We have been vastly excited about the election, did I tell you Jack made the enormous journey to London and back to vote?' Ada wrote to Mottram in February. According to Marrot it was Garnett who first suggested to Galsworthy that he should attempt a play for the newly formed Vedrenne-Barker management; at first the idea was rejected, but the notion stayed in his mind, and in the early months of 1906 he was at work. 'I've been writing a play,' he wrote to Mottram, 'hope to finish it this week. I should like to get it acted, but have little hope. All actor managers get about 40 plays a week to look at and I have no reason to believe I can write a play better than anybody else.'[7]

Galsworthy was pessimistic about his chances; the speedy acceptance of *The Silver Box* must be almost unique in the history of the theatre. The play arrived on Saturday, was read on Sunday by both Granville

Barker and Bernard Shaw, and accepted by Barker on Monday.

Galsworthy's decision to write a play at this moment may well have been the consequence of the difficulty he was having with his novel *Danae*. Reading the fragment of this book, which was unwisely published by Ada after his death, it is easy to see why he was disheartened: the novel drags along unhappily; none of the characters come to life; there are too many of them and they are all extremely boring (a few of them were resuscitated in much better spirit for *The Country House*). Young Jolyon lumbers on in his role of 'commentator'; he is an ex-suitor of the heroine Danae, but is now a real hanger-on with no part to play. At the dinner table of Anthony, Danae's father, he tediously holds forth on the failures of Christianity and Society. It was at this point that Galsworthy decided that the bonfire was the only place for this manuscript (though presumably not the only copy). Young Jolyon was also put out to grass for the next fourteen years; he undoubtedly bored his author as well as everyone else at Anthony's dinner party!

So it must have been with some relief that Galsworthy turned away from his novel to write a play. The writing went easily, and early in March Galsworthy is again turning to Garnett for his advice and criticism, which Garnett sent at once and in great detail. (Garnett had himself been writing plays for some time with no success at all. His friend's immediate success must have been slightly galling.) 'It would act very well *as it stands*,' he wrote, 'but much better, if you remodelled certain things.'[8] He then went on to list in great detail all the alterations he felt should be made. Some of these Galsworthy adopted and later, after the play's production, he was able to write to Garnett, 'I notice that two sayings you suggested to me in *The Silver Box* are those which receive the most regular laughter.'[9]

Galsworthy used his plays much more than his novels to be didactic; *The Silver Box* carries its message loud and clear, as did the later plays, *Strife, Justice, The Mob*, or *The Skin Game*. There was a danger that the play would become a sermon rather than an entertainment. Garnett saw this, though he certainly knew his friend too well not to realize that it was an essential part of his character. 'Scene 5 is all right and good technically, but somehow or other, to my mind, it *doesn't* prove your general contention. And I don't like your general contention either – that there is one law for the rich and another for the poor.'[10] But this 'contention' was basic to the whole play. Galsworthy had experience of the law courts. He was certain of his ground and determined, at all costs, to make his point.

The theme of the play is the stealing of the silver cigarette box from the house of John Barthwick, MP. The box is stolen by Jones, the husband of the Barthwicks' charlady. Jones, when drunk, follows the Barthwicks' son, Jack, into the house, has a drink with him, and removes the silver box and also the purse from the handbag of the woman that Jack has been out with, and which Jack has 'stolen' from her in fun. The woman comes to claim her property the next morning and thus the scandal of their son's behaviour is made known to his parents. Mrs Barthwick is a truly fearsome character, a real battle-axe of a woman, but possibly too much of a type to carry much conviction. Edward Garnett at least found her difficult to credit and Galsworthy has to defend her from his criticism: 'As to Mrs Barthwick, you don't seem familiar with the type – a fairly and increasingly common one in the upper-middle and upper class – the grey mare the better horse. The hard mouthed woman. You see them by the dozen in Harrod's Stores, and I could give you several instances from my personal acquaintance. They are uncompromising and have courage.'[11] The climax of the play is the trial in which through the use of influence Jack's theft is concealed from the court, while the wretched Jones who has no influential friends or lawyers is sentenced to imprisonment for theft. His last words are: 'Call this justice? What about 'im? 'E got drunk! 'E took the purse – 'e took the purse but it's '*is money* got 'im off – Justice!'

The play was finally produced at a matinée performance on 25 September 1906. 'You see the great event took place on Tuesday – the play was launched at a well-dressed and interested audience – there have been splendid reviews,' Ada wrote to Mottram.[12]

The success of a play or book, apart from its merit, depends to a great extent on timing; the time was right when John Galsworthy wrote his *Silver Box*; it was the kind of play that people were beginning to want. It was the kind of play that the comparatively new Vedrenne-Barker management were looking for to produce in their matinée bills at the Court Theatre.

C. B. Purdom, biographer of Granville Barker, has said that 'no theatrical enterprise of this century has left a deeper mark upon the theatrical history of London' than the Vedrenne-Barker experiment at the Royal Court Theatre. Granville Barker, a young and idealistic actor, conceived the idea of a theatre of uncommercial drama, a theatre of ideas, that would put on plays such as continental audiences were seeing in the works of Ibsen or Hauptmann (whose play *Biperpelz* was compared by reviewers to *The Silver Box*). He found a backer, J. H. Leigh, a rich amateur actor, who had already purchased the lease of the Royal Court Theatre, and with his manager, J. E. Vedrenne, he was able to put on Bernard Shaw's *Candida* in April 1904. The new drama came like a breath of fresh air blowing through the musty curtains and the stuffy auditoriums of the London theatre, and with the production of *The Silver Box* in September 1906 Galsworthy's name was at once linked with Shaw's as a dramatist of the new theatre of ideas. Critics applauded the realism of his plays, and the fact that they dealt with social problems, especially those which concerned the 'lower orders'; others complained that there was no theme of love or jealousy (*Weekly Dispatch*)!

The World, reviewing *The Silver Box*, went into the failings of the contemporary theatre at some length:

> The chief fault of the English Theatre from the point of view of the thoughtful playgoer, has been its detachment from the intellectual life of our time . . . The unpardonable sin in a playwright is to mumble over worn-out truisms instead of browsing among new ideas. Drama makes so direct an appeal that it calls for an instant response, and drama which is out of touch with the Spirit of the Age is to the mind eager for stimulus as flat as the fen Country, as dead as second-day champagne.
>
> Until Bernard Shaw came along the New Spirit was scarcely reflected by the English Theatre at all . . . Playwrights seemed to live in a world of their own – a world into which ideas never penetrated.
>
> Mr. John Galsworthy, author of the *Silver Box* exudes the new Spirit at every pore. His play is a trenchant criticism of the ideas which still govern the relations between the well-to-do and the needy.

And the *Daily Telegraph* welcomed the new playwright in even more dramatic tones, warning its readers, nevertheless, that he was not going to give them much fun.

Realism stern and gaunt, realism grey and sombre stalked across the stage of the Court Theatre yesterday afternoon, remorselessly dragging in its train a group of woeful characters. Cupboards were ruthlessly thrown open, and from their dark recesses emerged a long array of uncomfortable skeletons . . . this he [John Galsworthy] does with a precision, cleverness, and an honesty that demands the fullest recognition.

The review that gave Galsworthy most pleasure, and which he quoted with triumph to Mottram, was a rather coy piece in the *Lady of Fashion* headed 'The Coming Man': 'We have perhaps found the "coming man" who is to avenge, by his work, the universal slander against the English dramatist, Mr. John Galsworthy.'

These very few quotations, taken from pages of press notices in the book of cuttings that Ada kept for John, give some idea of the amazing reception that was given to *The Silver Box*. He himself was almost exhausted: he had personally supervised the casting of his play, had had endless consultations and correspondence with Granville Barker over the details of its production, and had been present at every rehearsal. (This he was to do during the productions of all his plays, even provincial performances, so that his life when in England tended to become a hectic rushing from one theatre to another.)

John's letter to R. H. Mottram a few weeks later reflects a sense of slight anti-climax: 'The play seems to have struck a good many people . . . the odd thing is I can't tell in the least what it's like. I lost one of my senses during rehearsals, but whether it was the sense of smell or not I don't know. I can't judge anyway.'[13]

Perhaps Galsworthy had already a suspicion that success, the sort of success he was now experiencing for the first time, was not going to bring him what he wanted most; it was going to deter him from his true purpose as an artist, it was going to fill his time and energies, it was going to place him in the public eye, when he longed to be a deeply private person, away on the wild open moors of Dartmoor, or the buttercup fields of Manaton.

But apart from his work on the play, Galsworthy had begun work again on his new novel *The Country House*. He worked steadily at it through the spring and summer, though when they were not travelling they led a hectic life in London. 'We have had a fairly busy week,' Ada wrote modestly to Mottram in January, 'bed about 1 a.m.

for eight or nine nights. We saw Shaw's *Major Barbara* a few nights ago, tremendously interesting, though not much of a play (not as good as *Man and Superman*).'[14] The spring they spent largely in Devonshire, at Ilkley and Manaton, then they were back in London again visiting their friends. 'Went to the Lucas's cottage near Edenbridge on Friday, stayed one night, walked over to the Garnetts, came back home at 11 on Saturday night, and had our dear Hudson to breakfast on Sunday. Since when I feel we're getting into the London treadmill again.'[15] This was mid June; by July they were packing up to go abroad again, once again to the Tyrol which they loved so much. 'Jack's mother goes with us and is going to prove one of those admirable travellers who produce everything from sticking plaster to mousetraps when required. I am one of the other kind.' At that time Ada may have been 'one of the other kind', but later in her life she was to surpass her mother-in-law with the amount of impedimenta she saw fit to carry about with her.[16]

Chapter 17

Writing or Ada?

The year 1906 Galsworthy's first biographer, H. V. Marrot, has called the *Annus Mirabilis* of his subject's life, the year in which the success of *The Man of Property* was followed by the even more resounding acclaim given to *The Silver Box*. It was a peak of artistic achievement such as Galsworthy was never to reach again.

Galsworthy had now proved to himself and the literary world that he had a talent that could take him almost anywhere; he had moreover captured the attention of the reading and thinking public. He was seen as the 'coming man' at this moment even more than those other writers of his generation with whom he was associated, and who saw themselves to some extent as a group, Conrad, Ford Madox Ford, Arnold Bennet, and H. G. Wells: 'Things have moved a little all round this last year,' he wrote to Garnett in August, 'and I feel that we must all rise (!) steadily, and stick together, and do something, for as far as I can see we have the nucleus of a movement, and there's no other moving power about anywhere. And don't let your d —— d literary pessimism brought from Unwin's etc. etc., stand in our way.'[1]

But first Galsworthy had to do something almost impossible to a man of his nature: he had to assert his independence as a writer, independence even from his beloved Ada.

He knew perfectly well what was the ultimate purpose of a writer; he knew that it was an immensely private, almost painful, function; it was the distilling of his most personal experience in such a way that it could be shared and understood by another.

If one comes to ask oneself why anything is written one finds, doesn't one, that it is because certain emotions have been passed through, certain thoughts thought and certain feelings felt, and because there is in us that inspiring and at the same time pathetic desire that others should also know of and share these emotions, and thoughts and feelings. The logical result of this is that to be true and real one must express only what each of us has felt . . . its value is its fidelity to ourselves, our convictions and our emotions, for only so does it go to the heart and convince others that a human being (a brother) like ourselves is speaking.[2]

Later, in 1910, in an essay about another writer, Joseph Conrad, he goes immensely deeply, almost religiously, into the motives behind a work of art. It is in itself a beautiful piece of writing, as well as being instructive as to Galsworthy's realization of what the deepest interpretation of a writer's function could be:

> There is present behind his [Conrad's] art . . . a certain cosmic spirit; a power of taking the reader down below the surface of the earth. He has the power of making the reader feel the inevitable unity of all things that be; of breathing into him a solace that he himself is part of the wonderful unknown. Shakespeare had this power, Turgenev had it, and Charles Dickens had it and Joseph Conrad not among the least.
>
> The Irony of Things is a nightmare weighing on man's life, because he has so little of this cosmic spirit. He has little and the little that he has he frequently distrusts, for it seems to him destructive of the temples that he builds, the gardens that he lays out, the coins that he circulates from hand to hand. He goes in fear of death and of the universe in which he lives, nor can he bear to think that he is bound up with a scheme that seems to him so careless of his own important life.
>
> If at the bottom of our hearts, below all our network of defences, we did not feel uncertainty, we should expire suffocated in the swaddling bands of safety; we could not breathe the stagnant air we try to fill our house with. It is the essence of this writer to let in the wind that blows around the world, bringing to all the savour of the mystery that let it loose.
>
> To understand nothing is to love everything. The moment that we understand, we are no longer curious; but to be curious is to be in love. The man who has the cosmic spirit knows that he will never understand, and he spends his life in love.
>
> The cosmic spirit is not in many men – but in each that has it, there is something of the unethical morality of Nature. They preach that things have no beginning and no end . . . The virtues of their

cosmic spirit are a daring curiosity and correlative courageous resignation.

The cosmic spirit's value to the world is in correspondence to its rarity. The irony of things is the disharmony of things. We jut out here, and jut out there, and there is no rest in us. We seek solutions, raise our flags, work our arms and legs loyally in the isolated fields that come within our vision; but having no real feeling for the whole, the work we do is departmental. The war of the departments is the game we understand, and we spend our lives in keeping up the ball and taking down the score.

Art inspired by cosmic spirit is the only document that can be trusted, the only evidence that Time does not destroy . . . The just envisagement of things is then the first demand we make of art.[3]

This strange but profound essay carries essentially one message: 'The moment that we understand, we are no longer curious; but to be curious is to be in love.' Galsworthy underlines the perpetual sense of mystery and wonder that must be always present in a writer, always alert, informing him like the antennae of an insect, and the death and stagnation that will surround the artist who has lost this sense of mystery and uncertainty: 'we should expire suffocated in the swaddling bands of safety.'

It was here that the dividing line came in Galsworthy's life, on the one side, deep in himself, his questing spirit, mysterious, unknown even to himself, and on the other Ada, 'the swaddling bands of safety'. Unaware that he had to do so, he had to make a perilous choice, himself or Ada. The two could go, as they both wanted, hand in hand, Ada always beside him to discuss and advise. In this path they would find a certain success: books would be written and plays produced; the man would rise steadily to a position of eminence. But was this all that Galsworthy wanted, or in fact what he really wanted? *The Man of Property* was a stepping stone, not the ultimate peak; he aimed to go further, not less far; he had mastered the medium of the novel, but he had not mastered the material within himself, or indeed explored it. But neither the circumstances of his life – the constant travelling, the ever-growing social round – nor in fact the character of Ada, who was to be his constant companion, encouraged him to do so. A determined effort against *her*, a ruthless assertion of self, would have been needed to make this leap into the inner world of his imagination; and it was not in him to do something that would have been not only in some senses selfish but also hurtful to Ada.

But it must be emphasized at this point, and again and again, that his devotion to Ada was real, that their companionship and love was as complete as a human relationship can be. That his two loves, his love for Ada and his love for his writing, were in some senses incompatible is perhaps the tragedy of John Galsworthy.

It is worth quoting the long description of Ada that he wrote in a letter to Garnett:

> I think of her sometimes as a piece of rare silk, with a bloom on it as delicate as that on grapes, but which you can't rub off and spun of filaments, each one of which shines, but subtly and so permanently blended that they can never come apart in colour or form. She is rare, but she is not rare with that obvious kind of rareness which jumps to the eye, and which consists in a person having certain qualities far more rare – it is the rareness and scent of the *fine fleur*, the perfect blend; no extremes in it, no violence. She has the grace and savour of the Cortina peasant woman, together with that something in Reynolds' Countess of Albemarle: both qualities are old. She goes back to Nature, in being as it were the last word of civilisation. She is complex, but you cannot see the complexity because it is so beautifully put together. Permanency is the word to use of her rather than change. She is nymphlike in her soul, and as you know nymphs have an elusive permanence.[4]

For John, Ada was almost a goddess rather than a woman; she was too exquisite, too perfect. He could not get over the fact that this deity had condescended so much for him, had come down from Mount Olympus and been his companion for ten years, and was now his wife. It was a pity for them both that his love had such a quality of worship; he also needed a human being, a warm, ordinary woman, but he scarcely would allow her to be that.

A porter at New College, Oxford, insisted on calling Ada 'M'lady' when John took her there to show her his old college; a child at a house where the Galsworthys were guests commented that Ada was the 'refinedest' visitor they had ever had![5] These two anecdotes tell their own story: the impression that Ada left on those who met her was aristocratic, almost queenly.

There can be no question either as to the sincerity of her love for

John; she was totally devoted and dedicated to him. At a distance, and writing from our own age of female emancipation, one might comment that her concentration on him was almost claustrophobic. He was her entire life; she had always wanted to be the woman behind a writer, to have a writer of her very own, and she had no other end but the success of her husband and his work. When she was not writing his letters for him, or typing his manuscripts, or playing the piano for his pleasure, she became bored, and because she was at times bored she needed distractions that he did not. At Manaton she became restless for the social life of London, or the varying scenes of foreign travel, while he, happy in the place he loved above all others, was totally content, riding his horses, walking on the moors, dreaming his dreams, writing. But Ada became ill; neither the life nor the West Country climate suited her.

Understanding the character of Ada must be a stumbling block to any modern biographer of Galsworthy. She was essentially a woman of her period; by the time Edward VII came to the throne she was nearly forty, thus she had grown up and matured during the latter years of Queen Victoria. She may have shared some of Galsworthy's modern ideas, particularly those relating to marriage, but she was never in any other sense a modern woman. It must be admitted that contemporary accounts of her, her own letters and writings, and Galsworthy's own picture of her as Irene Forsyte, present a character who is unattractive to today's reader. She appears as an artificial woman, delicate both in health and sensibility – what a fuss she makes, is the immediate reaction to Irene's outcry against Soames's ill-treatment, and our sympathies go out to Soames. Similarly, what a fuss Ada made about Major Galsworthy; how many women have married uncongenial husbands without making so much to-do. Was she never to get over her early experience and live happily with the man she loved? The answer to this is no, Ada never did.

But the people who knew Ada, and knew her very well, take an entirely different view. It has been my task to discuss this point with these people in great detail, and they insist that in the presence of Ada one's reaction would be completely different; there was something totally captivating about her, every movement was graceful and delightful. Galsworthy's goddaughter, Dorothy Easton, has described her as 'elusive' and completely unlike anyone else; whether she was welcoming a guest or pouring out a cup of tea she had a way of doing it that was entirely her own. John, of course, more than anyone, was delighted by her; he could not take his eyes off her; her presence was a constant joy to him.

Their partnership was no ordinary one. To Ada, John, in a world of brutal males, was a Sir Galahad, who had rescued her from her poisonous situation with Arthur Galsworthy; she needed protection and John gave her that protection. He had saved her from the vileness of his own sex, and it was of the utmost importance that he should spare her, who was already so wounded, from anything that was coarse or offensive. It is in this light that one should consider the statement made by Dorothy Easton, that it was firmly believed in the family that John and Ada, as Dorothy's grandmother put it, had 'never come together'. This is an astonishing suggestion and one that she herself finds hard to believe; on the other hand she maintains her grandmother was seldom wrong, and moreover it would explain much that is puzzling about John and Ada.

But on balance one must come to the conclusion that on this occasion Dorothy's grandmother must have been wrong: certainly Ada, still shocked by her encounter with Major Galsworthy, was probably always a frigid, even an unwilling lover, and John with his oversympathetic, gentle nature may have kept his demands down to a minimum. This is borne out by a strange symbol, a rounded capital A, that appears from time to time in the diary that John kept from 1910 to 1918; the most feasible explanation for this mark is that it was John's private record of the occasions when he and Ada made love; it was not very often. It is also a fact that they only shared a room in the early years of their married life – but again this was not as uncommon then as it would be today.

If this was their relationship, if it was one in which sex played little part, it may have been that quality that made it so special for Ada. That John could love Ada, as he undoubtedly did, that she could see him as the one man who could love her and yet honour her fastidiousness, may explain that strange aura of devotion and perfection that surrounded them, and of which others were so enormously aware.

Ada was an intelligent woman, and she believed that she wanted her husband to be intellectually free. But there were sides to Galsworthy's character that she did not understand, places in his mind where she could not follow; she did not care for things that were serious or sad, and yet the man she had married was nearly always serious and sometimes very sad.

It was in his poetry that the solitary, inward-looking, almost religious side of his nature found its most faithful expression, but it was in this medium that he received least encouragement from those on whose support he depended. In June 1901 he sent a long poem (some thirty-one verses) to Edward Garnett for his opinion; Garnett's reply must have been totally discouraging: 'I return *The Dream*, which certainly makes an effect on one; but personally I feel it altogether too *outré*. A meretricious method well worked out, would be my verdict. . . . P.S. I candidly own *The Dream* is clever – but I don't like its cleverness: It makes me feel old and prejudiced!'[6] The poem was in fact published in his first collection of verse, *Moods, Songs and Doggerels*, in 1912, but when Ada issued a volume of his Collected Poems after his death she omitted it. 'It dealt with a side of life Ada didn't care for,' Rudolf Sauter told me.

It is a deep, philosophically questing poem; moreover, it discloses the side of Galsworthy that was to have less and less voice in his novels and plays:

> I dreamed. Now God appeared to me,
> And beckoned. Forth, in night, we went
> To where a tall and lonely tree
> With ropes of yew-dark bough was bent.
> And, crowned by fiery sky of stars,
> God said: 'O man! confess thy faith!
> The word thou speakest saves or bars,
> For here are gallows of thy death!'
>
> Yet even while I strove to find
> Breath for my words, to make them live,
> There stabbed such pity thro' my mind
> That I my happy life must give –
> Give up my little day, my all,
> With this my unrepentant breath,
> And watch my choking body fall
> Condemned by my own words to death.

> For surely what I had to tell,
> The doubting story of my trust,
> Denying faith in Heaven or Hell,
> Would make me very gallows-dust
> To this dark God stark standing there,
> So like a tall black shadow flung
> Up high on misty midnight air
> By lighted lanthorn lowly swung.

Like his sister Lilian, Galsworthy had rejected orthodox Christianity as a young man, but he remained fundamentally 'religious' in his view of life. His novels and plays (with the exception of *Fraternity*) say little about his religious thinking; his clerics are on the whole dead characters: the Reverend Hussel Barter of *The Country House* is an overdrawn caricature, Edward Pierson the priest 'hero' of *The Saint's Progress*, whom Galsworthy has attempted to draw sympathetically, a weak and pathetic failure. It is in his poetry, his essays and his letters that we are able to glean an idea of his philosophical searchings, his need to come to terms with life, its cruelty, its pathos and its beauty.

'I am miserably read in Philosophy,' Galsworthy wrote to Thomas Hardy.[7] But this did not mean that he ever became unaware of or uninterested in the fundamental questions raised in his poem: what was the ultimate purpose of man; did it lie in his present existence or would he, in another life, be answerable to a deity? As 'The Dream' tells us, he opted for the former alternative:

> This life again
> I shall not live, and I would have
> My living soul in flower with love
> Of Harmony – that so my death
> Shall be no fall, and no remove,
> But reconcilement's very breath.

This 'love of Harmony' was basic to his whole thinking; he believed at the outset of his writing life that people were making progress towards this end, that they would become more understanding, more humane to one another. This was the end he longed for, this was the 'dream' that was for him irrevocably shattered in 1914.

It was the present moment that he believed in so intensely, the richness of the quality of life in itself: and it was his longing that those less fortunately placed than himself should have the opportunity to live their lives fully that lead to his enormous generosity and charity, a programme of giving and helping that was to reach almost saintly proportions, he pursued it with such determination. It was not good enough for the poor to have 'a pie in the sky'; they must live *now*.

> I would confess that human realisation of a First Cause is to me inconceivable. I am left to acceptance of whatever it may be. Out of mystery we come, into mystery we return; Life and Death, Ebb and Flow; Day and Night, world without end, is all I can grasp. But in such little certainty I see no cause for gloom. Life for those who still have vital instinct in them is good enough in itself even if it lead to nothing; and we humans have only ourselves to blame, if we, alone among animals, so live that we lose the love of life for itself. As for the parts we play, courage and kindness seem to me the only virtues, for they include all that is real in any of the others, alone make human life worth while, and bring an inner happiness.

This, the preface to the Manaton Edition of *The Inn of Tranquillity*, was written for the publication of the edition in 1923. Galsworthy has come a long way from the man who wrote 'The Dream' some twenty years earlier. There is a resignation and an acceptance that is not in the poem: the young man is asking questions, he is rebellious against his fate; the older man has accepted that there are no answers, only courage to live one's life, kindness to help others live theirs.

The war, as we shall see later, as well as age, had much to do with the changed mood with which he came to regard life. He lost heart; it became harder to believe after 1914 that mankind was essentially good. 'Don't abandon Shelton; he's your creation, your embodied conscious, your unrestful spirit going about on the earth,'[8] Conrad wrote to Galsworthy in a letter discussing the first draft of *Fraternity*, the novel which more than any other fictionalizes Galsworthy's philosophy. Galsworthy didn't exactly abandon Shelton, but his 'unrestful spirit' became less restless. 'As one gets older, one no longer takes such a serious and tragic view of things; rather one is struck by the irony, the humour in them,' Galsworthy told Leon Schalit.[9]

In fact this is not strictly true; his novels certainly became less serious and less tragic, but the writer himself became sadder and more stricken, and where his pen could, and should, have become an outlet for his inner feelings, which bordered on despair, it became a traitor to him, writing away about matters that were often trivial and insignificant; his books became lightweight, while an inner tragedy burned within him. It is here that Ada failed him: she was not to see the man suffering, and yet he could write nothing that she did not see; each page as he wrote it was submitted to her scrutiny. But again it would be wrong to blame Ada entirely or even largely. In his own character, in its very virtues, were inhibitions that forbade the writing that he needed to write for his own peace of mind, for his own growth as a writer. Courage, he believed, was the highest virtue, courage – which could be called, less kindly, the 'stiff upper lip' – and a courageous man does not pour his suffering over the pages of a book, or even speak of them to another human being; he bears bravely and silently that which is hurting him. Hardy, Henry James, Ford Madox Ford, could all fictionalize their sadness; Galsworthy could not.

Chapter 18

Success and Failure

The autumn of 1906 saw the Galsworthys back in London, their stay punctuated by visits to Littlehampton to escape the London fogs. Galsworthy was hard at work; his double success as novelist and playwright ensured that from now on there would be a ready market for anything he wrote. His new novel *The Country House*, having recovered from its false start as *Danae*, was going well, the play *Joy*, which was to follow up the success of *The Silver Box*, less so; it was destined to be a weak, lifeless piece.

The Galsworthys' lives were now set in the pattern that they were to follow for the next eight years, and those years were probably their happiest and most successful. In London they led an increasingly social life, mixing not only with other writers but with people from society and politics. Frequently they escaped from London, to Devonshire, where John, above all places, loved to be, to Littlehampton, the seaside place that appealed particularly to Ada, or abroad. Galsworthy's ability to write in any place and under more or less any circumstances has often been commented on, and when one considers the long train journeys that they made, even within England, and the many hotels in which they stayed, one realizes that this ability to work anywhere must have been the one factor that made his career and his enormous output possible. He could settle in almost any place, his blotter on his knee, his pen in his hand (he always used a J nib), and, cutting himself off from his surroundings, he wrote. For whether he was in America, in the south of France or at home in Devon, he wrote of England and English people; almost never did he use a foreign setting. He travelled as a tourist, observing the foreign scenes around him, but in his imagination he was still in England, with his very English characters.

The social whirl in London grew; they were entertained by London hostesses. E. F. Benson gives an amusing account of a dinner party given by Lady St Helier: 'Rarely, but very rarely was she not quite up to date, for once she leaned across the table to Mr. Galsworthy, who was sitting isolated between two divergent conversations and said, "We've been talking about plays, Mr. Galsworthy. Why don't you write a play? I'm sure you could." It was quite true that he could; *The Silver Box* had come out a week or two before, and we thought that he had already proved his capacity.'[1] In January (1907) they lunched with the Shaws and found 'G.B.S. very garrulous and affable'. 'He made me very furious,' Ada wrote to Mottram 'and I liked him much. It's impossible to put him down in words.' On Good Friday 1909 Arnold Bennet records in his diary: 'Dinner at Ford Madox Hueffer's [Ford's]. John Galsworthy and wife there. Slight gêne on my part on first encounter with Galsworthy, seeing my recent articles on him. However we did well together, and he asked me to dinner.'[2]

These are only a few social occasions of particular interest: it is worth quoting Ada's notebook both because of the interest and the length of her list of people they met, and because it mattered so much to Ada – she enjoyed social life and she was good at it. 'During the years 1905 to 1910, the literary men and others with whom J.G. most associated were: Joseph Conrad, Edward Garnett, Ford Maddox Hueffer [Ford], E. V. Lucas, W. H. Hudson, Granville Barker, Gilbert Murray, J. M. Barrie, William Archer, G. B. Shaw, John Masefield, R. A. Scott-James, A. J. Legge, C. F. G. Masterman, Gilbert Cannan, A. Sutro, Max Beerbohm, Arnold Bennett, H. G. Wells (last 2 slightly) Laurence Housman, H. W. Nevinson, H. W. Massingham, A. J. Hobson, W. J. Locke, H. Vachell, Anthony Hope, A. E. W. Mason, Ed. Gosse, Sidney Colvin, J. W. Hills, Charles Roden Buxton, Arthur Ponsonby, A. Birrell, Lord Crewe, Winston Churchill, Charles Trevelyan (last 4 slightly).' There is then a slight pause for breath, and Ada distinguishes the next batch, 'Acquaintances made of Asquith, Arthur and Gerald Balfour, Sidney Webb, Lloyd George, Sir Charles Dilke, Col. Seely, Lord Mc. Donnell, Robert Harcourt . . . Sir George and Lady Lewis, Mr. and Mrs. M. Crackanthorpe, Lady St. Helier, Mr. and Mrs. Daffarn, Percy Vaughan, Dr. and Mrs. Philpot, Mr. Herbert Gladstone, Sir A. Pinero, Duchess of Sutherland.'

It is a formidable list, which must include most of literary society during the first decade of the century, and it leaves no doubt as to the extent to which the Galsworthys had 'arrived', how little stigma can have remained of the scandal of their pre-marriage liaison.

It was always with some relief that Galsworthy left London for the country, leaving behind him the round of social entertainment or the strain of the production of a new play. 'It is nice to get to sea air and *The Country House* once more. I lose the sense of rehearsal at last,' he wrote to Garnett from Littlehampton.[3]

In the spring of 1907 they were travelling round Dorset: 'We enjoy ourselves quite well here, went a long walk on Thursday to Seaton along the cliffs; and then drove on to Beer – Seaton is rotten but Beer is a jolly little old-world place. Charmouth we went to and found very nice. Lyme itself we don't care for – it's too *grey*, and the natives are so d —— d ugly. In fact we miss the richness of Devon, and we're going to move on Tuesday.'[4] But this they decided against, for a few days later Galsworthy is writing from Littlehampton, 'Somehow we felt that this time of year is too dead and early for Devon, and came here in a negative spirit of certainty. At present it's blowing big guns from the NW. and quite discomfortable outside.'[5]

The winter's journeyings were not a great success; they failed to find a haven that suited Ada's delicate health. 'You're absolutely the only person who seems to realize that winter *is* a calamity to me. I believe everyone thinks I put it on a bit,' Ada confided to Mottram in January.[6]

Back in London they were able to take up their interests again. It was inevitable that Galsworthy, with his enormous concern for people, should take an interest in the current social movements for reform. He and Ada were always interested in and sympathetic to the Suffragette Movement, though her account of one of their meetings is not un-critical: 'We went to the Suffrage meeting on Friday night . . . a lady, Miss Christabel Pankhurst, ought to be muzzled for a hysterical muddler. She yelled for help from men in a perfectly sympathetic audience and then said, "if men won't fight for us we must fight for ourselves",' Ada wrote to Mottram in March 1907. And later in the summer they 'went to a Fabian Society soiree last night. I don't think I was much impressed. I would rather see Fabians at work than at play. But we had Morris dances and Somerset Songs which made the evening joyous.' Many of their circle were actively involved in the movement. 'Miss May Sinclair and myself,' wrote Violet Hunt, 'were drafted to hold collecting boxes for 3 whole days in High St. Station . . . We had asked all our friends and editors and readers to come and cheer us up as we stood pilloried and they backed us up splendidly. John Galsworthy sauntered along and tipped us immeasureably and gallantly & Mr L. Houseman & Mr F. MF [Ford Madox Ford].'[7]

During this year (1906) the work that Galsworthy completed is amazing; he had a new, almost dangerous, confidence in himself. *The Country House*, once a new start had been made, went along with exceptional ease; by November it was finished and dispatched to Edward Garnett, who at once heralded it as a masterpiece:

> It's *splendid*! Congratulations. I think *The Country House* is a great advance, artistically. I feel this chiefly because the author is so much more in sympathy with his characters, so much fairer to them than to the people in *The Man of Property*. Then the writing is brilliant. You've quite surpassed yourself in many pages. What I like specially is the romantic feeling in most of the chapters. You have a great sense of the poetry of life coming in all the time, like the wind from an open window.
>
> . . . Altogether my dear fellow I've never read anything of yours that has so convinced me. You seem to me to have purged away matter, and ethic – and to have shown us life through a very perfect medium. Your language is admirable.
>
> A thousand congratulations. The book should live.[8]

The criticisms he made were very few, and, with none of the agonizing months of revision that Galsworthy had experienced with his previous novels, the manuscript of *The Country House* must have gone straight to the printers. It was published by Heinemann on 2 March 1907, and re-printed twice that month, and again in April.

Generally the new novel was well received, but the letters from his other friends were more critical and less enthusiastic than Garnett's had been. H. G. Wells disliked it: 'I think you are much better as a play-wright than as a novelist because you paint into the corners so and have no illuminating omissions. And your range is narrow. You seem to look at things from the point of view of a very limited class indeed, and I miss your irony – '[9] And E. V. Lucas, though he enjoyed it, found it 'not so remarkable' as *The Man of Property*, 'but the air is clearer, and I have no doubt it will sell better'.[10] There was a characteristic letter from Arnold Bennett: 'You are one of the most cruel writers that ever wrote English. This statement I will die for. I don't know what made me read the book again, unless it was curiosity to penetrate your future . . . I tinglingly admire your stuff and that it enormously "intrigues" me . . . But I do seriously object to your attitude towards your leading characters.'[11]

Galsworthy himself was less certain about his new book. 'Garnett pronounces it the best thing I've done. I don't think I believe him. I want to, but I'm not able.'[12] Perhaps Galsworthy already knew that he had reached the summit of his achievement, that despite the acclaim he was receiving and was to continue to receive, the next book, the book that would truly be a step forward, would never be written.

Certainly *The Country House*, whatever Garnett thought, was a less good book than its predecessor. It had not the originality of *The Man of Property*, which created, as a certain type of great book does, a new world – for the world of the Forsytes was to take its place beside other great literary worlds. It was a new landscape, perhaps less powerful, or less moving, than that of Hardy or the Brontës, more comparable to that of Jane Austen or Trollope, where a certain class in society is looked at with a satirical eye, a picture drawn on a slant. In *The Man of Property* Galsworthy got the angle exactly right; it was neither so distorted as to promote disbelief, nor yet, as in the later Forsyte books, so little distorted as to give the books an ordinaryness that the first of the series had not.

The Country House is a good book, but not an exceptional one. The Pendyces, country squires of a family such as Galsworthy's mother came from, were people whom their author knew far less well than his town-living, property-developing Forsytes. There are some outstanding pieces of writing in the book – the character of Mrs Pendyce (based in some part on Galsworthy's mother) is beautifully and sensitively drawn – and the book has that essential quality of a good novel, that it holds the attention of the reader. It is a very professional piece of writing and a satisfactory successor to *The Man of Property*. But writers, unreasonably, expect each new book to be better than the one before it, and they are disappointed if it is not.

Essentially *The Country House* was to do for the country what *The Man of Property* did for the town. The dramatic situation of *The Country House* is similar to that in the earlier novel, the scandal arising from George, the son of the Pendyce family, falling in love with a married woman, Helen Bellow, and the way the characters react and ultimately deal with the situation. The Pendyce family are country squires, entrenched in the ways of the country and in their inherited position as rulers in a mini-kingdom; above all they are opposed to any sort of change, they are obstinate and determined to stick to the ways of the past; this attitude Galsworthy (rather irritatingly) calls 'Pendycitis'.

Galsworthy's obsession with the state of the unhappily married woman is both the wealth and poverty of his writing: it was the impetus which gave writing such as *The Man of Property* its strength, but it was also a crippling defect that he could seldom escape from the theme or find any other which he could treat with such effect.

But apart from this similarity of plot the two novels are entirely different in tempo and atmosphere. *The Country House* is altogether a mellower and gentler book, the ways of the country being treated with an almost loving nostalgia. This was the life that Galsworthy loved, the life that he would have led if his conscience and Ada had not bade otherwise; the race-course and the shooting field are treated by one who has experienced to the full the pleasures of such sports:

> George felt the ground with his feet, and blew a speck of dust off his barrels, and the smell of oil sent a delicious tremor darting through him. Everything, even Helen Bellow, was forgotten. Then in the silence rose a far-off clamour; a cock pheasant, skimming low, his plumage silken in the sun, dived out of the green and golden spinney, curled to the right, and was lost in undergrowth. Some pigeons passed over at a great height. The tap-tap of sticks beating against trees began; then with a fitful rushing noise a pheasant came straight out. George threw up his gun and pulled. The bird stopped in mid-air, jerked forward, and fell headlong into the grass sods with a thud. In the sunlight the dead bird lay, and a smirk of triumph played on George's lips. He was feeling the joy of life.

This is an autobiographical passage, recalling the pleasures Galsworthy had so often experienced as a young man, the shooting holidays in Scotland, the vacations spent on the grouse moors of his college friends. He had been an excellent shot, but the sport was not compatible with his compassionate nature and his love of animals. In the same account of the day's shooting he describes how a wounded hare cries out 'like a tortured child, which some men do not like'. He was himself such a person. In his sketch *Memories* about the spaniel Chris he explains what happened: 'It was strictly in accordance with the perversity of things, and something in the nature of calamity that he [Chris] had not been ours one year, when there came over me a dreadful but over-mastering aversion from killing those birds and creatures of which he was so fond as soon as they were dead.' But characteristically, aware of his dog's sporting instincts and training, Galsworthy sent the spaniel each year to Scotland to join a shooting party to indulge *his* pleasure in the sport that his master could no longer enjoy.

Arnold Bennett exaggerated when, having read *The Country House*, he called Galsworthy a 'cruel writer'. It is not a harsh book; in fact Galsworthy has considerable pity for his characters. He sees very clearly the smallness of their world, the pathos with which Horace Pendyce strides across the stage, completely unaware of the limitations of his character. As he reads the Lesson in church, 'he is hypnotized by the sound of his own voice, he was thinking: "This Lesson is well read by me, Horace Pendyce. I am Horace Pendyce – Horace Pendyce. Amen, Horace Pendyce".' Or later, as he receives the news that his son George is

A gambler!

To him, whose existence was bound up in Worsted Skeynes, whose every thought had some direct or indirect connexion with it, whose son was but the occupier of that place he must at last vacate, whose religion was ancestor-worship, whose dread was change, no word could be so terrible. A gambler.

It did not occur to him that his system was in any way responsible for George's conduct.

They are pathetic these Pendyces, so unquestioning of the scheme they are part of; and yet, in that scheme, in their ancestors and in their heirs, they have and treasure a certain immortality. Mrs Pendyce, as she sits in her morning room waiting to go to church, sees her husband as he is, sees the shallowness of his feelings, sees also the briefness and insignificance of their lives: 'She had sat there till her hair, once dark-brown, was turning grey; she would sit there until it was white. One day she would sit there no longer, and as likely as not, Mr Pendyce, still well preserved, would enter and say, "Now, my dear, you'll be late!" having for the moment forgotten.' The Pendyces, even more than their town cousins, the Forsytes, are people of a world that already seems to belong to a distant past. The 'changes' that Horace Pendyce dreaded came, and with two wars swept brutally across the landscape, sweeping away the country squirarchy, the Pendyces, the Cheshires of *The Eldest Son*, and the Hillcrists of *The Skin Game*.

The Silver Box had closed in London as it had begun, on a note of triumph, with the Prince and Princess of Wales attending the last performance in April. After such a success it is not surprising that Galsworthy was anxious to attempt another play; immediately *The Country House* was finished and sent off in November he embarked on his second play, *Joy*.

Joy must have been one of the Galsworthys' greatest disappointments; after such a reception as the last two novels and his first play had received, it would be hard for any author to realize that he was capable of the complete failure that *Joy* undoubtedly was. Favoured by critics and public alike, it says much for their integrity that they were still able to rap this new favourite over the knuckles. Ada was probably far more put out than John by the failure of the play; her cuttings book, which has pages of reviews for both *The Silver Box* and *Strife*, has not one single review of *Joy*. She was not prepared to place on record adverse criticism of *her* writer. And she wrote indignantly to Mottram to tell him of the play's reception.

> You see the critics won't have it – only A. B. Walkley sees its qualities, the rest miss the limelights beloved of their souls – Well! Well! It is quite true that the effects don't come out, they are too delicate mostly . . . I was indignant with the critics generally speaking; they opened their mouths and swallowed the whole Galsworthy qualities without a word, and roared at the G. defects . . .[18]

It was Galsworthy's great misfortune that those in his immediate circle were so often eulogistic and uncritical about his work. No doubt Ada had much to say about the minutiae of his writing, about the development of a character or the details of a scene; in that sense she was a helpful critic. But in the overall purpose and direction of his work it would seem that his intimates had nothing but praise for everything he did. His closest friend, R. H. Mottram, whose biography *For Those We Loved* presents a unique personal portrait of the Galsworthys, has much to say about Galsworthy's writing, but it is almost completely without criticism. He assumes that where writing was concerned his friend could not put a foot wrong. Conrad too never had anything but praise for everything that Galsworthy showed him – though as each work from *Jocelyn* onwards was greeted by long enthusiastic letters, this lack of criticism must have lessened the force of his friend's approval.

It is not necessary to go into the plot of *Joy* in detail: it is the story of a young girl's disillusionment when she discovers that her adored mother is in love with a disreputable bounder, and, moreover, that her lover is more important to her in her affections than her daughter. The girl, Joy, has then to find consolation with her own boyfriend, Dick. 'By George how staggeringly different it is to *The Silver Box*,' Galsworthy wrote when he sent a copy to Garnett for his approval.[14]

The play was soon accepted by the Vedrenne-Barker management, and was performed at the Savoy Theatre on 24 September 1907. Both he and Ada attributed much of its failure to a poor performance; the cast had 'no conviction or love of their parts', Ada told Mottram.[15] Even during rehearsals the play did not go well: 'Jack is all day and every day rehearsing, things go a little better but he is much worried and tired.'[16] But Galsworthy accepted that it was 'Quite a pleasant thing getting a bath of cold criticism'; in any case his new play *Strife* was already written, and Galsworthy must have realized that this too was 'staggeringly different' to *Joy*. As Conrad had said, consoling him for the failure of the play, 'Bad as it is to see one's work misunderstood, the murmurs against *Joy* shall be drowned in such a shout around *Strife* as this country has not heard for a hundred years or more. That is not only my conviction but my *feeling* – an absolutely overpowering feeling. You've got only to sit tight and watch your glory approaching.'[17]

Strife tells the story of an industrial dispute; a situation all too familiar in the 1970s, though Galsworthy's *Strife* has a personal quality unimaginable today. The two principals are John Anthony, the ageing director of the Trenartha Tin Plate Works, who is urging his fellow directors to give the men a better deal, and David Roberts, spokesman for the workers, who have now been on strike for four months. The dramatic situation develops when Roberts is told that his sick wife has died, a death that might well have been avoided without the hardships caused by the strike. He hurries to her death bed, and when he returns to the meeting finds that the other directors have turned out the sympathetic Anthony, and have made a settlement with the strikers in the absence of their leader. It is a poor deal for the workers, one that was offered them at the beginning of the dispute; their sufferings and Annie Roberts's death have all been for nothing. The dramatic tension of this play is perfectly pitched, a feat all the more remarkable when one considers what a difficult subject it was to tackle within the narrow confines of a stage set.

Chapter 19

The Social Reformer

During the years of Galsworthy's unmarried liaison with Ada, his chief preoccupation was with her and her predicament. His compassionate nature found in her suffering an object to care for and a subject to write about. Society he saw in the first place as her tormentor, the villain that had placed her in her wretched situation, that demanded that she should stay there and that finally condemned her for escaping from it. But from this first focus he saw its hypocrisy, its limitations, its self-satisfaction and its indifference to so much suffering and poverty.

Marriage to Ada liberated him to some extent from this first obsession, and his amazing début in London as a playwright and successful novelist, coming as it did at the same moment, found the Galsworthys suddenly respectable and part of that society that a few years before had rejected them. They were no longer outsiders but part of the establishment. Galsworthy was at once deprived of his original target, but he was also placed in a position from which he could champion new causes; he could write letters to the newspapers and they would be published; he could form committees and their members would consist of powerful and influential people; his pamphlets and essays would attract attention and respect.

Although his play *Strife* was not performed until March 1909 the writing was completed in the spring of 1907, and it marks a new development which was to come increasingly to the fore in Galsworthy's writing. The object of nearly all Galsworthy's work is, to put it bluntly, to moralize; Shelton in *The Island Pharisees* preaches openly, but this is because his author had not yet learnt the technique of keeping his characters' mouths shut; *The Man of Property* is equally didactic, but Galsworthy had now learnt to conceal his message in his fiction, so that it is in fact possible to read the story purely as a story, ignoring its moral content. So it is with *The Country House* or *The Silver Box*. But *Strife* is the first social treatise, it is the forerunner of *Justice* and the many documents and treatises that Galsworthy was to write on subjects of social injustice. The characters and the plot of *Strife* are far less important than the situation, and the situation is a universal one, the struggle between management and workers, between capital and labour.

It is not chance that immediately he had finished the play he set to work on a sketch entitled 'The Lost Dog', which he wrote for the periodical *The Nation*; 'The Lost Dog' was the first of a series for the magazine, which were ultimately collected into a book titled *A Commentary* and published in 1908. This collection is the first of a flood of essays and short pieces on every imaginable subject, from the caging of birds and the docking of horses' tails to solitary confinement or censorship in the theatre. It is worth quoting an undated list of causes made by Galsworthy, as it gives some idea of the enormous scope of his interests:

Abolition of the Censorship of Plays.
Sweated Industries. Minimum Wage.
Labour Unrest. Labour Exchanges.
Woman's Suffrage.
Ponies in Mines.
Divorce Law Reform.
Prison Reform: (Closed Cell Confinement).
Aeroplanes in War.
Docking of Horses' Tails.
For Love of Beasts.
Slaughterhouse Reform.
Plumage Bill.
Caging of Wild Birds.
Worn-out Horse Traffic.
Performing Animals.
Vivisection of Dogs.
Pigeon Shooting.
Slum Clearance.
Zoos.
Cecil Houses.
Children on the Stage.
The Three Year Average Income Tax.[1]

Galsworthy saw with a distressing clarity the numerous causes of suffering that existed for both human beings and animals; he also believed with an almost naïve innocence that man was progressing steadily towards a better and more humane society, and he saw it as the duty of every man to do all he could to further this Utopian end. Thus no appeal that was made to him, whether it was a circular from a social organization or a beggar knocking at his door, went unanswered. He was like his own character Wellwyn in his play *The Pigeon*, whose unbounded charity is ruthlessly exploited by its beneficiaries. Thus the reader of Galsworthy becomes swamped with fragmentary writings, crying out against the plight of human beings and animals. Agonized almost beyond bearing by any sort of suffering, Galsworthy was determined that his pen should work overtime to voice the cries of suffering humanity, to bring aid wherever it was possible. The writer became overburdened by the philanthropist; it was inevitable that it should have been so. It is in *Strife* that the scales begin to tip, and the humanist takes ascendancy over the artist, that what has been called by Marrot the first 'Crusade' starts to become the driving spirit of his whole life.

The two books written during this period reflect his increasing preoccupation with social injustice: 'In these two books, *A Commentary* and *Fraternity*, I sealed myself into communion with the world of dark and broken waters running beneath the bridges of great towns of shadows passing up and down alleyways and enjoying such life as God has given them.'[2]

A Commentary makes strange reading today, consisting as it does of brief sketches on a great variety of subjects. The 'sketch' is a form of writing that has long since gone out of fashion, but biographically these pieces are of some interest. Where another writer might have recorded his reactions to his experiences in the form of a lengthy diary, Galsworthy wrote sketches, sometimes amounting to very short stories. Thus immediately following his visit to Dartmoor Prison in September 1907 he wrote two sketches recording his experience and his appalled reaction to prison life.

A Commentary is the notebook from which much of his later writing sprang and should be read as such. There are portraits of the very poor, such as those in 'Demos' or 'Fear', showing their pride and resilience in the face of bitter circumstances; they also illustrate a difficulty with which he struggled repeatedly, his inability to bring these working-class characters to life in his fiction; they move on to the stage or the pages of a book to illustrate their pitiable condition or to play their part in a plot, but seldom live in their own right as people. They speak with accents and drop their h's, but they carry no conviction; they remain actors, dressed up to play a part.

Galsworthy has often been described as a sad, solemn or over-serious person. Except in his immediate family circle he was seldom light-hearted or amusing; he was not a man to make many witticisms or even to see quickly those of others. He cannot have been the ideal guest at a dinner party. Reading *A Commentary* one can see why. Not only was he uncomfortably aware of the suffering that went on around him – not in distant countries such as India or the Far East, but within a few miles of his own doorstep – but he was almost prophetically aware of the inherent dangers of modern society. Those things that he loved most and regarded as vital to man's survival as a rational, well-balanced human being – the countryside and a way of life that could give man the peace and solitude that he needed – were seriously threatened by modern technology.

> Motor-cars were crossing the Downs to Goodwood Races. Slowly they mounted, sending forth an oily reek, a jerky grinding sound; and a cloud of dust hung over the white road. Since ten o'clock they had been mounting, one by one, freighted with the pale conquerors of time and space. None paused on the top of the green heights, but with a convulsive shaking leaped, and glided swiftly down; and the tooting of their valves and the whirring of their wheels spread on either hand along the hills.

This passage, from a sketch called 'Progress' written in 1907, foresaw the traffic nightmare of the sixties and seventies! How wise is his shepherd who observes: 'There's some believes in them. But if they folk weren't doin' everything and goin' everywhere at once, there'd be no need for them rampagin' motors . . . Downs'll be left when they're all gone . . . Never been off the Downs meself.'

The next sketch, 'Holiday', enlarges on this theme of the pitiful restlessness of man and his pathetic attempts to escape from his own turbulence. It describes a crowded beach in holiday time.

> For nothing is so dreadful to this man as solitude. In solitude he hears the voice of the Nature he cannot understand . . . In solitude he feels so small, so very new . . .
>
> . . . And if, by unhappy chance, in their parks you find yourself alone, lie neither on your back, for then you will see the quiet sun-

light on the leaves, the quiet clouds, and birds with solitude within their wings; nor on your face, or you will catch the savour of the earth, and a faint hum, and for a minute live the life of tiny things that straddle in the trodden grasses. Fly from such sights and scents and sounds, lest terror for your fate should visit you; fly rather to the streets; fly to your neighbour's houses; talk, and be brave!

Twenty years later he could no longer hope that the menacing direction of a technological society could do other than go forward on its hopeless and destructive path: 'I think most modern unrest and despair come from the gradual discovery that there are no definite rewards or hopes to be had in the future . . . too much of town life has done us in; when we don't live (to some extent at all events) with Nature, we forget how to live at all.'

A Commentary provides the background of observation and thought from which campaigns against every form of injustice sprang. Galsworthy was not, as many writers and thinkers have been, content merely to state his views. He was a man of action, both on a public scale, actively organizing or taking part in movements for reform, and privately, endlessly giving to those who knocked on his door for help.

The first cause that he openly championed was against an injustice to his own profession, more than that to a personal friend, Edward Garnett. In the summer of 1907 Garnett's play *The Breaking Point* was officially censored. The question of the censorship of plays and the case for its abolition had already been taken up early in the year by William Archer, but this attack on the work of a friend brought the issue forcibly to the notice of Galsworthy. The possibility of forming a committee or a 'League' of literary men was discussed. Galsworthy now had influential friends; in May of that year he was dining at the House of Commons with C. F. Masterman, meeting at the dinner Winston Churchill, and now in July he sought their help. 'As to the H. of C.,' he wrote to Garnett, 'I've written to Masterman to see me, but Barker tells me by wire he doesn't think he'll do it; he tried him some time ago. I'll try and get R. C. Lehmann, if he refuses.'[3] Altogether circumstances were against immediate action; it was the summer, people were 'too scattered. I find Shaw in Wales and Archer at Cambridge.'[4] The theatrical manager, Vedrenne, refused to join them; it was 'too dangerous for *him* – he said – all right for authors, but not for those who like him made his living by leasing theatres'.[5]

It needed a new impetus, the censoring of Granville Barker's play *Waste*, to get the movement off the ground. At a dinner at 14 Addison Road, Galsworthy enlisted the support of his friend Gilbert Murray, who was persuaded to approach J. M. Barrie. The three writers formed the nucleus of a committee, aided by William Archer and Granville Barker, with 'the somewhat lukewarm assistance' of Arthur Pinero and Sir William Gilbert.

The committee was at least active if not successful in its purpose. A circular letter was drawn up and signed by '71 dramatic authors'; the Home Secretary, Herbert Gladstone, agreed to receive a deputation; finally a Bill was drafted and sponsored, first by Charles Trevelyan, and later by Robert Harcourt. Ultimately, in the autumn of 1909, a Committee of Both Houses considered the matter, and Galsworthy, as one of the principal witnesses, gave evidence.

The grievance was given an airing, playwrights had their say, parliamentarians played their part, and there the matter ended. Many years later in 1931, when the question was raised again, Galsworthy wrote to Mrs Dawson Scott, founder of PEN, the international writers' association: 'I have become reconciled to the evil as the least violent form of interference. Therefore if my opinion must be given, I should say leave the matter alone. For nothing anyway will come of a protest.' It was perhaps a sad end to his first campaign.[6]

Prison life, and particularly Dartmoor, had a strange, almost morbid, fascination for Galsworthy. Shelton, walking on the moors, receives a 'rude shock from the ultra-dreariness of the building', and contrasts it with 'the fantastic magic of his early morning walk across Dartmoor in a golden haze that had burned itself slowly away till the blue of the sky was as clear and fresh as the water of the stream'. These two feelings went very deep with Galsworthy, his almost sensual love of open spaces, of the country and nature, and on the other hand his horror, his sense of claustrophobia, at any sort of captivity.

I have a distinct and abiding aversion to being shut up or in any way controlled. If I were catechized by a psycho-analyst he would elicit the fact that at the age of five I was held down on the floor on my back by my nurse, which caused me acute terror. He would say: 'Here you are! This began that abiding aversion of yours.' I would say: 'Not so. Nine out of ten little boys might have been so held down without causing them anything but irritation. The tenth little

boy, myself, is so constituted that from birth on he has this characteristic, but no occasion occurred before that, to demonstrate that he
has.'[7]

This experience is described in *Awakening* when the child Jon is held
down on the floor by his nurse 'Da' as a punishment:

> This first interference with the free individualism of a Forsyte drove
> him almost frantic. There was something appalling in the utter help-
> lessness of that position, and the uncertainty as to whether it would
> ever come to an end. Suppose she never let him get up any more! He
> suffered torture at the top of his voice for fifty seconds. Worse than
> anything was his perception that 'Da' had taken all that time to
> realize the agony of fear he was enduring. Thus, dreadfully, was
> revealed to him the lack of imagination in the human being.

It was this depth of conviction that any creature has the right to be free
that led directly to Galsworthy's concern for every type of prisoner,
whether a human being in Dartmoor, a bird in a cage, a pit pony
working far under the ground, or even a woman such as Ada or Irene,
bound by the marriage tie in an uncongenial partnership.

The Galsworthys spent August 1907 holidaying in Devon and Corn-
wall, and undoubtedly one of the main objectives was for John to visit
Dartmoor Prison. 'We are here [Bude] till Aug. 30th, then to Two
Bridges, Dartmoor (where I'm going over the prison), till Sept. 2nd,
then Town again for Sept. It's *glorious* here – such air, such cliffs, sands,
downs and lanes, and skies. It's too beautiful to work and smells too
good.'[8] It must have been on this holiday that the Galsworthys decided
to make a semi-permanent home in the west. They returned to Manaton in October and again in the following spring, and that year they
took on a long lease of the farmhouse, Wingstone, or rather part of the
farmhouse, as the back rooms were occupied by the farmer Mr
Endacott, and his family.

But for the moment they were travellers. 'On Friday we journey to
Telverton, Devon. Jack has an order to go over Dartmoor prison,
gruesome, but he has long wanted to do it,' Ada informed Mottram
at the end of August.[9]

This visit must have been the first of many, and must merely have
given Galsworthy an impression of the horrors of the lives that were
led behind those walls; a vivid picture of what he saw is recorded in

'The House of Silence' and 'Order'. The inhumanity of the solitary conditions in which the prisoners passed their days (even after the official period of solitary confinement was over) was stamped on his consciousness so forcibly that he never forgot it.

> Within the circle of the high grey wall is silence.
> Under a square of sky cut by high grey buildings nothing is to be seen of Nature but the prisoners themselves, the men who guard the prisoners, and a cat who eats the prison mice.
> . . . Before he [the prisoner] was admitted to this House of Silence he had endured his months of solitude, and now, in the small white-washed space, with a black floor whence he has cleaned all dirt, he spends only fourteen out of the twenty-four alone, except on Sundays, when he spends twenty-one, because it is God's day. He spends them walking up and down, muttering to himself, listening for sound, with his eyes on the little peephole in the door, through which he can be seen but cannot see.

Once again Galsworthy's work for prison reform was undertaken in a totally professional way. He brought to it all his talents; as a writer he could imaginatively envisage what 'separate confinement' could mean to a man: 'Public Opinion has never yet succeeded in realizing what this so called separate confinement means.'[10] He made it his task to see that they understood, using his skill as a writer, both in the field of fiction and in articles and letters to be published in the Press. He was determined that people should understand to the full the horrors of the punishment they were inflicting on their fellow citizens. Moreover, his legal training enabled him to present and examine the whole matter in such a way as to preclude any accusations that he wrote with inadequate knowledge of his subject. He examined the case for separate confinement as well as that against; he made himself familiar with authoritative writing on the subject. His Open Letter to the Home Secretary, Herbert Gladstone, written in May 1909, is an impressive document.

Still more impressive is the letter he wrote in July to Sir Evelyn Ruggles Brise, of the Prison Commission:

> . . . I was at X. Prison on Tuesday, at Y. Prison yesterday. Saw all the officials and talked with twelve convicts . . .
> It was suggested to me at X. that I ought to stay some days there

and see every convict. I would be willing, if you would allow me, to stay some days at X. Prison, see every convict, and keep record of the answers obtained from each one as to the effect on him of separate confinement. I think they would speak to me freely.

Permission was granted, and Galsworthy's report on these interviews can be read in 'A Minute on Separate Confinement, Forwarded to the Home Secretary and the Prison Commissioners, September, 1909'. 'I visited these convicts in their cells, and conversed privately with each one of them for from ten minutes to a quarter of an hour . . . My object in the course of these conversations was to get behind the formal question and answer to the man's real feelings.' There follows an account of his interviews and a summary of the effects of the solitary confinement on the different types of people he spoke to. It must have been a harrowing experience for one as sensitive as Galsworthy to other people's troubles: ' "I've never felt right since – it's got all over me." (This man cried all the time . . .) "It's no life at all. I'd sooner be dead than here." (This man was very tearful and quavery).' But it should be remembered that Galsworthy had a certain courageous, almost hard, streak that enabled him to come face to face with the tragedies he deplored; he went out of his way to seek out first-hand evidence, into the prisons, into the slaughter houses, and into the slums. He always wanted to know, to see for himself.

Through the offices of his friend, C. F. Masterman, Galsworthy was able to present his case personally to Herbert Gladstone, Secretary of State for Home Affairs, who devoted much of his life to the reform of criminal law. Presumably Mr Gladstone had already received his report on solitary confinement, as he was able to tell Galsworthy that the authorities had agreed to reduce the term of separate confinement to a uniform three months for all types of prisoners. 'It is a big step in the right direction,' he wrote to Garnett, 'but it should and will, I hope before long, be done away with altogether.'[11] *

The play *Justice* was the culmination of Galsworthy's work for prison reform, his final great appeal for more humanity to be exercised in the treatment of prisoners. It is chronologically incorrect to discuss the play at this point; on the other hand it must be seen that it essentially

* Marrot gives the date for this interview as 7 September 1909. But as Galsworthy wrote on that date to Garnett from Manaton informing him that the interview was to be arranged, this seems unlikely.

belongs to his work as a reformer, that it was the direct outcome of the hours he spent talking with the prisoners and observing the conditions in which they lived.

He began work on the play in the summer of 1909; in July he had visited the gaols at Lewes and Chelmsford, and in September he was interviewing prisoners at Lewes. While these conversations were still in his mind, the atmosphere of the ordered, deathly silence in which they lived vividly before him, he sat down to pen his portrait of the pathetic Falder, the 'hero' of *Justice*. The cell that Falder occupies is the same as that described in 'The House of Silence' after his first visit to Dartmoor, the same 'small white-washed space'; the prisoners have the same meagre possessions, 'a black-bristled brush', and 'a little pyramid of godly books'. The conversations that take place within Falder's prison echo the notes and phrases that Galsworthy recorded immediately after each interview in Lewes. 'It's made me very nervous . . .' 'I keep picturing things and walking about. It sends "men up the pole!"' *Justice* was a 'documentary' play, a dramatized report of what Galsworthy had seen within the prisons he had visited. It was a painful task he set himself: 'It has been nothing but pain from beginning to end. It has cost me much peace of mind. I have written it, believing that what I have seen and thought and felt ought to be made known, and that I should not be true to myself or my art, and cowardly into the bargain, if I turned my back on the task.'[12]

The overriding theme and message of *Justice* is that a man who has been found guilty of a moderately serious crime – in the case of Falder altering the figures on a cheque – can by the process of 'Justice' be completely destroyed.

> Justice is a machine that, when someone has once given it the starting push, rolls on of itself. Is this young man to be ground to pieces under this machine for an act which at the worst was one of weakness? Is he to become a member of the luckless crews that man those dark, ill-starred ships called prisons?

Such is the argument put forward for his defence by Falder's Counsel, but 'Justice' takes its course, ending as was predicted by Falder's destruction.

Justice is an exceptional and unusual play. It was a cry from the heart, expressing the anguish that Galsworthy felt as he saw those captive people in their minute cells, driven mad by their silent world, and his anguish he communicated to his audience. Seldom can a play have had a more astounding reception than *Justice*, with the audience remaining long after the end of the play 'calling for the author, shouting his name, singing it, shrieking out their determination to remain all night until he came forward'.[13] Despite the efforts of the management, who plunged the theatre into darkness, 'the Gallery stayed on, shouting: "We want Galsworthy," "We mean to have him," and "We won't go home till we get him!" '[14]

Reformer or artist? Galsworthy repeatedly insisted that the two roles were completely separate. 'Honestly, though the public bangs the drum of *Justice* in connection with Prison Reform they so jolly well miss the main line of the play that one is more than ever discouraged from taking subjects which can be whittled down to one small issue by the practical – to the neglect of the fundamental criticism on human life . . . The public – bless them – take it for a tract on solitary confinement . . .'[15]

But whatever Galsworthy felt, the play could not have had the impact it did without being in a sense documentary. Its effect on its audiences was very like the effect on television viewers in this country of seeing the documentary about the homeless *Cathy Come Home*. People suddenly realized that Falder existed, that there were men like him enduring hour after hour of solitude, that solitude was driving them mad. 'I've lain awake practically the whole night thinking of that poor boy in the cell, going round the wall with his finger,' John Masefield wrote to him. 'I do think it is splendid of you to hold up this clear glass of yours to the ghastly things in life. I would to God I'd your sight and your hate and your truth.'[16]

The Press was uncertain as to what its response should be: *The Times* saw Galsworthy as a 'tragic writer' with 'a passionate yearning to put an end to what he feels . . . to be an evil thing'. *The Daily Mail* found the play's realism 'hideous and staggering'. Galsworthy felt the *Glasgow Herald* to be most sympathetic to his work (the play was produced simultaneously in Glasgow and London). The newspaper saw it as a 'play with a purpose . . . But *Justice* quite apart from its obvious social application is something very like a dramatic masterpiece, and has the austere beauty which arouses in our minds pity and terror.'

In practical terms the success of *Justice* was great. Winston Churchill was so much impressed by the play that he put into immediate effect certain measures for prison reform, including reducing the hours of solitary confinement. Galsworthy could write to Gilbert Murray that he believed his articles and *Justice* had 'helped to knock off 1000 months of Solitary Confinement per year'.[17] To which Murray replied: 'It is a fine thing to have achieved, a really great thing. Does not real life seem a tremendous thing as compared with art when one gets the two together? I mean, How much greater it is to have saved a lot of men and women from two months solitary confinement than to have sent any number of over-fed audiences into raptures!'[18]

Galsworthy was not certain. In one sense he had to admit that he was disappointed by the reception of *Justice*. In his notebook he recorded that the practical results of the play were more than he could have hoped but 'they had a good deal the effect of obscuring the main artistic conception of the play'. At a party given by Winston Churchill's mother in order to bring the dramatist and her son together, Eddie Marsh, the friend and biographer of Rupert Brooke, was also present and asked Galsworthy a direct question:

'If the Archangel Gabriel came down from heaven and gave you your choice; that your play should transform the prison system and be forgotten, or have no practical effect whatever and be a classic a hundred years hence, which would you choose?' Galsworthy did not answer at once, and his neighbour, who had fancied him more of a philanthropist than an artist, especially in present company, was impressed by his candour when he finally opted for the classic a hundred years hence.[19]

One is grateful to Eddie Marsh for asking such a question and to his biographer for recording it. Like his neighbour one must be both surprised by Galsworthy's answer and impressed by his candour. But was this really the truth or was it just his natural diffidence that led him to give this reply? Did he even know himself? However that may be, the dilemma is there.

Achieving a balance between the humanist and the artist was to be for Galsworthy an insoluble problem, but one to which he seemed strangely blind in his own work. He could see it in the work of other writers, in Tolstoy, for instance, who does not lose sight 'of the war between the artist and the moralist, that was always being waged, and the fusion of them that was always going on in his colossal spirit'.[20] Yet this was so agonizingly his own problem. 'In regard to my plays: it may perhaps be as well to bear in mind that I am not a reformer – only a painter of pictures, a maker of things – as sincerely as I know how – imagined out of what I have seen and felt. The sociological character of my plays arises from the fact that I do not divorce creation from life; . . .'[21]

He was overburdened by his social conscience; the injustices and inequalities of society weighed upon him as if he personally was responsible; his programme of giving increased with his earning power but it was never enough to assuage the guilt and distress that he felt. Politically he remained uncommitted: 'I do not consider I belong to any political party, neither Tory, Liberal nor Socialist and prefer to hold my judgement free.'[22] Party politics was not for him a way out of his dilemma, but he foresaw and welcomed the social revolution which he thought must inevitably come, and of which society as a whole was still happily oblivious. He was 'sure that thirty or forty years will see politics in this country a sheer fight of "haves" versus "have nots"', he wrote to Gilbert Murray.[23]

It was inevitable that such strong feelings should have overflowed into his writing, more than that, that they should often have become the entire subject of a play or novel. One may go further and say that as his spirits became more tamed his books became correspondingly weaker. The fire has died out in his post-war novels; like his character, Wilfred Desert, the 'hero' of *Flowering Wilderness*, written two years before his death, he finds there is nothing left to replace it.

Chapter 20
Manaton and 'Fraternity'

Without doubt the place where Galsworthy found most happiness was Wingstone, the farmhouse at Manaton in Devon, the place which he described in the story 'Buttercup Night', the 'rare spot' with which he felt an immediate affinity, set as it was in the heart of the countryside which he loved and from which generations of his family had come. For him it was escape from the social round of London; it was peace in which he could write and think; it was open spaces where he could ride and walk; it was above all an absence of the claustrophobia which he felt so strongly in the town. At Manaton he was free, mentally and physically.

Unfortunately his love of Wingstone was not shared by Ada. Sentimentally she was attached to it – it was the place where she and John had come the Christmas immediately after the death of John's father, in those first days of their freedom, to be together – but neither its remoteness nor its climate suited her. It was a rough, slightly comfortless life in those days, lacking both the amenities and the entertainments of the city; at Wingstone she was often ill and frequently bored. She longed to be back in London or travelling abroad in search of the sun and the distractions of foreign travel.

Manaton is a small hamlet on the edge of Dartmoor, lying roughly between Moretonhampstead and Bovey Tracey; it consists of only a few houses, a village post-office and shop, and, in those days, a pub. Wingstone farmhouse lies on the outskirts of the village, and is approached by a narrow lane lined with trees; the lane takes one straight into the farmyard and the back entrance of the house; the kitchen door would stand open, the children of the farmer, Mr Endacott, running in and out, dogs, chickens, farmcarts and all the paraphernalia of the farm cluttering up the yard. But this was not what the Galsworthys and their guests saw. In their day a drive swept round to the front of the house; carriages would bring them and their guests to the main door, where flower gardens led up to the veranda and long french windows fronted the house. This side, the Galsworthys' side, was very elegant; one would not have suspected that behind, in the same house, the vigorous life of a farm was in full play.

The Galsworthys had stayed at Wingstone on several occasions as 'paying guests' of the farmer Mr Endacott and his wife, and now, in the spring of 1908, they took over the lease of the front rooms of the farmhouse, the remainder of the house continuing in the occupation of the farmer and his family. Mrs Endacott looked after the Galsworthys and their guests during their visits there, and the farmer kept their horses for them.

The interior of the farmhouse has been described by R. H. Mottram; they had for their own use the two front south-facing rooms, which opened on to the long veranda; one of the rooms was the dining-room and also the study in which John worked, the other, the sitting-room, which also contained Ada's new piano: 'The little Bechstein "ran in" to Moreton . . . and journeyed thence on a little spring cart in its neat packing case.'[1] It was her one consolation, 'Jack writes and I potter and type and pretend to play on my dear little cottage Bechstein, which is our great new joy.'[2]

According to Ada's notebook they arrived at Wingstone early in April and stayed there for the next thirteen weeks, returning to London on 20 June. For Galsworthy it was a long unbroken stretch in which to tackle his new novel, which was at first entitled *Shadows* but which later became *Fraternity*. 'I seem to have been too immersed in writing to write letters,' he apologized to Edward Garnett for his failure to write to him. 'However we've managed to get glory out of the moors and the Spring. On sunny days now it's gorgeous.'[3]

Ada was less contented. In April she was envying Mottram's holiday to the Loire, 'and I just whisper to you *privately* this is no holiday to me – housekeeping and people and ordering rubbish from shops, no – not much . . . ssh!!'[4] And by June she is delighted by the prospect of their imminent return to London: 'for once I've had enough of the country, feel cosy and stale, and oh! the thickness of this Devonshire air, even when it is fine, which is not often . . . On Sat we had a real hurricane . . . early Sunday morning sheep got in and finished off everything practically. Give me little Addison Road garden where one does control things a little and there is very little to control.'[5]

It was a small tragedy for both John and Ada that they asked such different things of life: Ada was a very sophisticated woman, in her tastes, in her speech, in her way of dressing; she shone in the more formal life of the town. She enjoyed all the things it had to offer, its concerts, its theatres, and above all its society – for increasingly as John became famous the Galsworthys were invited to social functions, both private dinner parties and public occasions.

In the country those who knew Ada well admit that she was often bored and sometimes unhappy. However, long after they had left Manaton, as a widow, she wrote nostalgically of their life at Wingstone in her book of memories, *Over the Hills and Far Away*. Time had perhaps erased from her memory the rigours of an intemperate climate and the boredom which she confided in her correspondence with Ralph Mottram.

> Few diversions came our way on Dartmoor – very good for the soul of the writer were those spells of quiet and freedom, broken only by such guests as did not mind the simplicity of living. The long rides, the long walks, bird songs, farm sounds, the pageant of the seasons and their attendant events – lambing, sheep-shearing, hay harvest, *the* harvest, cider-making, threshing, all these simple things kept one in close touch with the earth, and were precious to us. An occasional cricket-match, a race-meeting, athletic sports, a concert of local talent, were often more enlivening than intended. A normal day's programme for summer would be: Writing for Himself and gardening for me from breakfast to near lunch-time. Then we would set forth on our horses for an hour's ride perhaps, and having found a likely spot for our Spartan picnic, we tethered the horses and had lunch. Then came the more serious riding: home towards tea-time, baths, tea, correspondence and miscellaneous duties and pleasures, dinner and then to a certainty – music, while Himself corrected proofs, read, or did secondary literary work – not creative, that is to say.

It was an almost primitive existence, especially bearing in mind that in those early days of the century the motor car was still a rarity. The Galsworthys and their guests would travel from London by train to Newton Abbot or Bovey Tracey, where they would be met by the farmer's horse-drawn trap or dog-cart; they and their luggage would then bowl along the country lane to the farmhouse. The farmhouse itself had no modern conveniences as we know them, no electricity, only oil lamps or candles, no modern plumbing or bathroom – a bath would have been taken in a hip bath before a fire, all the water having been carried up from the kitchen below. It was a life totally different from the commuting car-borne country life of today. They were more dependent on the amenities of the country itself; they walked and rode and took part in the affairs of the local community. Soon after his arrival John established a Manaton Rifle Range – 'the young folk (male) are quite excited,' Ada reported.[6] They kept their own horses, Peggy, John's favourite mare, and Skip, who was bought for Ada or their guests; they had an ever-growing number of dogs. Most of all they were dependent on the friends who came to visit them for their social life; Ralph Mottram was a regular visitor, as were members of John's family. And of course there were their literary friends, among them Edward Garnett, who kicked the dog Chris off an adder: 'it really was Edward G. who kicked Chris like a football from off the adder . . . I could not help wondering how often he had footballed a dog the action was so perfect.'[7] And one autumn they went on a short walking tour with the Granville Barkers; they 'proved capital walking pals; he is full of anecdotes, imitations, good stories and so on! And that leads me to say he plays the pianola (!) with genius – I heard two Bach toccatas played by him as I know I never shall by human hand.'[8]

But whether there were guests or they were on their own the routine of life at Manaton gave Galsworthy a steady background for his writing which he was seldom to find elsewhere. Through the spring months he worked on *Fraternity*. 'It's a queer book,' he wrote to Garnett. 'More intimate than anything I've done – I mean by that, that there seems less *machinery* of story, less history, more life.'[9]

It is an intimate book; probably no character in Galsworthy's novels is more autobiographical than Hilary Dallison. Like his creator, Hilary is a writer, a man of private means and almost exactly Galsworthy's age at the time of writing – forty-two; but of more importance than these factual similarities is his preoccupation with the troubles of others: 'how far was it one's business to identify oneself with other people, especially the helpless – how far to preserve oneself intact – *integer vitae?*' Hilary's dilemma is Galsworthy's own. In an undated note on the novel Galsworthy makes this revealing comment on the character of Hilary:

in Hilary the doom or curse of over-refinement was being revealed . . . The peculiar nature of English breeding and education tends when it gets the right kind of material to work on to produce a being so repressed, self-conscious, inhibited and hypersensitive that when life, as it sometimes will in the 'best regulated families', jerks him into contact with raw human flesh and blood he is simply paralysed . . . His is the tragedy of over-refinement, and a very real tragedy it is.[10]

The central theme of *Fraternity* is embodied in its first title *Shadows*: the 'shadows' of the cultured, well-to-do Dallisons are a group of impoverished people who live in a slummy street in Notting Hill Gate, a district immediately adjacent to the fashionable Campden Hill area where the families of the two Dallison brothers, Hilary and Stephen, and incidentally Galsworthy himself, live. The lives of the two groups become involved with each other, through the medium of the Hughs family (Mrs Hughs 'does' for Cecelia, Stephen's wife), with whom also the 'little model' lodges, who is brought in to sit for Hilary's artist wife, Bianca. Her extreme poverty arouses the compassion and interest of Hilary, who touchingly buys her a completely new set of clothes, even new underclothes, an action which not surprisingly arouses the suspicion of his family, and the jealousy of the drunken Mr Hughs.

This group of educated middle-class people, intellectually aware of social injustices but emotionally terrified of becoming involved, is ruthlessly torn apart, from the very young Martin and Thyme, who approach the problem with a naïve innocence, to the aged philosopher, Sylvanus Stone, who is writing the *Book of Universal Brotherhood*. ('I have an affection for him,' Galsworthy noted. 'He is . . . something of a prophet crying like a pelican in the wilderness and eating locusts and wild honey.'[11] In the case of Mr Stone cocoa and brown bread and butter.) The pathos of these characters lies in the virtue of their intentions but their inability to take any positive action – or when they do it ends in disaster; of this group Hilary is the most passionately concerned but the least capable of doing anything successfully. He is, as his nephew Martin points out, a modern Hamlet, 'weak and unsatisfactory because he's not in touch with life', and he accuses him directly: 'Ah, your precious delicacy! What's the good of that? What did it ever do? It's the curse that you're all suffering from. Why don't you act? You could think about it afterwards.'

Never since *Jocelyn* had Galsworthy allowed himself to enter so intimately into a character, or to explore the conflicts and limitations that were, at least to some degree, his own. The final defeat of Hilary occurs when he finds that his interest in the model is far from being purely philanthropic. He is panic-stricken, terrified by her devoted love for him, horrified by the prospect of any sort of union with someone whose difference of class and outlook would doom from the start their relationship. 'The scent of stale violet powder came from her, warmed by her humanity. It penetrated to Hilary's heart. He started back in sheer physical revolt.'

'The stale violet powder' was, taken to an extreme, the difficulty the whole group of Dallisons felt. 'They knew that these people (their "shadows") lived, because they saw them, but they did not *feel* it – with such extraordinary care had the web of social life been spun.' Hilary had felt their existence – and was revolted.

In some ways this was Galsworthy's most crucial book: less satisfactory as a novel than *The Man of Property*, it was nevertheless a more ambitious piece of writing. Hilary Dallison is the most complex character that Galsworthy ever attempted, and in so far as the book is the story of a character *Fraternity* can be seen as a modern novel in a sense that his other books were not. One may go further and say that had Galsworthy pursued this vein of writing with any confidence he would have found a more secure place among the post-war writers of the early twenties. It may well be that the 'modernness' of Galsworthy's approach to Hilary explains why Conrad, who read the book in manuscript, took such violent exception to the character.

> H. has no individuality as above defined, he is refined into a special monster. I don't think, my dearest Jack, that in the glow of inspired composition . . . you have realized the harrowing atrocity of his conduct. All the way along you show him as absolutely betraying his clan in the whole course of his inner life, of his intimate relations – in thought, in half speeches, in his silences. Why? For what object? (except as a secret gratification) is undisclosed to us. He is so. There is nothing positive about him. He is perfectly faithless, he is so from the beginning.[12]

Galsworthy put Conrad's reaction down to his complete lack of understanding of 'the special cultured super-sensitive English type which Hilary represents'. This is undoubtedly true, but more than that Conrad failed to see the point of Hilary or the part he played in the novel: he was cast as the hero, but his behaviour is constantly unheroic. It was a departure from the tradition of the novel as he saw it, and as he believed Galsworthy should see it.

The critical reaction to the book was, as Galsworthy saw it, 'curious', ranging from the highly appreciative to the *Saturday Review*'s opinion that it was 'a very dangerous and revolutionary book. *Fraternity* is nothing more or less than an insidious and embittered attack on our social system.' It is interesting that Francis Hackett of the *Chicago Evening Post* should have praised it for those very qualities that horrified Conrad. He liked 'its individual version of life, which must owe much to experience, but an experience transmuted by art and by the life of that imagination which is not frequent in English fiction. English writers so seldom tell what they *think*, or aspire to, or proudly, shamefully feel.'

Galsworthy believed *Fraternity* to be, after *The Man of Property*, and possibly *The Dark Flower*, his best novel: 'I think it is, perhaps, the deepest of them all . . .'[13] The year of its publication was 1909. Could he have guessed or even suspected that little more than a year later he himself would undergo an experience strangely similar to that of Hilary's passion for the little model, an experience that would be for him even more traumatic, and ultimately damaging to his progress as a writer of modern novels?

The year 1909, like 1906, was a year of achievement: not only was *Fraternity* published in February, but the following month his play *Strife*, written two years earlier, was at last produced. It had, Ada recorded, 'visited various intelligent managers',[14] but without success; the Vedrenne-Barker partnership at the Royal Court Theatre, which had proved such a ready market for *The Silver Box* and *Joy*, had broken up, and it was in consequence harder to find a management prepared to take on plays of an experimental nature such as *Strife*. However Charles Frohmann, a manager of foresight and enterprise, put *Strife* on at the Duke of York's Theatre for Six Special Matinees; the play proved such a success that it was transferred to the Haymarket and Adelphi Theatres, a run that was only ended by the cast having previous engagements. '*Strife* . . . was the "talk of London",' Ada wrote to Mrs Mottram, 'just as *Country House* was in its day . . . Its last night was its biggest audience, and they seemed to be the very fashionable, well-dressed, much-jewelled people, who I suppose dared not stay away for fear they should not be able to talk about the play! It's a really great thing, but immensely serious.'[15]

Strife not surprisingly attracted a good deal of critical attention. It was an unusual subject to attempt in dramatic form, particularly at a time when troubles of industrial unrest were still comparatively rare. To have made such a subject so dramatically exciting would have been a triumph for any playwright, but for Galsworthy, whose *Silver Box* had been followed by the disappointing and lifeless *Joy*, the success of *Strife* must have been particularly pleasing. 'It is the English play for which we have been waiting,' the *Evening Standard* wrote of it, while the *Court Journal* and the *Glasgow Herald* called it a 'masterpiece'. It was indeed an occasion, as the *Westminster Gazette* recorded: 'Yesterday afternoon it almost seemed as if the Vedrenne-Barker management had come to life again. Mr. Vedrenne was in the house, Mr. Granville Barker had produced the play, the cast contained at least half-a-dozen people, some of whose best work was done at the Court Theatre . . . and the author was Mr. John Galsworthy author of the admirable play *The Silver Box*.'

Chapter 21
The Price of Success

With the success of *Strife* the Galsworthys can have had no doubt that they had, to use an unpleasant modern phrase, 'made it'. It does, however, exactly describe what had happened. John would have had no illusions as to his real achievement in his chosen career as a writer: he still had far to go; he had only begun to show his promise. But as the writer of two novels and two plays that had been enormously well received by the public, he was a 'success', and this had given him and Ada a certain standing in society. They were public figures, the scandal of their unmarried liaison was forgotten; they were received and entertained everywhere. And what was almost certainly of far greater importance to John, he was now in an even stronger position to forward at least some of the causes that were so constantly appealing to his compassionate heart and purse.

What with parties to be attended, letters to be written, appeals launched, speeches written and delivered, the demands on his time and energies were enormous, and all these things had to be done from a background of constant mobility: they would be at Manaton for some weeks and then in London, then down at Littlehampton, or Ada would pine for the sun and they would be away for several months on the continent. And, increasingly, the demands of John's work necessitated travel both in England and abroad; in December they went out to Cologne for the German performance of *Strife*; 'it did not translate to advantage,' Ada wrote, 'some spirit seemed to have leaked out of it.'[1]

Ada's correspondence with her old friend Ralph Mottram tells of much of the discontent she felt while at Manaton, and also of the pleasures (to her) of their journeys abroad. 'We had one day in Paris, very muddy but always nice. We went as always to the Louvre and were in a very picture mood . . . also to the Cluny and found many treasures. In the evening to hear Orpheus at the Opera Comique . . . Did I tell you I flirted with the Poet Laureate [Alfred Austin] at Costabelle? and then went off without even saying good-bye, as I hear he has bitterly complained! He was an Anti-Suffrage so you understand the whole episode.'[2]

A summer visit to the Tyrol was planned but cancelled at the last minute. John was feeling the strain of his exhausting life: 'Jack is feeling so unable to work too lately [*sic*], the sunlessness is telling on him, poor dear. I don't really love the country in the middle of the summer – it's too thick and green and fat.'[3] They went instead to Yorkshire, where, at Ilkley, Ada had treatment 'boiling my bones'[4] for rheumatism. It was here that Galsworthy began the writing of *Justice*, and also wrote the first two chapters of his new novel *The Patrician*. But London, which Ada loved, was always a place where Galsworthy found it impossible to work; 'We had a wild week at Addison Road. I liked it but Jack seems glad to be back here [Manaton],' she wrote to Mottram in June,[5] and again in November: 'Jack is steadying down to work. London was disastrous this time. He never had a chance, for one reason or another.'[6]

'When I'm there I would be here; but when I'm here I would be there,' Lamond, the traveller in the allegorical play *The Little Dream*, laments. Galsworthy wrote this play at Easter 1909, when he and Ada had completed their first year as tenants at the farmhouse at Manaton. For John it had been a period of comparative happiness: after the years of travelling with Ada here at last was a place where he could put down roots, where he could settle and work steadily at his writing. But already it must have been apparent that Manaton, like other places, could only be a temporary haven. The wandering pattern of their lives was to continue, from one hotel to another, from Dartmoor to London; the Galsworthys were always to be birds of passage.

The Little Dream has something in common with Galsworthy's earlier poem 'The Dream' (which was incidentally the first title of his new play). It hasn't the strength or the sharpness of the poem; it is pessimistic where 'The Dream' is optimistic; it is in a sense a play of defeat. Seelchen, a mountain girl, is torn between the temptations of the town and the peace of the country; two lovers, Lamond and Felsman, represent the town and the country, and she is helplessly divided between her love for both of them. The message of the play is that there is no way of life that can satisfy a man; he needs both the country and the town, he must forever be wandering between the two.

One needs to consider what the town, the Wine Horn of the play, signified to Galsworthy. It was a life led in public; it was dinners, speechmaking, committees, rehearsals of his plays (though there were of course compensations, his family and friends, and the many people he needed to see about his many projects); this was his London life, and increasingly his life on the continent and in America. Manaton was in every way the complete opposite; it was a totally private life, walking and riding over the moors, the company of a few close friends, and above all time without interruptions in which to write. For Seelchen in her dream the only escape from her dilemma is the Great Horn – death:

> Wandering flame, thou restless fever
> Burning all things, regretting none;
> The winds of fate are stilled for ever –
> The little generous life is done,
> And all its wistful wonderings cease!
> Thou traveller to the tideless sea,
> Where light and dark, and change and peace,
> Are One – Come, little soul, to MYSTERY!

Galsworthy's dilemma was far greater than Seelchen's; not only was he divided between the life of the town and the country, but he must have begun to realize that he and Ada, in so many respects ideally matched, were in other ways extremely different. Life would never be easy, it would always be a matter of seeking compromises that would work for them both; but would this way of life be possible for him as a writer? Could his talent develop, or even survive, in the sort of life that was to be his? *The Little Dream* is a play of defeat; Galsworthy could for the moment see no escape from his dilemma, except the Great Horn.

On the other hand it is essential to emphasize how deeply Galsworthy believed in life itself: 'Life is good enough in itself even if it lead to nothing.'[7] Nor should it depend on place or circumstances to be fulfilling. Courage was a virtue he admired perhaps above all others; there is a little jingle by Adam Lindsay Gordon that he often quoted (Mr Paramor quotes it in *The Country House*) which he said was 'hard to beat as a summary of what keeps most of us going under the wear and tear of life':[8]

> Life is mostly froth and bubble,
> Two things stand like stone:
> Kindness in another's trouble,
> Courage in your own.

He would and did despise any weakness in himself, therefore he was determined that his need for a settled background and Ada's need for the very opposite should be resolved in a compromise that would to some degree work for them both. Ada would travel and find the climate and distractions that suited her health, and he would write; however difficult the circumstances, he would establish a routine of writing that would not be dependent on place or situation; he would write on trains, in strange hotels, or on ocean liners, somehow the difficulties would be overcome. That he believed in courage did not necessarily mean he always had it; his standards of personal behaviour were higher than could possibly be achieved. There is a revealing entry in the diary which he began to keep in 1910.* 'Interrupted at 12.15 by an old lady who came to ask me to provide her with courage. Told her had not enough for myself. Poor old thing – she wept.'[9]

Such moments of self-revelation are rare. John Galsworthy was not a man who believed in discussing or writing about what he felt, except under the guise of fiction, nor of course was it 'done' in the age in which he grew up, in which reserve, especially in men, was regarded as an admirable quality. His cousin and goddaughter, Dorothy Easton, who as a young girl stayed regularly with the Galsworthys and had a particularly intimate and charming relationship with her uncle, has described how as a young writer herself she confided her literary aspirations, the plots of her stories, even her diary, to her Uncle John. He helped and encouraged his young niece, giving her a small allowance to give her the independence which would enable her to write. But she was sometimes frustrated and miserable because she longed to discuss her 'feelings' with this uncle, whom she hero-worshipped. It was never allowed, she said, 'books, we could discuss, feelings, no'.

Nevertheless the pattern of life that John and Ada established for themselves worked tolerably for them both during those early years of their official marriage. In his writing Ada was for him, what she had always wanted to be, an ideal amanuensis; she read and criticized everything he wrote, and then patiently typed out his manuscript, often several times before he was satisfied. Their marriage was a companionship but not an intimacy; the cold and formal character of Ada, which has been commented on by those who knew her best, reinforced the reserve that John had cultivated within himself since boyhood;

* John's diaries from that date are preserved; it seems likely that earlier ones existed but have been destroyed, and a résumé made from them by Ada.

except in his writing, and most of all in his poetry, there was no outlet for his deeper feelings, no one to whom he could confide his internal conflicts.

This itinerant pattern of life must explain why Galsworthy worked on so many different pieces of writing concurrently, while most writers (his friend, Conrad, is an example) would work consistently on one book. During the year 1909 he wrote *The Little Dream,* he revised and partly rewrote *The Eldest Son,* he began that same spring two other plays *The Mob* and *The Winter Garden,* and, then, abandoning both these two, in July at Ilkley he started to write his play *Justice* and the novel *The Patrician.* As well as these larger works he wrote many of the short stories that were collected and published as *A Motley* in June the following year.

These works range over a great breadth of society and conditions of life, from the hopeless clerk Falder in *Justice,* to the opulent, high-living 'Patricians'.

But it was with these 'Patricians' that the Galsworthys found them-selves mainly associating (to Ada's secret delight): 'Generally speaking rather "after" *Patricians* at this time. Met a good many.' 'Made acquaintance with Mrs. Asquith at dinner with Duchess of Marl-borough . . . lunched with Asquiths a little later. Met Lord Morley. Also met Ilchesters at Holland House. Also Lord and Lady Ridley.'[10] Ada once said to Mottram of *The Patricians*: 'Ah, that was *my* book.'[11] She could equally have said 'that was *my* time'. This was indeed the life that Ada loved; fashionable dinners, high society, and above all a lot going on. It must to both of them have seemed a time of almost bewildering success, with performances of *Strife* in Germany and Manchester, and *Justice* about to open in London.

But was this really what John became a writer for, to be lionized by the fashionable, to be travelling hither and thither like a spinning top? Would it ever be possible in such a climate of activity to write the novel that would fulfil the promise of *The Man of Property* or *Fraternity*? 'We are now half the week between London and here,' Ada wrote to Mottram in January 1910 from Littlehampton. 'He has been tidying up many sketches for a volume to come out in March [*A Motley*], is now writing a paper to read at Oxford and I hope will soon be able to go at the long neglected novel again.'[12]

At last the Galsworthys returned to Manaton, and at the end of March Ada wrote regretfully to her confidant, Mottram. 'Littlehampton was perfect – the sun and sweet air with the larks in it, and the gentle sea. Wingstone will be the devil in this coldness. I do shrink from it.'[13]

And so the seesaw of their tastes continued. John, back at Manaton, took up his novel again: 'and now I settle down to the drag of my novel – having got to that stage, which requires my heart hardened for the full stream, and the pull in,' he wrote to Edward Garnett at the end of April;[14] and a few weeks later: 'The novel progresses in a way – forwards, backwards, sideways, and at times stationary.'[15] But for Ada it was the domestic, uneventful life that she so thoroughly disliked. 'Longings for a far-away holiday are simply gnawing me,'[16] she was writing to Mottram early in June, and in her next letter: 'J. is pegging away very hard and is pretty tired in the head. I as usual typing, sewing, gardening and writing his unimportant letters.'[17]

However, the domestic tedium was broken by the visits of friends; Galsworthy's sister Lilian Sauter and her son Rudo stayed with them in April, and later in the month Professor Gilbert Murray. Murray's visit was happily timed; he took an immense interest in the progress of the new novel, which during the summer he read twice in manuscript, offering enormous encouragement and also criticism. When it finally appeared Galsworthy dedicated *The Patrician* to him.

The Patrician, as its original title *The Patricians* suggests, is concerned with the ruling class, the aristocracy. 'The germ of The Patrician is traceable to a certain dinner party at the House of Commons in 1908, and the face of a young politician on the other side of a round table,' Galsworthy recalled in his Manaton preface to the novel. He was to be Eustace Miltoun, son of Lord Valleys. Miltoun's fortunes follow the well-trodden path of so many of Galsworthy's heroes: he falls in love with a married woman, Audrey Noel, who is living apart from her husband. He is determined to risk everything for his passion, for, like Galsworthy and Bosinney, he loves a woman who is chained to a husband who refuses to release his wife by divorce. But in the end wisdom prevails, and Miltoun accepts that his political ambition is the dominating force in his life, and he allows Audrey Noel to disappear tactfully.

The other major work that was completed and finally revised in November 1910, his play *The Eldest Son*, has much in common with *The Patrician*. Both works are concerned with the aristocracy and the importance of inheritance: Bill Cheshire, the eldest son, is to inherit his father's title and position as country squire, just as Miltoun, as his father's son, is expected to follow his father into the world of government; both of them are expected to make marriages that will not jeopardize their position in life, and both are in danger of doing so. Bill Cheshire has had an affair with his mother's maid, Freda Studdenham, and she has become pregnant with his child, just as, on a different plane, Miltoun has fallen in love with a married woman; in both cases it is the women who voluntarily release their lovers from their inconvenient attachments.

At last, on 18 August, Galsworthy was able to record in his diary that *The Patrician* was finished, 'having taken from start to finish in the actual writing 14 months, broken by the writing of *Justice* and its production, and by the writing of several short studies'. It was the end of the series of five social novels that he had set out to write nearly ten years earlier, the completion of his satirical picture of society that began with *The Island Pharisees*. It was a natural break, as, in the course of writing the series, his novels had moved a long way from the hard-hitting satire of *The Man of Property*. '*The Patricians* is less satiric than the others,' he wrote. 'There has been a steady decrescendo in satire through the whole series, and, I think, a steady increase in the desire for beauty. This may be a sign of age; or it may be a good sign; or again it may be only that there is so much that one can't express in dramatic form that one tends naturally in the novel to make up to oneself and write out one's feelings for beauty more and more in the novel form.'[18]

Galsworthy's search for 'beauty' was too self-conscious; the book has a softness that is almost cloying. The heroine, Audrey Noel, so similar to Ada in many ways, is drawn with a feather pen; she is over-delicate and feminine, and has a preciousness that is intolerably refined. There is only an occasional glimmer of the old sharpness, a touch of the whip that could, if more liberally applied, have given strength and structure to the novel. 'Lady Casterley was that inconvenient thing – an early riser.'

At the time Galsworthy seemed unaware of the defects of the novel, or of the general trend in his writing that it represented. The year 1910 ended leaving Galsworthy in a reasonably complacent mood; as he recorded in his diary, he had written 'about 100,000 words that stand', and of his novel *The Patrician* he wrote on 21 December, 'On the whole I think it may be the best of my novels.' The same entry concludes with a view of his work as a whole as considered in relation to his contemporaries:

The book [*The Patrician*] discloses me finally as an impressionist working with a realistic or naturalistic technique. Whereas Wells is a realist working with an impressionist technique, Bennett a realist with a realistic technique, Conrad an impressionist with a semi-impressionistic, semi naturalistic technique, and Forster an impressionist with a realistically impressionistic technique.

It was a complicated over-simplification. And it is hard to believe that even Galsworthy can have believed such sweeping statements about himself and his fellow writers.

When Galsworthy reconsidered *The Patrician* for his preface to the Manaton Edition of 1923 he found himself much less happy with the book. 'Aesthetically speaking I consider that a certain forcing of the "beauty" note rather self-conscious in the latter part of the book, a sort of softness in the love stories detracts from its merits . . . did not give me the same satisfaction when I read it through for the purpose of this preface as *Fraternity* or *The Dark Flower*.'

But Professor Gilbert Murray, as well as Ada, was effusive in his praise and enthusiasm for the book. 'I think for beauty and poignancy together it is the finest of your novels. . . . It is much more like a poem than a prose novel,' Murray wrote to him after his second reading of the manuscript.[19] Thus Galsworthy was completely unprepared for the unfavourable reaction of Edward Garnett to his new novel when he sent it to him in September.

> I'm not complimentary to *The Patrician*. I'm not going to be. I send you the notes I took as I read the pages . . . I'm afraid that this book will, in the public mind, draw a line round your talent and will circumscribe it definitely – and will let the light in on – not chiefly on your strength, but a good deal on the blanks at the back of the strength.[20]

The correspondence that ensued between Garnett and Galsworthy is basic to the whole situation: Garnett, who was not by any means always a wise critic where Galsworthy's work was concerned, realized that in this book his former protégé's work was veering in a disastrously wrong direction. 'I don't regard this book as *vital* to you, or deeply of you,' he wrote to him, and accused him of writing of a world, the world of the aristocracy, of which he knew nothing.

The latter accusation worried Galsworthy so much that he ultimately presented Garnett with a list of no less than 130 titled people, whom he claimed to know tolerably well, a list that he said did not include 'as many more' untitled but nevertheless aristocratic persons. It was not therefore, he argued, through lack of knowledge that his book failed, but lack of artistry.

The mind boggles, not only at the size of Galsworthy's circle of acquaintances, but at the naïvety of Galsworthy in believing that this superficial association with people would necessarily give him insight into their character. In fact this whole correspondence between critic and author, ostensibly attacking and defending the new novel, goes much deeper. Garnett saw a superficiality in the book which he disliked and feared for its damaging effect on Galsworthy's reputation; Galsworthy was forced to defend not only the book he had written but his whole way of life. He had not written a book that was 'vital' to him or deeply himself, but could he do so? He had deliberately turned away from satire, and he declared himself to be searching for 'beauty' in his writing. But without depth beauty floats unanchored like a flower without a plant; it is flimsy and insubstantial. He had to delve deeper into himself than he dared, he needed quiet and solitude and time in which to think. He had to go forward with the depth of *Fraternity* and the power of *The Man of Property*. He could do neither.

Chapter 22

Margaret Morris

John Galsworthy was by nature an uncomplicated and direct person. He saw the spectrum of the world around him as a scene painted in black and white, and the activities of his fellow human beings as good or bad, right or wrong. His deeply felt views on love and marriage were similarly naïve; that people should be bound to uncongenial and loveless marriages appalled him; that people, such as his own character Miltoun, should be prevented from marrying the people they loved because of social taboos was also abhorrent. What he failed to see was the essentially complex nature of marriage or any other relationship, that those that appear to be unsuitably partnered might in fact have their own sort of contentment, or that others, apparently much in love, could be unhappy; even less could he imagine that people who loved, as he and Ada loved, could ever be unfaithful to their partner. His own characters fell in love again only when they were unhappily married.

Thus Galsworthy, at the age of forty-four, was totally unprepared for his encounter with the young and beautiful dancer, Margaret Morris. So unprepared, in fact, so incapable of imagining that he could be susceptible to the charms of any woman other than Ada, that for the first months of his acquaintance with the young dancer he was completely unaware of what was happening to him, or indeed to her.

Galsworthy met Margaret Morris for the first time in the autumn of 1910 on the stage of the Savoy Theatre. She was only nineteen, an extremely vivacious girl with dark hair and lively brown eyes. As a physical being she was exceptional; she had a lovely body and her training had taught her to move with graceful ease. She had also an innocence which would have appealed to Galsworthy, a youthfulness, which, whatever her other qualities, he had never known in Ada. The occasion was the first night of Marie Brema's production of Gluck's *Orpheus and Eurydice*, for which Margaret Morris had done the choreography and designed the costumes and scenery; such a commission for so young a girl was in itself an amazing achievement. Galsworthy was delighted by her dancing, and enormously interested, for Greek dancing was something new to the London stage, something that Margaret had herself learnt from Raymond Duncan, brother of the famous Isadora. He was so much interested that he at once asked her to come and meet Ada at Addison Road. Only a few days later she came to tea with them and told them more of her new ideas about dancing.

The meeting was a success on both sides. Margaret Morris, in her book *My Galsworthy Story*, has described the enormous impression the Galsworthy home made on her: 'the peace and beauty of that little house, the magnolia tree, the spaniel "Chris" . . . the whole effect was harmonious and restful.' She was struck by the simplicity of Ada's furniture, the white walls and white paint, the unclutteredness of the furniture and ornaments. It was so different from her own much more Victorian, and much less rich, home. Her father was an artist; her mother cooked for her family, and they ate together in the basement kitchen. She also devoted herself to the training of her enormously talented child, and much of the time, Margaret Morris tells us, she was 'touring with her mother, living in cheap theatrical "digs"'. Margaret Morris, it would seem, was immediately captivated by Galsworthy's charm, as she records in her book: 'to see him was to love him – he had such a gracious, kindly personality and a most charming smile.' After that first tea party at Addison Road she was so excited that that evening she absent-mindedly went on to the stage to dance in her 'red felt slippers'.

For Galsworthy the meeting had an additional significance: Margaret Morris's dancing was exactly what he was looking for for the production of his play *The Little Dream*. He lost no time, and as she hurried away from the tea party in Addison Road he asked her to lunch the following week to discuss the play, which was already scheduled to be produced by Miss Horniman at her theatre in Manchester. At lunch he described his play to Margaret and it was agreed that she, with a group of children trained by herself, should dance the 'Death by Drowning' and 'Death by Slumber' sequences.

It was Galsworthy's sister, Mabel, now married to Tom Reynolds, whose house in Holland Park had become a centre where musicians such as the young Myra Hess met and played at informal soirées, who introduced her brother to the composer Wolfgang von Bartels. He agreed to write the music for Galsworthy's play. 'Music could not be better,' John wrote to his sister, '. . . little von B. is as pleased as Punch. I owe you a great debt for getting me this music; the greatest stroke of theatrical luck I am ever likely to have.'[1] The arrangement with von Bartels must have been finalized by the time of this first lunch with Margaret Morris, as, on this occasion, Galsworthy was also able to tell her that the music for the play was being specially written by the Austrian composer.

By February they were meeting regularly to discuss the play. On 5 February he notes in his diary: 'Margaret Morris came 12. Read *The Little Dream* and discussed the dance thereof. A picturesque young critter. She stayed to lunch.' A few days later (9 February) he wrote arranging for her to meet the producer Iden Payne, and on the 22nd to tell her that he had got the dance music in manuscript. 'It is rather hard to read. and requires a little talking over. I wonder if you could come to us here at about 4 o'clock tomorrow?'

At this time Margaret Morris was dancing in Maeterlinck's *Blue Bird* at the Haymarket but during the day she was free to work on the dances for *The Little Dream*. She saw a great deal of John and Ada, who both took an active interest in the progress of her dances for the play. Then, three weeks before the play was due to open in Manchester, Margaret, with two friends, went into lodgings in the city and re-hearsed the play at Miss Horniman's Little Theatre. In April the Galsworthys came up to Manchester to supervise the rehearsals, staying close by at the King's Coffee House at Knutsford. 'He [J.G.] and the young composer of *The Little Dream* music are just gone off to Man-chester for a preliminary tug at the various troubles connected with that little play . . . then we all go and tug together from the 2nd April to the 15th when it appears.'[2]

It was a magical time for the young dancer, training her children for the play, enchanted by Galsworthy's constant interest in her work, but probably not yet fully aware of the depth of her feelings for him. Galsworthy was, as always, almost over-considerate to his actors, paying them more than was required for their performances, paying their taxi fares home when they stayed late rehearsing. On one oc-casion, Eleanor Elder one of the dancers recalls, overhearing them dis-cussing what they could afford to pay for their meals, he insisted on paying for their meal. 'I would hate to think of you going hungry, would you please allow me to help you out?' And he gave them all the silver he had in his pocket, apologizing that it was not more. On

Sundays Margaret was invited to spend the day with the Galsworthys at Knutsford.

For Galsworthy anxiety over the success of his play marred those days: '. . . rehearsals in evening very bad. Most gloomy journey out to Knutsford. Things (mechanics and lighting) looking hopeless,' he wrote on 14 April. But the next day all was well for the first performance, though in the afternoon 'Things looked fairly gloomy.' But he admitted 'Performance *very good and a great success. Many calls.*'

On 20 April, his play going well, he and Ada returned to Addison Road. With the Galsworthys' departure Margaret found that Manchester was no longer the sparkling city it had seemed while John was there; it was a dark and gloomy place, that had been transformed into 'the most desirable spot in the whole world' by his presence. She knew now that she was deeply in love, though she had not the slightest idea that John would ever return her feelings. Margaret Morris has always emphasized that at no time was there any question of the depth of his feeling for Ada, or of that feeling altering in any way. And yet without knowing it John was already in love with Margaret; back in London he was busily engaged in writing a new part for her. This time she was not to dance, but to act the part of Mrs Megan in his new play *The Pigeon.*

This play is the story of a philanthropist, Christopher Wellwyn, who cannot prevent himself from giving away all that he has. Mrs Megan, a flower-seller, is in desperate straits, so also is Ferrand, who appears again from *The Island Pharisees*, a Frenchman and Galsworthy's spokesman from the suffering poor, and a third, a cabman, Timson; these three have been given a card by Wellwyn giving his address and telling them to call on him if they are in trouble. They do, and Wellwyn is himself ruined by his own charity.

To many people the possibility of sexually loving more than one person at a time is difficult to comprehend; we have been educated to believe that one love excludes another, that for a married person to fall in love again is automatically an act of infidelity. John and Ada were both totally committed to the idea that love should not be possessive, but, tragically, when their principles came to the test neither was strong enough to live out their belief.

In those early days Margaret was still the protégée of both the Galsworthys; her friendship, she insists, was with both John and Ada.

After the success* of *The Little Dream* they decided that Margaret's talent in training children to dance should be developed; if she could find a suitable room to start a small school of dancing they would give her all the support she needed. A small room was soon found in Bloomsbury; the Galsworthys paid the rent, and furnished it with lino and curtains and a piano. The Margaret Morris School of Dance was advertised and an audition held (attended by John) at which six children were selected to be the first pupils at the new school. The school was so successful that within two months Margaret transferred to new and larger premises in Endell Street, once again with the backing of the Galsworthys. By now Margaret was so confident in the general usefulness of her method that she offered to give the Galsworthys some lessons! (In the text of her book she comments unromantically that, as her theory of movement was particularly valuable to people after middle age, it would have helped John and Ada.)

Most of the summer of 1911 the Galsworthys were out of London, at Wingstone or travelling to Ireland to visit the John Masefields or to Ilkley for some more hot baths for Ada's rheumatism. They were in Ilkley for the coronation of George V and 'watched coronation sports and saw 54 children dance Morris dancing and very little tots sing and hop about in the songs London Bridge etc'.[3]

Revivals of his plays in the provinces and London meant more travelling about and distraction from the new play John was working on, *The Fugitive*: *The Silver Box* in London, *Justice* in Manchester and *Strife* in Liverpool where 'J.G. made 2 speeches, an unheard of innovation, for he loathes speaking'.[4] Galsworthy was also beginning to make plans for the production of *The Pigeon*: the theatrical manager J. E. Vedrenne decided to produce the play early in the new year, and Galsworthy kept his promise to Margaret Morris and suggested her for the part of Mrs Megan.

On 27 May she lunched with the Galsworthys at Addison Road and John 'read her the Pigeon with a view to seeing if she could play Mrs Megan. Think she will do.'[5] Vedrenne was at first less happy at the prospect of using an untried actress in so important a part, but after he

* 'The Little Dream, though I think only understood by one in ten, impressed people and was quite a success in its way. Anyway the little actress [M. Morris] got 7 bouquets and a full house in the last performance. London hangs back naturally being too bloated to take the slightest risk.' J.G. to Mottram. 13 June 1911. •

had auditioned Margaret his opposition was overcome, and after the first rehearsal Galsworthy wrote to reassure her: 'A hurried line to tell you that Vedrenne thinks you have the right temperament, and are intelligent (!) Be very intelligent and do not reply to any suggestion of his with; "Oh! I thought I was to do this!" or "Mr. G. said I was to do that." If things are going wrong leave me to pull them back again.'[5]

It was during these rehearsals that John and Margaret began to meet frequently, usually at long lunchtimes spent talking in her studio. Naïvely they both still thought of it as a triangular friendship that included Ada, though one cannot help suspecting that Ada already had some idea of how deeply the other two had begun to feel about each other. It was for her one of the saddest and most distressing winters of her life. On 19 December their spaniel, Chris, died. John recorded the event in his diary: 'Chris is gone. Ada prostrate. Oh! So sad a day.' In a letter to Margaret he told her: 'We have been and still are very sad. Don't mention him in letters or by mouth, please.' As we have already said, Chris was no ordinary dog to the Galsworthys; Mottram has said that he was more like a child than a pet to them, and certainly, though they had many other dogs, no other one meant as much as Chris had done. There was something almost symbolic about the dog's death coming at this moment in their lives, as if the event heralded the end of what had been a perfect and intensely romantic relationship – at least for Ada. Chris, their 'child', was dead, and John was in love with another woman.

The 'affair' between John Galsworthy and Margaret Morris must have been one of the briefest and most touchingly innocent relationships in history. Margaret, despite her success both as an actress and as a dancer, was by her own account exceptionally unsophisticated and innocent. In her book she describes how during a rehearsal for *The Pigeon* she was kissed by Denis Eadie in his role of Ferrand, and Vedrenne, who was sitting beside Galsworthy, watching the performance, called out from the stalls: 'Miss Morris, haven't you ever been kissed before – can't you try and look as if you liked it!'[7]

Later, during a dinner at Kettners, apparently still not suspecting her feelings for him, John asked if she had ever been in love. She lied, and told him no, deeply fearful lest he should guess the truth. To which he replied: 'What a pity! To love is the most marvellous thing in the world. It will be wonderful for the man who can awaken you.'[8]

The intimacy of such a conversation, so utterly uncharacteristic of Galsworthy, who was usually formal and correct to the point of stiffness, shows how far the friendship between him and Margaret had already gone. It is not therefore surprising that on the next day, returning from a visit to a theatrical costumier in search of suitable clothes for Margaret to wear as Mrs Megan, the situation at last came out into the open. To use her own words:

It was horrible weather, and in the taxi back to the theatre John said, 'You look terribly cold,' and he put his arm round me. That was too much – he had never touched me before. I snuggled up against him, and he suddenly said: 'Look at me.' I did not dare, but buried my face in his coat – I can still feel the soft texture of the deep pile of the overcoat he wore; but he insisted, saying, 'I must know, you must look at me.' So I did, and he knew, and of course he kissed me and the whole world was transformed.[9]

During the weeks that followed Margaret and John openly discussed their situation – and Ada. They intended to become lovers, but how and when, and particularly how to avoid any hurt to Ada, was still vague in their minds. These meetings took place in Margaret's flat in Castle Street, and John insisted that they remained rigidly apart, sitting at opposite sides of the room. They talked endlessly, Miss Morris has said, of their own situation, of their lives, and of the future that John planned for Margaret in the theatre. And all the time she begged him to say nothing to Ada; it was Margaret's belief that Ada would be able to accept a *fait accompli*, that she would be able to see that Margaret as John's mistress was no threat to her own life with John, or John's love for herself. It was a naïve hope: few women in 1912 – or indeed 1976 – could accept the idea of shared love.

It was inevitable that a crisis should come. Margaret, not surprisingly, had abandoned her visits to 14 Addison Road, for though the couple tried to convince themselves that Ada might ultimately accept the situation, while it was still secret the strain was intolerable, and particularly for John. Signs of the strain he was under began to show, and when Ada asked him outright why Margaret no longer visited them, though John tried unsuccessfully to cover the truth, Ada broke down.

In his novel *The Dark Flower* Galsworthy has described, with what

appears to be astonishing accuracy, his affair with Margaret Morris
Mark Lennan is the hero, whose three experiences of love are described
as 'Spring', 'Summer' and 'Autumn'. As a very young man in Spring
he falls in love with his tutor's wife; she ultimately rejects him telling
him to find a partner of his own age. In Summer he falls in love with
a married woman. In the last section, Autumn, having been married
happily for many years to an early love, Sylvia, he becomes infatuated
by a young girl, Nell. Miss Morris by her own account never read the
book until very much later, in fact when she was arranging her
correspondence with Galsworthy for her own book. Of it she writes:
'When I read "Autumn", I was startled by the accuracy with which he
quoted almost word for word whole passages of dialogue that actually
took place between us.'[10]

The Dark Flower is in fact much more than an account of Galsworthy's infatuation for Margaret Morris. It is, like an earlier novel he
attempted to start in the summer of 1911, *The Book of Youth*, a recapitu-
lation of the emotional life of a man. And, just as it is possible to
identify Nell with Margaret Morris, so Ada is painted both as the
dramatic and vital heroine of 'Summer', Olive Cramier, who sym-
bolically is drowned at the end of the section, and who is undoubtedly
the real passion of Mark Lennan's life, and also as his wife Sylvia of the
third episode, whom he still loves and cannot bear to betray. But in
Sylvia something is dead that was alive in Olive Cramier.

It is impossible to ignore the implications of this novel. We know
from Margaret Morris that 'Autumn' is an almost exact account of her
affair with Galsworthy; the passionate love that Mark Lennan felt for
the married woman Olive Cramier in 'Summer' fits in exactly with
his other fictional accounts of his affair with Ada. Olive Cramier has
much in common with Galsworthy's other unhappily married heroines,
Audrey Noel of *The Patrician*, and even more Irene Soames. There is
a scene in *The Dark Flower* remarkably similar to that in *In Chancery* in
which Soames pleads for Irene's love, and to which she replies: 'You
may hunt me to the grave. I will not come.' Robert Cramier begs
Olive to love him: 'Have Mercy! Love me a little!' to which she
replies: 'Mercy? Can I *make* myself love? No one ever could since the
world began.' There is a hardness about these women with which it is
difficult to sympathize, and yet Galsworthy always sees *them* and not
their wretched husbands as the suffering and injured partners. Ada
must have given John the most lurid account of her life with Major

Galsworthy, and from these descriptions his vindictive heroines must have taken their colour.

It is legitimate to see that Sylvia is, even if unconsciously, to some extent a portrait of Ada some fifteen years after their first passionate meeting. Mark's marriage he describes as 'Happy enough – gentle, not very vivid, nor spiritually very intimate – his work always secretly . . . remote from her . . .' And later he says of her: 'Sylvia would not understand passion so out of hand as this [Oliver Dromore's love for his cousin Nell].' But throughout this story of a middle-aged man's passion for a young girl, Galsworthy is never deluded into thinking that this new obsession can be compared with his love for Olive Cramier, the Ada of fifteen years ago, a love to which he is constantly harking back. 'There *she* [Olive] had lived; there was the house – those windows which he had stolen past and gazed at with such distress and longing.'

Matters came to a head in the last week of January: on the 26th the Galsworthys went to Littlehampton. 'Neither of us well,' John wrote in his diary, and the next day: 'Cursed *The Little Dream*.' It must have been at Littlehampton that John at last told Ada of his feelings for Margaret, begging her to understand that they in no way replaced his love for her.

Ada struggled to do what she believed she should do, to be generous ✷ and unpossessive. She wrote, replying to a letter from Margaret: 'You must not be unhappy, but very happy – first love at your age – can there be anything more holy! And you must not think of me – I am content. Just at present physical weakness dominates me and makes a bad impression, but the spirit is well-meaning and strong.' And she ended her letter: 'The world is not a dreadful place – presently you will know it. Everything shall and must be turned to *good*.'[11]

But though Ada undoubtedly meant what she said in her letter, this 'physical weakness', which always distressed John so much, in fact doomed any continuation of his friendship with Margaret. As he began to see, their friendship could only be at the expense of Ada's health and happiness. An earlier arrangement for Margaret and her mother to come to Addison Road for tea had to be cancelled at the last minute: 'A. would not be fit to talk to or see anyone, and I should feel a little distracted, and I don't want to be now that the last chance of altering anything has come,' he wrote to Margaret.[12] But there was no real chance of altering anything. In *The Dark Flower* he describes the desperate dilemma: 'Could Sylvia not let him keep both her love and the girl's? Could she not bear that? She had said she could; but her face, her eyes, her voice gave her the lie, so that every time he heard her his heart turned sick with pity . . .'

It must have seemed for Ada as if the Nemesis of her childhood was once again catching up with her; rejected from the first by her mother, unloved during her girlhood and adolescence, followed by her loveless marriage to Arthur Galsworthy, now was John, the one person she had trusted, the person who had given her stability and security, was he too to reject her?

The affair of the novel ended in exactly the same way as that between John and Margaret: an almost overnight decision to take Ada abroad and himself away from the temptation of Margaret Morris. After the first night of *The Pigeon* on 30 January, which John attended without Ada and without going backstage to see Margaret, he sent her a brief note:

> To Margaret:
> Forgive me if you can for going without seeing you. Neither you nor I are capable of taking any happiness over such illness and suffering. Be a brave child, and think of brighter days that will soon come, believe me. Write if you like.

The Galsworthys travelled first to Paris, from where John wrote to Margaret on 1 February, telling her that Ada was 'already feeling better; so do not feel despairing and too sad'.[13] From Paris they travelled on to the South of France and stayed at the Grand Hotel, Grasse. From here Ada wrote with forced cheerfulness to Mottram: 'Paris was very flattering: numbers of intellectuals who quoted J.G. by the page and seemed to know his work better than we did.'[14] Ada, John reported, was still improving in health, and she herself sent messages to Margaret telling her to write 'when and *what* you like'. But, John added, 'her spirit is still I think too willing for her strength, so perhaps not all you would like'.[15] The couple continued to correspond, though John told Margaret 'to burn these scraps of mine or keep them on you and give them to me when I see you'.[16] A piece of advice Margaret fortunately ignored. By now John was writing from a Post Restante at Beaulieu, and it was here on 18 February that he at last wrote announcing that he and Margaret must give up all hope of their friendship ever continuing. The letter is so moving it is worth quoting in full:

Beaulieu
Feb. 18, 1912

Dear dear child,

In my letter to you I have kept on saying 'She is better', 'She is better'. It was wrong of me, but while I could still hold on to hope I didn't want you to despair. But in very very truth there is and can be no better for her unless all ends between us. I have watched it day by day and night by night – such torture and misery I have never seen and never could bear to see again. There is only one thing for it, we must give each other up, and utterly. Her life and mine together has been such and our love has been and is such as to make. it a sacred trust; and you are too dear and good not to feel with me that we cannot take happiness out of her despair and misery. Then there is all the secrecy and the yearnings for more than Fate would have let us give each other, and I don't feel that underground life and starvation are right for your dear self. Better nothing at all, better to root up this feeling for me. A finer mate, who can give you a sweeter and fuller life will soon come to you. And if it's any joy to you to know that I loved you, as it is still joy to me to feel that you could have such a feeling for me – well there it is and will always be, even when we have both got over it. So my poor dear it must be Goodbye – a real lasting Goodbye, and God bless you! Forget, forget and forgive me!

That fortnight in France must have been one of the most difficult and testing times that Galsworthy ever had to face. Ada was ill and suffering desperately because of his defection. She wanted to give John the freedom he needed; at the same time she was shattered and bewildered that *he*, whom she had believed to be so different from other men, should want such freedom, or in fact want any other intimate friend than herself. How much were they able to discuss their situation? Or did they face it in a terrifying and painful silence? There are hints in John's diary that some sort of discussion about their future did take place: on 17 February he wrote: 'Going away made definite. Resolution to go to New York and produce *Pigeon*, thence travel and return about June.' And on the following day, the 18th, he wrote the letter which is quoted above. In his diary he wrote: 'Spent afternoon lying out on the promontory of St. Jean over the sea. It was nice. Evening to Monte. Between us we lost £2.'

It is not difficult to see the pattern of that day. No doubt his letter was at least thought out, if not written, as he lay on the grass overlooking the sea; he must have seen that if his life with Ada was to continue with any sort of happiness he must finally cut Margaret out of his life completely. But the implications of his decision went far deeper than at first appears: his nephew, Rudolf Sauter, has said that after the events of the past few months, which Ada saw as an unforgiveable infidelity to the virtually sacred trust that was between them, their marriage was to continue, but on different and less intimate terms. We have raised the possibility that sex played a very small part in the Galsworthys' marriage; now there was to be none. John, as he lay stretched out in the hot southern sun, rejected the passionate love of Margaret Morris and accepted a life that would from now on be entirely celibate.

The decision, once made, must have brought relief as well as pain, and the evening at the Casino in Monte Carlo, losing their modest two pounds, must have made a welcome escape from the tension of the weeks that had gone before. As the roulette wheel spun so the Galsworthys set out on a new and less happy epoch of their lives together.

Chapter 23
America — Convalescence and Recovery

In all this chaos what of his work? Could he ever have peace of mind for it again? . . . To have had the waters broken up; to be plunged into emotion; to feel desperately, instead of stagnating – some day he might be grateful – who knew? Some day there might be fair country again beyond this desert, where we could work, even better than before. But just now, as well expect creative work from a condemned man. It seemed to him that he was equally destroyed whether he gave Nell up, and with her, once for all, that roving, seeking instinct, which ought, forsooth, to have been satisfied, and was not; or whether he took Nell, knowing that in doing so he was torturing a woman dear to him! That was as far as he could see to-day. What he would come to see in time God only knew![1]

Galsworthy saw his predicament with amazing clarity; in his rejection of Margaret Morris he was perhaps doing irreparable damage to himself, both as a writer and as a person. But he had no alternative: a man who could not bear to see a horse or a dog in pain could scarcely stand by and see the suffering of his wife and do nothing to alleviate it.

It is perhaps at first sight strange that at the height of his crisis, on 7 February at Grasse, he should have begun to write the second story of his novel *The Dark Flower*, 'Summer', the story that deals with his passion for Olive Cramier. But on further consideration it was the most natural thing for him to do: he needed most urgently to persuade both himself and Ada of the far deeper significance of his love for her; he needed, once again, to write the story of Irene and Bosinney, of his own great love for a woman who in law belonged to another. But his mental distress was too acute for any sort of sustained work; the story, begun in Grasse, was not taken up again until their return from America in May, and the final story of the book, 'Autumn', was not written until January 1913, a whole year after his final break with Margaret Morris.

Because it is biographically so relevant to this period of Galsworthy's life, it is necessary to jump on a year and consider this novel, *The Dark Flower*, from which we have already quoted so liberally, but which was not in fact finished until the spring of 1913, and not published until October of that year. It is important to remember that though factually the story told in 'Autumn' is a fairly accurate account of his relationship with Margaret Morris, his reflections and conclusions were those of a man who had had time in which to think more calmly of the affair, to come to terms with what had happened, and to see it in the context of his life and philosophy.

The experience he had gone through was, he came to believe, an inevitable stage in the life of a man. 'It had begun with a sort of long craving, stilled only when he was working hard – a craving for he knew not what . . . They said that about forty-five was a perilous age for a man – especially for an artist.' But nevertheless he bitterly resented his inability to resist the temptation when it came to him: 'he felt in the grip of something beyond his power to fight against; something that, however he swerved and backed, and broke away, would close in on him, find means to bind him again hand and foot.' And then finally the utter despair he felt, torn between the two women whom he loved so differently: 'between these two, suffering so because of him, he felt as if he had lost his own existence.'

Dorothy Easton, his goddaughter, has said that with the writing of *The Dark Flower* the whole experience of his love for Margaret Morris was purged from him and finished with. But was it? Could it have been? Just as a new relationship emerged between him and Ada, that would never be the same as the old, so John Galsworthy was a different man after the experience of 1911 and 1912. He lost faith in himself; he found it almost impossible to forgive the hurt he had caused to Ada. As Mark Lennan at last gives up the struggle to fulfil his love for Nell, he reflects on the injury he could do to Sylvia: 'I, who believe in bravery and kindness; I, who hate cruelty – if I do this cruel thing, what shall I have to live for; how shall I work; how bear myself? If I do it, I am lost – an outcast from my own faith – a renegade from all that I believe in.' John Galsworthy did not abandon Ada; he gave up his friendship with Margaret completely, but he still did not escape from the consequences of his passion. The hurt to Ada could not be undone; he did find himself 'an outcast' from his own faith, 'a renegade' from all he believed in. From now on Galsworthy was to keep an even closer guard over his feelings; never again would he allow himself to be carried away by his emotions. Thus a man, already inclined to be formal and stiff in his relations with people, was to become more so. This was the man whom his young goddaughter, Dorothy Easton, grew to know at about this period of his life, and who said of him that he would never discuss his, or anyone else's feelings.

But at this point the Galsworthys had to escape, from England, from Margaret, hopefully from their own distress. Their decision to go to America was put swiftly into action. They returned to England by the *Rapide* on the 19th, spent the next two days frantically packing for what was to be a long absence, and on the 23rd took the train to Liverpool in time to board the SS *Campania* the following day.

As they set sail from Liverpool on 24 February, the Galsworthys were indeed in low spirits. Apart from the appalling cloud that had come between them, John's play *The Pigeon* was having only a very moderate success in London. In view of this it is perhaps surprising that one of the objectives of the American visit was a production of the play in New York. But the American public had already shown itself to be a sympathetic recipient of Galsworthy's work, and in the future America was to be a place where the Galsworthys could always be certain of a warm welcome.

The voyage, a period of enforced inactivity, was a trial to them both. 'The whole voyage was the apotheosis of monotony. One has got too much accustomed to employing one's time to tolerate inaction,'[2] Galsworthy wrote in his diary, and in a letter to Gilbert Murray: 'I suppose I've got out of the way of steamer travelling, but the enforced and utter vacuum is appalling. I am reading *The Moonstone* for the third time – it seems to be the only thing I can do except eat Mothersill [a seasickness cure], and Ada is in the same condition.'[3]

They arrived in New York on 3 March, where they 'Escaped all reporters but one. This unfortunate encounter brought on me a pack of others during the next week.'[4] Ada immediately began to feel better, and after a week was able to write a typically cheerful letter to her sister-in-law, Mabel Reynolds. 'We are having a brisk, hustling merry time! Jack has been interviewed about sixty times, I should think . . . I've been undertaking a mild rest cure in a jolly country place [Lakewood, New Jersey] among pines, and calmly added 11 lbs. to my weight in the week.'

While Ada was relaxing and recovering her strength, John got to work at once on rehearsing this new production of *The Pigeon*. Released from the inactivity of the voyage, John was only too glad to throw himself into the work. 'Fourteen hours rehearsal the first day . . . Rehearsed *The Pigeon* from noon till two at night. It improved wonderfully, especially the second act. We went through each act three times.' The Press was more enthusiastic than their colleagues in England had been; 'Has Humour and Heart-Beat,' the *New York Times* headed their notice.

Immediately after the opening of the play the Galsworthys set out for a few days' visit to Boston, and from there, via New York, they went on to Chicago. On the train to Chicago on 20 March, they both wrote letters, John to Gilbert Murray, Ada to Mabel Reynolds. In his letter John outlined their plans; they were booked to return to England on 11 May, on the *Titanic*, and suggested that the Gilbert Murrays, who were also in America, should lose no time in taking bookings on that fated ship, 'for she's new and popular'.[5] (In fact the ship was doomed never to reach America, sinking with much loss of life on 15 April.) Both letters were enthusiastic about the country, especially Ada's. She was already feeling better, and had found 'New York . . . the brightest place, not only mentally; the air makes one feel as light as a feather. We were dined and lunched and spoiled generally, and went off to Boston last Friday, where the same sort of thing awaited us . . .'[6]

The American journey of 1912 was exactly what the Galsworthys needed after the emotional traumas of the winter; not only were they distracted by the many sights they saw, but everywhere they went they were welcomed with receptions and hospitality, and Galsworthy was gratified and reassured to see for himself what an enthusiastic public he had on the other side of the Atlantic. 'I expect Chicago will be rather a staggerer, but we are told Jack is more widely read there than anywhere else.'[7] 'One feels that (over here) they are just longing to make a spiritual leader of him! and a little hurt if they don't see signs of his stepping on to his throne! . . .'[8]

Of the sights it was the Grand Canyon that made the deepest and most lasting impression on Galsworthy. 'The most wonderful sight and masterpiece of Nature in the world I think. Morning and afternoon walking and gazing at that marvellous, mysterious, beautiful piece of shifting form and colour.'[9]

It was also here, according to Rudolf Sauter, as he stood at the edge of the Grand Canyon, that John finally resolved to be faithful to Ada.

Until this moment the issue was, in his own mind at least, not quite decided; to have Margaret as well as Ada was now obviously impossible; to take Margaret with all her youth and vitality for his own – could he inflict this final devastating wound on Ada? For his happiness, even for his fulfilment as a writer, it was perhaps the obvious course; Margaret could give him the freedom he needed to develop his talent and to explore the depths within himself. To live with Ada must be to accept the essential superficiality and limitations of her character; it meant a restless life, wandering from one place to another in search of new distractions. This is not to say that he did not love her; he did. But he must have realized by now that she would never recover from the wounds of her early life; that she needed endlessly to be reassured and pampered, to be given the love and care that life until she met John had denied her. Now as he viewed the marvellous landscape of the Grand Canyon, 'one of those few wonders of Nature that are real masterpieces of art', he was struck perhaps by his own insignificance, by the comparative unimportance of his own suffering; one is 'a midget representation of this inspiring marvel before you and you get a sense of cosmic rhythm and Deity which one is always looking for and so seldom catches'.[10]

From the Grand Canyon they went on to San Francisco, Santa Barbara and New Orleans. At Santa Barbara Galsworthy began to do some writing, and while journeying round America he wrote the study 'For Love of Beasts' and also *Memories*; and of course there was work to be revised, this time his play *The Fugitive*.

Memories, the story of the dog Chris, like 'Summer' in *The Dark Flower*, is a nostalgic tale, in which Galsworthy indulged his need to dwell on a life which had in a sense gone for him and Ada. 'I am trying to write my "Memories" of our beloved Chris. As they grow they carry with them such a lot besides – so much of oneself and Ada all these years. I want to get something large into them,' he explained to Margaret Morris.[11] For an undoubtedly sentimental story about an animal, it is remarkably successful; Galsworthy has caught the essence of the dog, and even to a non-dog devotee it is a story of great charm.

John and Ada were animal lovers of a very extreme kind; their devotion to their pets must at times seem over-sentimental and even far-fetched: 'If *we* have spirits that persist – *they* have. If *we* know after our departure, who we were – *they* do. No one, I think, who really longs for truth, can ever glibly say which it will be for dog and man –

persistence or extinction of our consciousness. There is but one thing certain – the childishness of fretting over that eternal question. Whichever it be, it must be right, the only possible thing.'[12] In a similar vein he wrote to Dorothy Easton on 16 August 1912. 'I take it death is always terrible only to the living, who are left. I incline more and more to the feeling that to dwell on death and what comes after it, with anxiety and even with curiosity, is childish. We do not, or we should not, dwell on the hazard of each to-morrow with fear and trouble. Why then on that to-morrow which is death? For that particular to-morrow is only one more link in the chain of continuity – as obvious and necessary a link as is every fresh one of our sunrises and the day it brings. Whatever is, is right, whether it be extinction of our consciousness or persistence of consciousness; or, as I suspect with you, some thing that is neither life nor death, as we know them.'

Ostensibly the American trip went well. At Santa Barbara they stayed at San Ysidro ranch, and here Galsworthy was able to write in a 'sun-trap hut in a quiet spot'[13] in the mornings, and in the afternoon they went for long walks, or for one whole day they walked up La Campe Trail, a walk of some eighteen miles, but they still failed to reach the summit. On the way down 'coming to a secluded stream, Himself, disgusted (by ticks) threw off his clothes and bathed heartily in a pool. On coming out he was found to be decorated with many more ticks than before.'[14] Ticks were not their only adventure at Santa Barbara, they also experienced a small earthquake: 'It was at the dead of night, and I was sitting up in bed in the grip of an attack of asthma, when the quite unmistakable heaving began. This time it was as if some huge beast were stirring under the house; at each roll the cottage rocked from side to side. I had just said, "One more, and over we go!" when the movement lessened, then ceased.'[15] From Santa Barbara they went on to Washington, which they found a pleasant and sociable place, and their activities ranged from a baseball match – ' "Ra!" Ra! The Queerest exhibition of underbred hogs you ever saw'[16] – to an attendance at the hearing of the Titanic Disaster Commission, 'the public all agog to fix the blame on some unhappy shoulders'.[17] They then ended the trip at New York, where Galsworthy met Theodore Roosevelt: 'He is full of vitality and has for me no charm.'[18] On 9 May they joined the Gilbert Murrays and the party embarked on the SS *Baltic* and sailed for England.

But though Ada regained her spirits and put on weight, John was still desperately unhappy; of this the long letters he wrote regularly to Margaret Morris leave no doubt. These letters are some of the most personal he ever wrote, full of his hopes and forebodings, hopes which included plans for Margaret to take part in the plays he was writing or intending to write. From the *Campania* on the outward journey he told of the 'terrible monotony, especially when thoughts are not cheerful . . .' and that it was 'impossible to do anything but brood'.[19] It was to Margaret that he was most vividly able to describe the effect America and the Americans had on him. 'Such a queer place this [New York] and such queer people. In the streets are to be seen fat fallow soggy men with helpless feet – feet, very flat and broad and put on at a sort of side angle so that to run is impossible for them. I do like useful feet that belong to the animal that wields them. The women look much more alive than the men on the whole.'[20] 'The people . . . are groping for standards and far too much in a hurry ever to have them. Everything in America is grabbed at and swallowed before they know what it's really made of or why it really exists; the result is indigestion.'[21]

Or he would write personally of his ideas and thoughts:

I feel such a humbug about religion. I have such good theories about the whole and being part of it and all the time feel how extraordinarily strong is just one's ordinary vital selfish grasp on life, so that almost one could feel that outside oneself nothing matters. As a boy I remember often having the feeling, that if one died the whole world would die too and disappear – that everything existed just for oneself.[22]

And all the time there is concern for her happiness and the sadness he has caused her. 'I wish I could make you happy – I wish – I wish I could. You *must* not be unhappy – do you hear, my dear – you must not, because it makes me unhappier.'[23]

These letters make it abundantly clear how intimate and relaxed the relationship between Galsworthy and Margaret Morris had been, something, except possibly in the early days with Ada, he never experienced with any other person. But these letters marked the end of the intimacy between himself and Margaret. In her book Miss Morris comments that after his return to England in May 1912 there was a marked change in the tone of his letters; he no longer wrote to her as 'My dear Child' but as 'My dear Margaret', and the later letters have not the warm intimacy of the American ones. Back in England he was determined that there must be no weakening of his resolution not to see her. As she says, 'I feared he was gradually but determinedly shutting me out of his life.'

Chapter 24

'A Lot of Travelling'

On their return to England the Galsworthys went straight to Wingstone and were back there on 18 May. It is impossible not to observe the difference, at least outwardly, in the mood of Ada and John. John, as we have already said, had found the American journey greatly overshadowed by his parting from Margaret Morris, and now, back in his beloved Devon, he found it hard to settle back to his writing: 'He [John] doesn't manage to shut his mind away from all on earth as he used to do. I don't know whether it's a good thing or bad thing, but I know work doesn't go quite so quickly,'[1] Ada wrote to Mottram, and 'J. is working rather heavily, I mean, not very willingly.'[2] But of herself Ada wrote with extraordinary cheerfulness: 'I never felt so well in my life as over the other side of that beastly ocean. Insolently well and able . . . America does brisk one up so nicely, and I can eat huge breakfasts, drink coal black coffee and gobble ices in a way I never thought to do.'[3] For someone who had been so completely shattered and thrown by her husband's infidelity, her enjoyment, coming so soon afterwards, seems almost indecent.

During this brief summer's stay at Wingstone (18 May – 9 July) Galsworthy returned to work on the middle section of his novel *The Dark Flower*, 'Summer'. Possibly in an attempt to make Ada more content at Wingstone, he bought a horse for her, a chestnut gelding called Jane; she would use the new Mexican saddle (brought back from America) and a riding habit he had ordered to be made for her while they were at Santa Barbara.[4] The venture was not totally successful; while riding the saddle slipped and Ada was thrown from her horse. 'A great shock,' John noted in his diary.[5] He was also 'a little distracted by visitors', among whom was Frank Lucas, the writer and critic. Lucas, Galsworthy noted, was 'the life and soul of the party'.

In the meantime John was writing to Margaret Morris about a new production of *The Little Dream* which, he wrote, is 'to be entirely your affair as far as production is concerned, the matinées being yours and yours only'. He was, however, to finance the venture and advise over the music. The plans for the new production renewed Margaret's hopes of seeing John again, but about this he was adamant. 'Peace is too precious,' he wrote to her,[6] and in his next letter, five days later, he urged her 'to let me sink away by sheer blankness, by sheer starvation of your feelings. What are you going to get out of life if you let the thought of me hold on to your heart indefinitely?' And once again he harped back to his tenuous hold on peace: 'Peace is not in my own control, nor in yours.'[7] The tension between them increased when he and Ada came up to London early in July. 'I made a great mistake to come up at all before we go to the Tyrol which we do in a few days. It is only putting an unnecessary strain on you, and on Ada,' he wrote to Margaret in answer to a letter from her asking for his help over the play. And he continued with great firmness: 'If you think that *The Little Dream* will put a greater strain on you in respect of the wish to see me – better give it up! I must not and will not any more play with fire to Ada's grievous hurt, as well never have been through these months.'[8]

One must admire the determination with which Galsworthy refused to allow Margaret Morris to enter his life again, despite her entreaties to be allowed to see him. They continued to correspond about the play, however, and Margaret never completely gave up the hope of seeing him again. She felt too, not unreasonably, that it was extremely difficult to produce his play without his ever appearing to give advice on such matters as lighting and scenery, about which he felt so strongly. And when the production was, in her opinion, a failure, she blamed it in part on his refusal to co-operate except by letter. But for Galsworthy greater issues were at stake:

> You have forgotten, or never have realised the reasons for nothing-ness. It is not you, it is not me – it is someone whom I love and value more than either; and more and more profoundly regret to have made suffer. What I want you to realise is that suffering and terror such as that was is never forgotten and waits like a veiled thing to uncover itself again on the slightest provocation. Reason has nothing to do with these things – no more than it has to do with life and death.[9]

And then again, after the failure of her production of *The Little Dream*, Margaret felt that in 'killing' his play she had 'killed' his child, and she wrote and told John of her despair. Why, she must have written, couldn't they have met in secret? To which he answered: 'As to going to see you unbeknownst that day instead of writing – you don't understand in what absolute community we live: you don't understand how *anything* kept back, however harmless, poisons existence when people live like that.'[10]

This unhappy interchange of letters during the autumn of 1912 must have made Galsworthy realize how hopeless even a correspondence between them was. In the following year his letters came at infrequent intervals, and were shorter and less personal; finally, on 13 August, he sent her a last cheque for the rent of her studio accompanied by a note that is painfully curt, and in which he specifically asks her not even to acknowledge it. The Margaret Morris incident was, at least outwardly, over.

During the summer of 1912, as well as working on his new novel *The Dark Flower*, Galsworthy was putting together a collection of essays and sketches, written over several years, which were to form the volume entitled *The Inn of Tranquillity*, a collection of 'nature and life sketches which should bring out the side of one which acquiesces and is serene'.[11] It was published by Heinemann in October 1912. These included the sketch *Memories*, and a paper 'About Censorship', written in 1909, when he had been actively involved in the campaign to abolish censorship in the theatre, but of much the greatest interest is the last essay in the book, 'Vague Thoughts on Art'. This essay is more than any other piece of writing a summary of Galsworthy's personal philosophy as it was at this time. It shows the optimism he still felt, that man and his civilization were rising towards a new peak of achievement, an optimism that was to be eroded, first by what he saw to be his own personal failure, his betrayal of Ada and his own ideals, and in 1914 by the tearing up of civilization in a war of unprecedented horror and destruction.

The essay, written in the summer of 1911 at Wingstone, has as its background the countryside of Manaton. It was inevitable; the beauty of nature and its mystery were fundamental to Galsworthy's philosophy. 'Once in a way, in those trees against that sky I seem to see all the passionate life and glow that Titian painted into his pagan pictures. I have a vision of mysterious meaning, of a mysterious relation between that sky and those trees with their gnarled red limbs and life as I know it.'

I cannot help thinking [he wrote] that historians, looking back from the far future, will record this age as the Third Renaissance . . . now Orthodoxy fertilized by Science is producing a fresh and fuller conception of life – a love of Perfection, not for hope of reward, not for fear of punishment, but for Perfection's sake. Slowly, under our feet, beneath our consciousness, is forming that new philosophy, and it is in times of new philosophies that Art, itself in essence always a discovery, must flourish.

New philosophy – a vigorous Art! Are there not all the signs of it? In music, sculpture, painting; in fiction – and drama . . .

And how has it come, this slowly growing faith in Perfection for Perfection's sake? Surely like this: The Western world awoke one day to find that it no longer believed corporately and for certain in future life for the individual consciousness. It began to feel: I cannot say more than that there may be – Death may be the end of man, or Death may be nothing. And it began to ask itself in this uncertainty: Do I then desire to go on living? Now, since it found that it desired to go on living at least as earnestly as ever it did before, it began to inquire why. And slowly it perceived that there was, inborn within it, a passionate instinct of which it had hardly till then been conscious – a sacred instinct to perfect itself, now, as well as in a possible hereafter; to perfect itself because Perfection was desirable, a vision to be adored, and striven for; a dream motive fastened within the Universe; the very essential Cause of everything. And it began to see that this Perfection, cosmically, was nothing but perfect Equanimity and Harmony; and in human relations, nothing but perfect Love and Justice . . .

I have felt it worthwhile to quote from this essay at considerable length because it describes so well the optimism that was so basic to Galsworthy's life both as a writer and as a man, the belief that the world was steadily progressing towards a greater state of 'Perfection'. It also makes it possible to appreciate the shattering effect of the two calamities, the one personal and the other international coming so soon one after the other, that left him, after the Armistice of 1918, a disillusioned and greatly saddened man.

America had improved the situation between John and Ada, but it was by no means a complete cure. The return to England, and particularly their visit to London, had renewed the strain. Ada, Galsworthy wrote to Margaret Morris, was not well, she had a bad chill and neuralgia and rheumatism. 'We shall go [abroad] the first moment we can.' This was on 7 July, but on the 11th they were lunching with the Colefaxes, the day after they went to 'Sonning rowing down there from Reading in a skiff',[12] and on the 12th they went with Rudolf Sauter to Lord's for the Eton and Harrow match, an annual event of the greatest importance to Galsworthy: 'Harrow made plucky stand . . . but were beaten by six wickets; when will they ever win?'[13] All this activity suggests that Ada was perhaps not so very ill.

They left for the Tyrol on 15 July and made straight for their favourite place, Cortina, where they found 'our dear old haunts looking same as ever but weather poor'. Like his writing of *Memories* and 'Summer', it was another bid to return to a much happier past. Here were old associations and memories of times of great happiness; this was the country they had wandered in as lovers, where they had come for much of that year of their first release, following the death of John's father, while they waited for Ada's divorce. Surely here they would still find something of that past?

Possibly because of the bad weather, Galsworthy was able to work fairly steadily, following the pattern he had established at Wingstone, writing each morning, and probably revising between tea and dinner. He finished, revised and re-revised 'Summer', the middle section of *The Dark Flower*, and wrote the first two chapters of 'Spring'; he corrected the proofs of *The Inn of Tranquillity*; he also worked on his play *The Patriot* (finally called *The Mob*).[14]

On the last day of their stay at Cortina he had a birthday: 'I am forty five. Confound it!' he wrote in his diary on 14 August. And he was relieved to find that despite his age he and Ada 'are both still as good walkers as we were'. For at Bremmerbad, where they went from Cortina, they had 'scrambled up the hill at the back and down again in 2 hrs & a quarter. Quite an athletic feat.'

At last, on 6 September, they were back in Wingstone, and Galsworthy could return to his writing of *The Dark Flower*. By the middle of October he had finished 'Spring' in rough, '36000 words written in about six weeks all told'.[15] Galsworthy sometimes had an almost mathematical approach to his writing, carefully recording the number of words written, or, during the war, the exact amount earned by each piece of work.

By now nearly a year had elapsed since Galsworthy's break with

Margaret Morris, and during this period Ada and John had spent comparatively little time in England, and only a very few weeks in London. The house in Addison Road, where they had once been so happy, had become a place of poisoned memories: Chris, the spaniel, was dead, and it was to that house that Margaret had come so often in the early days of her friendship with the Galsworthys. It is not therefore surprising to find the Galsworthys house-hunting as soon as they returned to London at the beginning of November. They looked at two flats, one in the Temple, and the other 1a Adelphi Terrace, which they decided to take. It was the same building in which the J. M. Barries also had a flat.

While they were at Cortina Ralph Mottram had written to Galsworthy with the suggestion that he should undertake a biographical study of him. Galsworthy agreed, but made the proviso that there should be no personal detail, and that his work should simply be a literary criticism. Ada, who knew Mottram so well, was his chief source of information: 'I am secretary and caretaker,' she wrote to him.[16] Mottram's book never reached the stage of publication,* but some of the information she gave him in letters throws an interesting light on Galsworthy's life at this time, and particularly the criticism he had to face:

> As to public work, you will not again suggest for instance that J.G. may be said to have stood aside from public questions! It is true that he makes a point of not belonging to 'Parties' Societies, Unions, etc. and always retains his independence . . . Why! The critics have labelled him a fighting man, cannot bear him to write poems, Little Dreams, Inns of Tranquillity. Anything great or small that occupies itself with Beauty. They fear at once that he is laying down his lance.[17]

It was a difficulty from which Galsworthy could never escape, his wish to be a creative writer and at the same time his inability to refuse to espouse any cause that moved him. Even his fiction tended to contain a message, as Conrad complained when Galsworthy sent him his story 'The Windlestraw': 'Almost everything you write I feel like that pool which the Angel came down to stir. I become troubled.'[18]

* This early abortive work should not be confused with the study R. H. Mottram wrote of the Galsworthys after their deaths, *For Some We Loved*, published in 1956.

And now it was suggested to him that he investigate the conditions of slaughterhouses, a task that, with his love of animals, would be particularly repugnant to him but would also invoke all his sympathies. He approached it with characteristic thoroughness, flinching from no part of the grisly investigation, but he found it a great strain: 'Have just started my slaughterhouse job and it sits on my head,' he wrote to Margaret Morris. 'Was at Islington Abattoir on Tuesday – a gruesome business indeed. I never quite realised how gruesome.'[19]

His report, originally published in the *Daily Mail* and later incorporated in a book of miscellaneous writing called *A Sheaf*, shows that he carried out an investigation very similar to the searching enquiries he had made into the prison system several years earlier. As usual he approached the subject with mathematical calculations: 1,850,000 'beasts' (cattle), 8,500,000 sheep, and 3,200,000 pigs were slaughtered each year. He allows that his figures may be a million or so out; nevertheless, they show that a very large number of animals were killed for food, and there was virtually no legislation to see that this was done in a humane fashion. He visited a large number of slaughterhouses, including some continental ones, and he interviewed butchers; he then described exactly the methods of slaughter he had witnessed, the amount of suffering he saw, and how, by quite simple means, much of this could be avoided. For anyone it would have been an extremely disagreeable task, for a sensitive man almost unbearable, but he investigated everything, and then unstintingly exerted his time and energy to see that the facts were carefully reported and publicized. As he wrote in a letter to his old friend J. W. Hills, 'I want a very short simple Bill embodying, roughly speaking, the proposals in the articles, with possible extension of Local Authorities' powers to build Public abattoirs and close private slaughter houses in places where there are public ones.'[20]

Galsworthy's articles drew public attention to the problem, but his work did not lead to any new legislation. For Galsworthy it had been a major distraction, involving as it had much of his time and energy. Each year it was becoming more difficult for him to conserve his time for his main purpose as a writer, nor was Ada willing, or perhaps able, to protect him, as she wrote to Mottram on 12 November: 'After *For Love of Beasts* booklet [an article written in America for publication in the *Daily Mail*] there are various odd trends – the sort of thing editors are continually asking him for – Certainly not a week passes but he is

asked for some expression of opinion, and few days pass without requests for interviews, articles, speeches, presidings, what not!'

Productions of his plays were also making demands on his time:
The Eldest Son was at last produced, at the Kingsway Theatre on 23
November, and at the same time Galsworthy was down in Oxford
rehearsing a new production of *The Pigeon*. Ada always thrived on a
rush of activity, but John, one suspects, was already beginning to feel
the wear and tear of his hectic existence: 'I feel rather mad at not being
at *The Eldest Son* again tonight, but he is tired, poor dear . . .'[21] The
play suffered as Galsworthy feared it might, by its similarity to *Hindle
Wakes* by Stanley Houghton. The reviews were, as Ada said, a 'motley
collection',[22] but nearly all saw the underlying seriousness of its tone:
'the author's personality is there . . . You find it, perhaps, in the per-
sistent tone of sadness . . .' (*The Times*, 25 November 1912). Other
newspapers, less kindly, saw it as perhaps 'too grim and grey and un-
romantic' for the ordinary playgoer (*Standard*). 'Fairly good success
d'estime, and the usual commercial failure,' Ada summed up the play's
achievement in her notebook.

December was the usual Galsworthy rush. On the 5th they went
down to Bristol: 'He a-lecturing tomorrow night. I accompany my
silly songs the night after.'[23] (Some of these 'silly songs' had been
written on the American trip: 'I've set 17 of Jack's lyrics to music, so
there. I did 9 in America of all places.'[24] They had been accepted for
publication in America but failed to find a publisher in England.) And
on 20 December they again left England, this time for Paris, where they
spent Christmas at the Maison Garnier. It proved to be anything but a
quiet Christmas: an artists' 'reveillon ball' kept them awake the whole
night, and the following evening they dined with the Arnold Bennetts.
'Bennett, who is a good fellow, was rather naïvely beginning to enjoy
full expansion. Mrs Bennett makes a quaint foil, so very French is she,'
were Ada's rather patronizing comments in her notebook.

One may sympathize with Galsworthy, when, summing up the year,
he wrote: 'A lot of travelling this year.'[25] It had indeed been in every
sense extremely exhausting.

Chapter 25

The Successful Author

The first days of 1913 found the Galsworthys settled at Moulleau, near Areachon, where they had gone from Paris immediately after Christmas. The south-west Basque corner of France, Ada wrote, 'appealed to us so specially, that we seldom strayed beyond it'.[1] Ada had an attack of influenza during their first week at Moulleau, but on the whole they found the place, and their hotel, so agreeable that they remained there for ten weeks; 'never have been ten consecutive weeks in any hotel before – nor ever so comfortable,' Galsworthy recorded in his diary as they were about to leave.[2]

The success of their holiday was in part due to the proximity of their friends the André Chevrillons, who were staying in a villa nearby. Chevrillon was assisting his niece with a French translation of *The Man of Property*, and naturally the progress of the work was followed with considerable interest by Ada and John; the two couples met constantly, and Chevrillon read aloud to them from the new translation; on one occasion the Chevrillons prepared for the Galsworthys 'the identical Soames dinner out of the *Man of Property*'.[3] But apart from their friends the Galsworthys found that the country had much to offer:

The view from our little sitting-room extraordinarily Japanese: little squat pines with big roots on a sandy soil, blue water beyond, many curlews flighting in curiously beautiful hieroglyphic formation. Excellent riding in the great wood that covered all the country, and on our little horses Tapageur and Jupiter (a *froid caractère*) we covered many miles of sandy tracks among the trees. But the great attraction were our friends the André Chevrillons, in a villa at Areachon, with whom we fed, and talked. In our hotel was the very pleasant French family of the hotel-keeper, Fournier, M. & Mme. Rolan-Gosselin, and Mme. Verde-de Lisle, with a fine voice. d'Annunzio had a villa close by, but though we saw him on his bicycle, followed by borzois, we rather avoided making his acquaintance.[4]

Galsworthy now started work once again on what would still have been an extremely painful piece of writing for him and Ada, the third episode of his novel *The Dark Flower*, 'Autumn', that part which deals with his love for Margaret Morris. It must have been a considerable strain for Ada, who typed out his finished manuscript and no doubt listened to readings at the end of each day's writing. On 22 January John wrote in his diary, ' "Autumn" nearing the end,' and the next day triumphantly, '*Finished it.*' But on the 20th Ada had been 'seedy' and had had a bad night; it is hard not to connect the two events.

But on the whole it seems to have been a successful holiday for them both. They walked and rode on the sands – 'The soft sand riding is delightful.'[5] On one occasion Ada was thrown from her horse, Jupiter, but she was none the worse for her fall. One day they walked into Areachon and 'saw a most monstrous case of cruel use of a horse. Never saw such knees in my life. Instructed Bronstet, our riding man, to buy horse for me and have it destroyed . . .'[6] Unfortunately the Galsworthys' intervention was to no avail; the owner, perhaps irked by their interference, refused to sell. Altogether they spent three months in France, ending their stay with a few days in Paris, during which they visited the Moulin Rouge for the first time and were 'not impressed. Vice is a dreary business.'[7]

Back in England they started to arrange their move from Addison Road to 1a Adelphi Terrace, the flat which they had taken in November. Since the unhappy events of the winter of 1911 the Galsworthys' mode of life had changed: they were spending even more time abroad than before; Ada, when travelling, was in every way a happier person; her health was better and she enjoyed the distraction of new places and new people. The new flat would not only be an escape from painful memories but was more suitable for a life in which they planned to spend only short periods in London or Devon. As Ada wrote in her notebook, '1a Adelphi Terrace, a flat on the top floor, whither the feeling that we were spending too much money in a house which we inhabited so little, constrained us to move. It was rather sad after eight years, but when Chris departed, the house was never the same again, nor the garden.' They finally moved on 22 July, spending the days of transition in the Hotel Cecil. 'Melancholy getting out of the little old house. Sorry when one has time to think of it; but the heart went out of it when Chris died,' John noted in his diary. Chris had become the symbol of their past happiness; in the future they would be content, but they would never again experience the carefree joyfulness of those early years.

Apart from their move the summer of 1913 was an unusually hectic one; after so long an absence there was much to catch up with, friends to be seen, business matters to be attended to. 'Wading through accumulations of papers and correspondence.'[8] The next few days were taken up with visits to friends, the Granville Barkers and the Conrads. 'Conrad looking v. worn,'[9] Galsworthy noted, and a few days later, 'He wants me to be his executor. No joke.'[10] For the last ten years of his life Conrad was to suffer almost continuously from ill-health and depression. They waited on in London until the first night of *Strife* on 3 May and then went down to Wingstone on the following day. While in London Galsworthy had been rereading his own *Man of Property*; 'It really isn't bad,' he wrote in his diary. 'Can only hope my next book may be as good.'[11]

His 'next book', *The Freelands*, was already in his mind, and immediately they had settled in at Wingstone he began the new novel, underlining the entry recording the fact in his diary.[12] But it was a summer of too many distractions and the actual writing of the novel made little progress. However, he and Ada made a journey to Malvern to explore his mother's birthplace, and generally research the background of the novel, which was to centre round a family, the Freelands, who were undoubtedly based on the Bartleets, his mother's family: 'motored out to Castle Morton, where Mother's family lived from the 14th Century at least till about 1750 . . .'[13]

Apart from the active social life which he and Ada led, two plays, *The Fugitive* and *The Mob* (originally *The Patriot*), and his novel *The Dark Flower* were in the stage of final revision before production and publication. *The Mob* had been accepted 'with enthusiasm'[14] by Lawrence Irving (this project was later dropped), and *The Fugitive* had been accepted for production at the Court Theatre in the autumn. These three works had been in various stages of writing and rewriting for the past two years, and illustrate very clearly the uneasy progress of Galsworthy's work at this time. He lacked both the time and the confidence to pursue a piece of work to its end; he was constantly switching from one thing to another, then returning to the earlier piece of writing, and, finding it unsatisfactory, beginning once again with an extensive revision, but almost never was a work entirely discarded. Like a dog with a bone, he would dig up his writings, worry at them and then bury them once again.

The Fugitive, yet another play on the subject of marital unhappiness, provides a particularly good example of the way he worked. The first mention of the play is in January 1911: 'Finished the play in rough. Began it beginning of December. Started as a satiric comedy it has come out as drama. This is like me. If I write a single scene that goes deep the rest will have to conform before I'm through with the job. Comedy requiring almost trivial subjects is very hard for me. The subject for this play was never right for comedy, not even satiric comedy.'[15] He mentions in his diary that he is working on the play during the spring of 1911, and again in October of that year. In his résumé of the year's work for 1912 he says that 'a lot of work was done on *The Fugitive* and *The Patriots*', though the only mention in the diary of these plays is of revision done on board the SS *Baltic* in May on their return from America. It is in the spring of 1913 that he finally 'retackles' the play 'on a bigger scale', and on the 23rd May he records having finished the new version. He seems at last to have been satisfied, for there are no further mentions of the play apart from 'readying *The Fugitive* for the Ld. Chamberlain' at the end of July. It then opened at the Court on 16 September. 'Not bad and well received.'[16]

Reading it some sixty years after it was written, it is difficult to see why this play, in its theme so similar to much of Galsworthy's other work, should have been seen by its author as so controversial, and why it should have caused him such difficulty to write. The heroine, Clare Dedmond, because of her distress at being married to a man who physically repels her, commits suicide. Gerald du Maurier, to whom it was first sent with a view to production at Wyndham's Theatre, wrote that 'It depressed me, angered me, and I have come to the conclusion that I do not understand it . . . I positively *dislike* it . . .'[17] When it was produced in September at the Court Theatre the critics also found the play depressing and the *Daily Chronicle* and *Daily News* complained of its lack of humour.

'The thing has gone out for better or worse – generally worse, and there is an end of illusion; an end of one's own vision; and generally a taste of ashes in the mouth . . .'[18] Increasingly, irrespective of its public reception, Galsworthy was dissatisfied with his work; he gave so much time and thought to everything he did and still the final result fell far short of what he hoped to achieve. But there were other productions in the pipeline, making demands on his time and keeping him away from his writing: in August he was in Liverpool rehearsing *The Eldest Son*; Esme Percy was to produce *Joy* in Manchester in November, and in December Granville Barker was reviving *The Silver Box* at the St James Theatre; and abroad *Justice* and *Strife* were to be produced in Vienna.

It was a fantastic record for any playwright, but for Galsworthy it meant endless travelling and a complete disruption of his writing: 1913 was a year in which he achieved particularly little. He and Ada were at Wingstone for only a few short weeks during the summer; he started his novel *The Freelands*, but gave it up and turned to shorter works, a long short story called 'The Stoic' and another book of essays, *The Little Man*, which he himself described as a 'whimsy'. He reread his earlier novels, *Fraternity* as well as *The Man of Property*, as if seeking consolation and encouragement from his previous successes.

Foreign travel took an even greater toll of the Galsworthys' year than usual, starting with nearly three months in France at the beginning of the year. At the end of July, on the first day in their new flat, they decided quite suddenly to accompany Lilian and Georg Sauter on a visit to Switzerland, leaving two days later on the 29th, a holiday that could just be fitted in before rehearsals started for *The Fugitive*. Galsworthy, seeing the Matterhorn for the first time, found it 'a very fine creature – alive as no other mountain that I know of . . . It is very pleasant to watch it . . . and to think that when we and the little backfishes and all have vanished, and the earth is cold as that moon, it will still stand there and offer its defiance to the sky.'[19] But with this one exception they found Switzerland a great disappointment, as Ada wrote in no uncertain tone to Ralph Mottram. 'I do soundly hate this Switzerland, and we mean never to see it again except on the way to somewhere else. Material-minded, exploited, lacking in dew and sweetness and everything that's worth having. Its spine is a cog-wheel railway, its torso a tunnel.'[20]

Later in the year, in October, they went out to Vienna for the productions of *Strife* and *Justice*. The plays were 'very warmly received in Vienna, and so was I,' Galsworthy wrote to Dorothy Easton.[21] The play was undoubtedly a great success – 'seventeen curtains: unfortunate me much hauled before curtain' – though Ada found the 'standard of acting was not up to that of our own country, neither so natural nor so subtle'.[22] From Vienna they travelled on to Frankfurt and Wiesbaden, 'where J. had baths and massage for a shoulder damaged in June, by the swinging back of a heavy gate, which he was holding with a riding whip at an awkward angle'.[23] Neither this treatment, nor that of a bonesetter in England, seem to have been successful in curing the shoulder, which continued to cause trouble, and was one reason why Galsworthy was declared unfit for service in the war.

While they were in Vienna *The Dark Flower* was published in England (on 9 October), and according to Marrot its appearance 'fluttered the dovecotes'![24] The only fluttering he records is a long adverse review by Quiller-Couch in the *Daily Mail* in which he was accused of advocating, as Shelley had done, ' "free love" and philandering'. On the whole his friends, Gilbert Murray, John Masefield and Hugh Walpole, found the book 'a beautiful thing'. The dove who was really disturbed was Ada, as twenty years later she leant over the shoulder of her late husband's biographer, and wondered how the world should not be told of the true origins of the final episode of *The Dark Flower*. 'If, when he was attracted to a woman, it amounted to nothing that mattered, it was not because he was married, but because he loved so profoundly the woman he had married.' Thus Ada emerged with flying colours on the pages of Marrot's biography.[25]

During November Ada's mother died. Mrs Cooper had in fact refused to see Ada since her marriage to John, which, as a friend commented, was strange as 'Ada was only doing what Mrs Cooper had been doing all her life.' 'She kept her life apart from mine in these later years, and to be quite honest, I must say that I am truly glad it was so,' Ada wrote to Mottram. At the same time she declared her intention of not going to the funeral. 'What the rest of the world may feel about it seems to me unimportant. I do not mind their comments or condemnation.' And later she refuses the offer of her mother's motor car: 'any other motor on earth would be preferable and I hope to keep clear of any such luxuries for some time yet.'[26]

This year neither of them seemed to survive the winter well, and on 17 December they were packing and nursing their colds in preparation for their departure for a long winter holiday in Egypt. The next morning they left London for Marseilles, the first leg of their journey to Port Said, which cannot have been an enjoyable voyage, as they were both still 'heavily water-logged with colds', and found it a 'horrible crowded journey'.[27] It was an unpromising beginning to what was to be their last foreign holiday before the war.

Given our incurable aversion from sightseeing Egypt seems a strange choice to have made for our winter quarters in 1913–1914. But we were in great need of sunshine and warmth, and thought it the safest of climates. For those reasons, therefore, we settled ourselves at the gorgeous hotel at Heliopolis, whence the sun was visible from morning till night.

Thus Ada began the chapter on North Africa in her book *Over the Hills and Far Away*. The Galsworthys may have believed themselves to be averse to sightseeing, but travelling as much as they did they could not avoid seeing a great many 'sights', and from their letters they seem to have enjoyed doing so. They travelled in a manner that guaranteed them a certain privacy, staying in the best hotels, or even hiring a complete villa for their party, and they were thus protected from the mainstream of tourism, though in 1913 that stream was a mere trickle compared to the tourist scene in the second half of the century. But though they sought privacy, congenial company and a certain amount of social life always added greatly to Ada's enjoyment; in the last years of their life together they always took with them Galsworthy's nephew, Rudolf Sauter, and his wife Vi. On this particular journey the Galsworthys had been fortunate in meeting up with H. W. Massingham and his wife, quite by chance, at Marseilles, and the two couples remained together for the greater part of the Egyptian journey. 'One could not wish for a better travelling companion,' Ada wrote of H. W. Massingham,[28] the editor of *The Nation*.

They spent the first two weeks at the Heliopolis Hotel, during which they 'recovered gradually' from the 'poor condition' in which they were on their arrival. They explored Cairo, and were entertained by the society of the town: they lunched at Lord Kitchener's, whom Galsworthy found 'a bloomin' autocrat', though he 'was affable to A., contrary to his reputation', and on another occasion 'dined native fashion with an Arab Sheik of great wealth and importance'; in addition 'Ada and Mrs Massingham had their first sight of a harem'![29] Galsworthy also found time to write, and he began work on a new play, *The Full Moon*, which eventually became *A Bit o' Love*.

On 5 January they left Cairo for Luxor, and spent a week sightseeing; even so they 'were happier there than anywhere else in Egypt except in the desert'.[30] They saw the Tomb of Kings, which John found 'Remote and splendid, but underground things are trying to the spirit'.[31] Back again in Cairo at the end of the month they began preparations for their journey into the desert, the party to include 'A. self, the Massinghams . . . an Egyptian cook and 12 other Arabs'.[32] A photograph of that expedition is an amazing sight: the two Galsworthys in the centre of the picture mounted on camels (Ada became greatly attached to hers, which was called Daisy Bell), the Massinghams less grandly mounted, on two donkeys, the four Europeans surrounded by their retinue of twelve Arabs. But most surprising of all is the luggage that the party took with them: judging by the photograph almost a houseful of furniture appears to be loaded on two camels – chairs, tables, beds, and we know, because Ada fed her camel out of it, a travelling rubber bath.

The desert journey was as well ordered as their equipage suggests, and a domestic routine was soon set up: 'We start about 10. ride till 1.30 lunch of eggs and things, ride again till 4.30. Set up camp, have tea; lounge in a chair watching the sun down; then a bath and dinner. A great life to rest every faculty except that of doing nothing with joy.'[33] In a more reflective mood Galsworthy describes in a letter to Frank Lucas the enormous impression his first experience of the desert made on him – this time an earlier excursion they made from Cairo.

> Desert – a great moon rising pale – the little trees like men amazed below her – a light moving across – the sky lavender, and some stars creeping out in it – a line of date palms crossing space like a caravan of Arabs – one dog barking – the smell of burning maize-stalks – a dhow sailing up, and the shadows of her crew dark in the gold water.[34]

On the desert trip the travellers were also entertained by an Egyptian dancing girl: 'An experience,' Galsworthy noted in his diary. 'Her dancing was just primitive love-making to us all women included.'[35] Ada is more explicit: 'Her dancing was good, but I think not remarkable; her acrobatic and balancing feats were much more striking. Late in the evening she made a little tour of her audience, perching first on Himself's knee, then on mine. I hope we behaved quite suitably.'[36]

After their return to Cairo on 10 February the Galsworthys and the Massinghams parted company, the Galsworthys travelling on to Sicily, where they spent another two weeks, writing and exploring the sights of Syracuse and Taormina. And at last, on 28 February, they started on the journey back to England, travelling slowly via Genoa and Paris.

It had been a long absence, and Galsworthy had often thought of England with nostalgia. 'The stupendous sunniness of this land [Egypt] frightens one, 29 days and not a smell of rain – how return to Dartmoor? And yet I'm homesick sometimes.'[37]

This long winter's journey was, though they were still completely unaware of it, the end of an epoch for John and Ada, as it was to be for countless other Europeans; the sun was setting rapidly on the world of the Forsytes – though ironically the family of the novels had not yet achieved the height of its popularity. As yet Galsworthy had no idea of prolonging the fictional lives of his Forsytes: *The Man of Property* was so complete as a novel that to continue with it must have seemed pointless. Moreover, in 1906 Galsworthy saw it as his first successful book, to be superseded by others, perhaps even more successful, at least achieving for him a closer proximity to what he wanted to say in his writing. Now, with four more major novels published, as well as a series of successful plays and shorter works, one can detect an increasing dissatisfaction with his work and achievement. His creative strength as a writer was already failing.

Chapter 26
Outbreak of War

The summer of 1914 followed the pattern of many others, the Galsworthys shuffling between Wingstone and London, or further afield to Manchester to supervise the first production of *The Mob* at the end of March, or back once more to that constantly comforting place, Littlehampton. Most of those months Galsworthy worked on his novel *The Freelands*, begun the year before but abandoned for their Egyptian holiday. Even now he worked unsteadily, interrupting the progress of his novel by writing short stories or articles, and in the middle of May he was toying with the idea of abandoning the novel altogether: 'Full of the idea of a new novel and laying aside *The Freelands*.'[1] But a few days later, having read through the manuscript, he had a new idea for the book which gave him new determination to complete it: 'Shall not lay it aside, *on the contrary*.'[2]

But the summer was full of interruptions: the Manchester production of *The Mob* was moved to London, where it opened at the Coronet Theatre on 10 April, and in May *Justice* was revived at the same theatre by Miss Horniman's company. Towards the end of June Ada was confined to bed with neuritis in her neck: 'At once the soul of the place vanishes, no work, nursing,' Galsworthy wrote in his diary.[3] During the last few years, since his brief liaison with Margaret Morris, John had become increasingly more dependent on Ada; and he was quite unable to work without her constant encouragement. In July Galsworthy and his nephew Rudolf made their annual pilgrimage to Lord's; this too was a disappointing occasion: 'Beaten for the 5th time running. I walked about Lord's like a ghost cast out. Shall give up this match.'[4]

It was the last month of peace, and though there is no mention in Galsworthy's diary of the political situation until the end of the month, he seems to have been depressed and restless, dining alone at the Savoy and the Petit-Riche – 'wretched dinner' – and visiting Barrie who was laid low with a high fever.[5] On the 21st he dined at the Square

Club and left forgetting to pay the bill.[6] He was also preoccupied with social ventures, going down to Old Ford and visiting the homes of 'sweated workers' with one of the parish workers: 'Some gruesome sights. Poor People.'[7] As the following day he was seeing Pinker and Granville Streatfield about cottages at Manaton, one must assume that he had in mind some scheme similar to that which he carried out at Bury years later, building and making available at extremely low rents good cottages for the villagers. But July 1914 was no time for such altruistic plans: by the end of the month he was back in Wingstone working on his novel, and also writing a sketch for *Le Temps* of 'my favourite spot in England – that is here' (the article was never published).[8] The next day, 29 July, there is the first mention of the political situation: 'These war clouds are monstrous. If Europe is involved in an Austro-Servian quarrel one will cease to believe in anything.'

Day by day his diary records the increasing horror he felt as the outbreak of war became more imminent. That the war was a universal catastrophe is obvious, but for Galsworthy it was something more personal than that. For all his adult life he had put his entire faith in the essential goodness of people. Now as war approached he saw that goodness would not necessarily prevail; man's knowledge was to be used for destruction and not construction, and the world would become a harder and more evil place in which to live.

Friday July 31st. Things going on working up for this awful catastrophe . . . The suddenness of this horror is appalling.

August 1st. . . . Blacker and blacker! Little or no chance now!

August 2nd. War is declared between Austria and Germany v. France and Russia. Too ghastly for words. The European war has come true. The nightmare of it. We rode to distract our thoughts. I wish to Heaven I could work!

August 3rd. A miserably anxious day . . . I hate and abhor war of all kinds; I despise and loathe it. And the thought of the million daily acts of its violence and hateful brutishness keeps riving my soul. I try not to think of all the poor creatures who are suffering and will suffer so terribly; but how not to? Wrote some words of Peace; but shan't send them anywhere. What's the use of whispering in a hurricane?

August 4th. *We are in* . . . The horror of the thing keeps coming over one in waves; and all happiness has gone out of life. I can't keep still, and I can't work. Ada manages to behave better, bless her. The temper of England seems finer than I thought it would be. There is little or no bluster, and much unity of resolution. If this war is not the death of Christianity, it will be odd. We need a creed that really applies humanism to life instead of talking of it.

The war came quickly even to a village as small as Manaton. On 5 August a constable came to inform Galsworthy that his favourite horse, Peggy, must be taken into Moreton for the 'horse muster', where horses would be requisitioned for the army. Fortunately Peggy was rejected as unfit. The local men of military age went to the war, and Ada set about organizing the making of clothes for the war effort. 'Young Eric and Clifford Endacott are gone off to the Yeomanry from Wingstone. Eric is a first-rate rider and shot, the other one just good enough.' 'I am feeding my dressmaker's least well-off girls with flannel which they make up and forward where wanted. As far as I can see ordinary flannel shirts for well men are more wanted than hospital things . . . Jack is hard at work on all sorts of things. He gets a considerable jolt twice a day when newspapers arrive, but is wonderful at readjusting the work apparatus.'[9]

As always Galsworthy turned to his pen for consolation, and in the first week of the war he was writing a piece entitled 'Thoughts on the War'. These 'First Thoughts', as they were published in *A Sheaf* in 1916, are confused, almost incoherent reflections on war, and one cannot but blame a too unselective publisher for committing these writings, and many other fragmentary pieces to print. In his despair Galsworthy flits hopelessly from one idea to another: somewhere there must be a scapegoat, some thing, some creed, that can take the blame for the catastrophe; orthodox Christianity, that at least can never survive the war; now at last people must see how hollow are its values. And of despotic governments, Germany, Austria or Russia: 'they are doomed in theory, if not as yet in fact.' Then with no apparent reason he recalls his visit to the poverty-stricken homes of East London; how will these people fare under the conditions of war? And he concludes, 'There is only one national necessity – to have from roof to basement a clean, healthy, happy national house.' And so he rambles to his final paragraph, which is really what all his distress is about, 'This is the grand defeat of all Utopians, dreamers, poets, philosophers, idealists, humanitarians, lovers of peace and arts; bag and baggage they are thrown out of a world that has for a time no use for them.'

This indeed was the crux of the matter. A man of Galsworthy's imaginative compassion could not but feel despair at the suffering which was now inevitable, a despair which was increased by his own apparent helplessness to do anything very positive to help the war effort. He was filled with self-doubts: would he, even had he been younger and more fit, have had the courage to take an active part in the war? It was in his diary entry of 15 November that he fully accepted his terrible agonizing misgivings.

> The heart searchings of this War are terrible; the illumination of oneself rather horrible. I think and think what is my duty, and all the time know that if I arrived at certain conclusions I shouldn't do that duty. This is what comes of giving yourself to a woman body and soul. A. paralyses and has always paralysed me. I have never been able to face the idea of being cut off from her . . .
>
> I say to myself: 'If I were young and unmarried I should certainly have gone! There is no doubt about that!' But there is great doubt whether if I had been of military age *and married to A.* I should have gone. Luckily for my conscience I really believe my game shoulder would not stand a week's training without getting my arm into a sling. Moreover I suppose there is no one yet training as short-sighted as I am. Still I worry – worry – all the time – bald and grey and forty-seven and worrying. Funny!

His solution to his despair was to write with renewed energy and determination. From now on all money earned by his writing would be devoted to the war effort; in this way, he argued, with reason, he could do more for the war than by serving in some active capacity.

It was not an easy task; his writing never came easily and what was written had to be subjected to so many revisions. But now he had to write against time. He turned again to his three-quarter finished novel, *The Freelands*. 'Started my spurt to finish *The Freelands*. A big price is promised from Scribners for the serial. So much American money will come in handy for relief funds . . .'[10] Always mathematically minded he began to see his life as a series of figures: 'Sent off £250 to Various War Funds, making £1250 to date. i.e. Motor Ambulance £400. Belgian Relief £300. Cigarettes £250. Prince of Wales £200. Authors and Actors £100. Small Funds £50. M.E.R. £50. Devon £50. Queen's Women's £25. Belgian Refugees £25.'[11]

Any other attitude to writing would have seemed to Galsworthy unforgiveably selfish at a time of national crisis; he seemed to forget that creative artists are not machines and cannot be treated as such, that work churned out with the first aim of producing money, and that as quickly as possible, would inevitably be work of poor quality. On 1 October he finished *The Freelands* in the rough. 'It has been a pull to concentrate on it since the war began, but I have earned £1500 for the serial rights and Scribners, and this was the most substantial thing I could do for the Relief Fund.'

The Freelands, published in August 1915, was not a success, nor was it the right novel for that particular time, with the landed gentry and their feudal rights as its subject. Nevertheless it won the approval of his friends. Gilbert Murray, always an appreciative admirer of Galsworthy's work, found it a 'consolation and joy'. It was the worst seller of all his novels, and Marrot reports that the original edition was still far from being sold out nineteen years later.

The book was envisaged as being the last of Galsworthy's social novels. With the exception of Frances Freeland, an elderly lady, the mother of the four Freeland sons, a portrait of Galsworthy's own mother, the characters are too much 'types' to carry conviction: Felix, an author and intellectual, John, a civil servant, Stanley, a 'captain of industry, possessor of the Morton Plough Works', and Tod, the good, simple man dedicated to the life of the land, with his wife, Kirsteen. The story of the book is how the younger members of the family espouse the cause of the farm labourer, Bob Tryst, who is threatened with eviction from his cottage because his moral conduct is displeasing to local gentry and squires, the Mallorings, as he wants to marry his deceased wife's sister, thus breaking a law of the church.

The agonizing, ever-worsening political situation apart, Galsworthy had family problems: his mother, now an old lady of seventy-seven living in Torquay, became seriously ill, and the winter was punctuated by constant journeys from Wingstone to Torquay. This vigil ended on 6 May 1915, when Blanche Galsworthy died. 'Dear Mother passed away at 11.45 of the morning, Lily and I with her . . . Her last words to me were, "Now darling, I think I'd like to sleep." Dear soul! The long sleep be good to her.'[12] Two days later she was buried next to her husband in the family vault at Highgate. Some years later Galsworthy wrote a short story, 'The Grey Angel', a fictional portrait of his mother; it would suggest that the old lady who died in Torquay had mellowed considerably since the days when she tormented her children by her fussiness, and finally left her aged husband because she believed him to be unfaithful to her.

Another even more painful situation was that of his brother-in-law, Georg Sauter, now officially classified as an enemy alien, and as such subject to new legislation which sought to intern all 'aliens' resident in the country. In the course of the war, despite the efforts of Galsworthy to prevent it by pointing out to the authorities and the Home Office how much Georg Sauter had done for English painters, and their recognition abroad, Georg Sauter, and, later, his son Rudolf were both confined in internment camps. For the Sauter family the wretched injustice of such an act had distressing consequences: the painter, permanently embittered by the British government's treatment of him, never again felt able to live in England. This in fact meant a lasting separation from his wife, Lilian, who was herself shattered by her husband's internment and whose health would never have stood the rigours of life in post-war Germany. In fact Lilian never recovered from the separation and trauma of the war. The short story, 'The Bright Side', written in 1919, tells the story of Georg and Lilian Sauter, of how a good citizen, just because he is German, can be victimized by society, imprisoned, exiled and ultimately broken – in Galsworthy's words 'buried under the leaves of despair'.

In the meantime the Galsworthys prepared for their first winter in England for many years; in fact, though Ada had 'flu from mid February until May, she still found the winter on Dartmoor surprisingly beautiful. 'The Moor is looking more beautiful than you can think. I always felt pretty sure winter was wonderful there, now I know, such bloom and blue and purple and deep rose and brown and gold – you can't help gazing and gazing.'[13] Apart from the visits to Torquay, there were a number of visitors to Wingstone that winter, among them the Frank Lucases, William Archer, Pinker the literary agent, and, for several stays, Galsworthy's nephew Rudolf. The scene was undoubtedly brightened by the presence of the young boy, who rode every day with his uncle, and played music with them in the evening. The diary records a typical day: 'January 28th. Novel. Rudo. Stunts in the evening. Larks. Music.' The part of the house at Wingstone occupied by the Galsworthys was so small that it is surprising they found room for their guests; for their own use there were only three bedrooms, one scarcely more than a cupboard, and two living-rooms of very modest size. And, of course, one room, the dining-room, was used also as Galsworthy's study.

Galsworthy began a new novel at the end of December 1914 – having raced through several short pieces, including working on a long short story called 'The First and The Last' – 'I can earn £300 with it for Funds quicker than any other work will earn anything.'[14] The novel *Beyond* was written, he recorded when he finished it on 2 January 1916, in 'One year and seven days work; length 120,000 words – the longest book I have written'. More than any other work it suffered from his desperate feeling of writing against time to raise money; he clocked up the words, as if to get something down on paper, no matter the quality, was the only thing of importance. 'July 11th. Novel. Walk with A. Novel. Reached the 200th page of MS. written in 38 days. Since returning to Wingstone May 28th. With sketches – 35,000 words in 44 days.'

Beyond is a highly romantic story. Gyp, its heroine, is the love child of Charles Winton; she makes a disastrous marriage to a Swedish musician, from whom she ultimately breaks away to join her lover, Bryan Summerhay, who is then tragically killed in a riding accident. But the relationship with which Galsworthy is really concerned is that between the father and his daughter; like Fleur and Soames in the later Forsyte novels, this is the true 'love affair' of the book. Later, when Galsworthy came to write his preface to the book for the Manaton Edition, he too saw its defects, calling *Beyond* his 'longest, worst written novel'.

The tempo of work continued throughout the year. His writing was a 'refuge', he wrote to Hugh Walpole, and so also was Wingstone. 'We've clung to Manaton pretty closely since the War began. I can't write in London, and one hasn't much heart in being anywhere in particular.'[15] Once again Ada's letters to Ralph Mottram give a good picture of their day to day life at Wingstone. 'Jack working hard and collecting shekels which go at once to war. He keeps it up mercilessly, thank goodness, and we live as skimpily as may be. Till just a week ago all the clothes I'd bought since last May were 2 pr. gloves 7/-, 1 pr. shoes 15/6, but now colder weather has broken down my resolutions a little. I had meant to have nothing new for one year – but I really don't know how better to help. I'm nothing like strong enough to take up any public work. I knit like a demon, of course, all the time.'[16] And then, three weeks later: 'J.G. is working like a slave, making very heavy weather just now – He will *not* take a day off, feeling that would be shirking. We do really both go at it as hard as we know how. I do lots of mechanical piffling work saving his time for more valuable efforts.'[17]

Even the production of his play *A Bit o' Love* at the Kingsway Theatre on 25 May did little to alleviate the gloom. Galsworthy did not even bother to attend the first night. 'They say it went well,' he wrote in his diary. 'I did not go. But walked about in Trafalgar Square, and watched the searchlights and a couple of lovers, and a drunken woman.'[18] His detachment from the production is strange, for Ada noted in her notebook 'that it was a play that J. is fond of, feeling that it has more colour and sense of place than any of his others'. They did, however, go to it two days later and Galsworthy found it 'a good performance'.

But it was a relief to return to Wingstone at the end of May and to be able to work uninterruptedly through June on his novel *Beyond*. For the Galsworthys, accustomed to a life that had consisted so largely of foreign travel or the hectic social round of their London life, these war years spent at Wingstone must have seemed very quiet indeed. The long hours of working were punctuated by riding and walking on the moors, there was more time for reading, and Ada was herself working on a translation of some Maupassant stories. 'I do love translating,' she wrote enthusiastically to Mottram.[19] In June Galsworthy was rereading his old favourite Whyte Melville, 'to see what the stuff was like that I loved so as a boy. Queer but something in it. Naif.'[20]

By September 'bad headaches' forced Galsworthy to take a brief rest from his writing. At the end of the month he and Ada left Wingstone for a short period, which they spent in London and visiting friends. As well as being exhausted by the constant pressure of work, they may well have felt that now that Lilian and Rudolf Sauter had come to Wingstone as permanent guests the small farmhouse was uncomfortably crowded.

They visited Thomas Hardy at Dorchester – 'Nice, dried up, alert old fellow; liked him,'[21] – and then went to Tunbridge Wells, to the Spa Hotel, where Ada was to take the baths. This gave Galsworthy an opportunity to visit Conrad at Capel House, Ashford: 'found them all well, much talk with dear Conrad . . .'[22]

After a brief visit to London, during which they saw the damage done by a Zeppelin raid,[23] they returned to Wingstone and another spell of hard work at *Beyond*. As the months of the war grew longer so

Galsworthy's despair deepened; except for writing there was nothing he could do, but was this enough? As well as his novel he was writing numerous articles for publication in newspapers and journals, ultimately to be collected into two volumes of essays, *A Sheaf* and *Another Sheaf*. 'First Thoughts on This War', which first appeared in *Scribner's Magazine* in 1914, was followed by 'Second Thoughts', written for the same magazine, for the next year, 1915. By the end of the year he was exhausted and despondent. 'Felt weak and done so paused before the run in [end of novel].'[24] And on the last day of the year he wrote: 'An unhappy year; but a terrible lot to be thankful for considering what others have gone through. My God!'[25]

It is impossible at this point not to become increasingly aware of an ever-widening rift in Galsworthy's character: the man and the imaginative writer are not one, but two personalities. The man is totally preoccupied by the disasters of the war, the needless suffering, the appalling waste of life. According to Rudolf Sauter, he was completely broken by the war years, experiencing an anguish that could only have been alleviated in a brutal fashion by active participation in the combat. We know from the passage in his diary for 15 November 1914, already quoted, how he was tormented by doubts as to whether he was shirking his duty, whether he lacked the courage to volunteer. It is interesting that right at the end of the war, on 17 July 1918, he did in fact volunteer for the Army Reserve, and was granted a certificate of discharge on the grounds that he was 'permanently and totally unfit for any form of Military Service'. (This certificate is carefully copied out in Galsworthy's handwriting and reproduced in Marrot's life.) All these feelings are poured on to paper in the numerous articles he wrote concerning the war, often repetitive and unoriginal, but always showing the anguish he felt. They are on the whole pieces of writing that have no permanent value or interest, such as could have been written by any good journalist.

So we must see Galsworthy the man as quite divorced from Galsworthy the creative writer. He clocked up the hours of writing and counted the words of his fast-growing novel, *Beyond*, but none of his feelings went into the book; while he thought of war he wrote of love and trite romance. It is hardly surprising that the book he wrote carries so little conviction, and was in the end, by his own admission, a failure.

Of greater significance than the failure of one novel, however, was the growing divergence between Galsworthy's writing and that of the generation of younger writers who were to re-shape the novel in the post-war years, such writers as Virginia Woolf, James Joyce and E. M. Forster. While Galsworthy's novels were becoming less concerned with the inner life of his characters (one has only to make a brief comparison between *Beyond* and *Fraternity*), the new novelists were increasingly preoccupied with ideas rather than actions. Galsworthy found it difficult to understand or sympathize with their aims, and was inclined to be hyper-critical of their work. (To be fair they underestimated his work even more than he did theirs; Virginia Woolf's scathing comments on Galsworthy are well known, and to have bracketed Wells, Bennett and Galsworthy as 'those three materialists' is a gross distortion of truth.) Nevertheless, there was sadly a touch of bitterness when Galsworthy wrote of his contemporaries in the post-war years: 'the plain and rather depressing fact is that the "new" Western Fiction is being written about over-sophisticated people by over-sophisticated people for over-sophisticated people. It is and will remain I feel "caviar" to the general.'[26]

There was, however, one medium in which Galsworthy was still able to express himself as a whole person, and this was in poetry. His poems, particularly during the war period, expressed the feeling of both the artist and the man; here there was no division. In poetry he could still use words with the skill of a craftsman, and at the same time voice the agony of his spirit. His best poems are a continuation in style and genre of that long early work, 'The Dream'; they still present a totally personal statement. Though in style they are a long way from what we now think of as modern poetry, they have a conviction and a depth of feeling that give them their own validity. One such poem written during the war he called 'The Valley of the Shadow':

> God I am travelling out to death's sea,
> I who exulted in sunshine and laughter,
> Dreamed not of dying – death is such a waste of me!
> Grant me one prayer: Doom not the hereafter
> Of mankind to war, as though I had died no –
> I who, in battle, my comrade's arm linking,
> Shouted and sang, life in my pulses hot
> Throbbing and dancing! Let not my sinking

In dark be for naught, my death a vain thing!
God, let me know it the end of man's fever
Make my last breath a bugle call, carrying
Peace o'er the valleys and cold hills for ever.

And another 'Youth's Own':

Out of the fields I see them pass,
Youth's own battalion –
Like moonlight ghosting over grass,
To dark oblivion.

They have a solemn tryst to keep
Out on the starry heath;
To fling them down, and sleep and sleep
Beyond Reveille – Death!

Galsworthy's reputation as a poet has never been great, and few examples of his work appear in modern anthologies. Nevertheless it was the form of writing he took most seriously, and certainly as the years wore on it was the one medium of creative writing in which he felt able to express himself without restraint.

Chapter 27

The French Hospital

The winter of 1915–16 was the first that the Galsworthys had ever spent entirely at Wingstone. Ada gritted her teeth and wrote to Mottram early in December: 'stern Fate says we've got to stay here. J. can't write ever very well in London; so there's one home empty, and this isn't a winter climate, but he *can* work steadily here, so here we stick in home no. 2.' 'I keep on knitting and typing and generally driving along as hard as possible. The one thing one mustn't do in these days is to *brood*.'[1] One cannot help feeling sorry for Ada: her role of knitting and typing must have been a very dull one indeed for someone used to a much more interesting life, someone who needed diversions, new scenes and new people.

For John these long months of uninterrupted writing were what he had always longed for, but, ironically, now that the time was his he was able to use it to little advantage. On 2 January he finished *Beyond*, 'the longest book I have written . . . with the exception of *The Country House* written in less time than any other'. Even the revision of this long rambling novel took far less time than usual: by 24 January it was finished and sent off to 'Miss Pugh for typing'. Then Marrot records that 'five days were devoted to reading the whole of *Beyond* aloud to his wife'! It is a daunting thought both for John's voice and Ada's patience, and one could wish that some constructive criticism might have resulted from the five days' reading: unfortunately *Beyond* was just the sort of story that Ada liked. Like her favourite book *The Patrician*, it was romantic and mentally undemanding, and it still had undertones of her now distant adventure with Major Galsworthy.

Galsworthy himself, even at the time of writing, was not convinced of its merits: when on 22 March he received the cheque for the serial rights in the magazine *Cosmopolitan*, the editor, Edgar Sisson, thanked him 'for its superb quality'. 'This is comforting,' Galsworthy added.[2]

With *Beyond* out of the way Galsworthy devoted his energies to two long short stories, 'The Stoic' and 'The Apple Tree'. The latter is one of the most successful of his later pieces of work, highly imaginative, and written in a style that is reminiscent in atmosphere and lyrical quality of one of his earliest stories, 'The Man of Devon'. In fact Galsworthy bracketed the two stories in the collected edition of his short stories, *Caravan*. 'One of my best stories,' he noted in his diary on the day he finished it, 8 July 1916. 'The Apple Tree' was inspired by Jay's Grave, which is still one of the sights of Dartmoor, and is even today usually decorated with flowers. The legend of Jay is that of a girl crossed in love, who then committed suicide and was therefore not permitted burial in consecrated ground. Galsworthy's poem 'The Moor Grave' is also on this subject:

> I lie out here under the heather sod
> A moor-stone at my head; the moor-winds play above
> I lie out here . . . In grave-yards of their God
> They would not bury desperate me who died for love.
> I lie out here under sun and moon;
> Across me bearded ponies stride, the curlews cry.
> I have no little tombstone screed, no 'Soon
> To glory shall she rise!' But deathless peace have I!

Despite Galsworthy's determination to make writing his war effort, no novel was published between *The Freelands*, coming out in August 1915, and *Beyond* which finally appeared in August 1917. This fact is at least partly explained by the increasing restlessness he was experiencing, a nagging need to do something more actively concerned with the war than his work as a writer could be. It is noticeable that once *Beyond* was completed the sense of urgency that drove Galsworthy to produce page after page of written material lessened. Writing wasn't enough to satisfy him; it was also becoming a considerable mental strain.

The year 1916 began with an unusually hard winter – in February there was a 'tremendously heavy snowfall, lasting long' – and both the Galsworthys had prolonged attacks of influenza. Galsworthy, confined to his bed, read Hardy's *Dynasts* straight through, and found it a 'very fine affair', also some Stevensons, 'to which he ever turneth when indisposed', Ada commented in her notebook, in the rather arch language she tended to use.[3] They went to St Ives to convalesce, and there saw much of W. H. Hudson, to whom they were both devoted. 'He is not really so ill, I believe, as he thinks himself. Quite the strangest personality in this age of machines and cheap effects. Like an old sick eagle.'[4] During May, they made a visit to London. 'Alack! we must go back to Wingstone on Thurs. or Fri.,' Ada wrote to Mottram on 2 May. 'It is criss-cross of things. This old London is too distracting just now; J. is getting unable to work and coin money for the realm.' Galsworthy was arranging for publication under the rather unsuitable title *A Sheaf of Wild Oats* all those articles and papers which he had written during the past few years. The 'Wild Oats' were finally dropped and the volume appeared simply as *A Sheaf*; 'a book of published humanitarianism and other writings,' Galsworthy described it in his diary.[5]

As Ada rightly commented to her correspondent, the summer of 1916 was one in which 'Jack had to rush about a good deal',[6] while she, somewhat unhappily, braved it out at Wingstone. 'We've gone back to fires and heavy rain – and spirits to match.'[7] On 14 May John was in Liverpool for a new production of *The Silver Box*. Revivals of his early plays must have been reassuring for their writer; earlier in the year *Justice* had been revived in Boston – 'Great success, notices superb,' he was cabled from America. Later in May he was in Leeds visiting his wretched brother-in-law, Georg Sauter, in Wakefield Camp,[8] and then in June he spent a few days with the artist, William Rothenstein, and sat for several drawings – 'the last is admirable'.[9]

July at Wingstone was a more tranquil month, during which Galsworthy spent long days working in the fields helping with the hay harvest. They also entertained seventy wounded soldiers to tea. But their time at Wingstone was curtailed, and for once Ada seemed to regret leaving the farm: 'I believe we shall be in the wilds of Wales (in Aug) some of the family [the Sauters] want us to turn out of here for Aug. and we're not brave enough to say "You be d —— d" to them.'[10]

When Galsworthy arrived in London from their Welsh holiday he was impatient to do something more immediately concerned with the war effort than writing. One of the first things that occurred to him was to offer the Red Cross the old Galsworthy family home, 8 Cambridge Gate, as a Wounded Soldiers' Club, and with it £400 to fit it up for this purpose. It was while he was at the Red Cross headquarters that he met Dorothy Allhusen, and she suggested to him that he and Ada should come out to France to her convalescent hospital for wounded soldiers at Die near Valence, John as a masseur, and Ada to superintend the care of the linen. At first sight it seems a most extraordinary idea, especially as it was never seen as anything but a very temporary break from writing, to last, as it did, for about three

months. He was immediately enthusiastic, and two days later, on
11 September, she came to tea with the Galsworthys to discuss her plan
in further detail. Within days Galsworthy had embarked on a course of
lessons in Swedish massage. Ada as usual enlarges on their activities in
her correspondence to Ralph Mottram:

> . . . he is rapidly becoming a good masseur in preparation for our
> jaunt to France. We go to a small hospital near Valence in early Nov.
> he as masseux [sic] for rheumatic and neurasthenic French soldiers,
> I to look after linen and garments . . . His monetary value to his
> country will go down sadly, but he does badly need a change and
> nothing would induce him to stop work. We think to be there for
> 3 or 4 months and then he'll go on writing and handing over all
> proceeds here. We go up for a fortnight's more hard training in the
> work, at which he's already rather good, having long ago taken a
> good course in the English method (to work on my rheumatism).
> Muller exercises also come in handily and at them we're both
> experts.[11]
>
> I don't believe I'll wear any 'costume' . . . commonsense tells me
> that an ugly washing overall is all that is wanted in connection with
> the care of house linen.[12]

Galsworthy himself had many misgivings as to his suitability for the
work: 'Do the baths at your Hospital include electrical installation?
I'm rather scared of mechanical appliances, which are not "in my
character", and I'd like to know, that I may see (if they are there)
whether I'm fit to deal with them,' he wrote anxiously to Dorothy
Allhusen on 12 September. Happily his worries were unfounded: 'I'm
relieved about the electricity. I think I shall be decently all right for the
massage – in fact, mean to be.'[13] But by October he was still uncertain
about whether the project would work. 'It seems a little absurd,' he
wrote to André Chevrillon in Paris, 'and I'm afraid I shan't be much
good; but I badly want a rest from the head and pen, and one can only
rest from that by working with the hands.'[14]

During the last weeks before their departure Galsworthy worked
furiously finishing off various pieces of work on which he was engaged:
a new play titled *The Foundations* was completed, a short story called
'Defeat', and numerous articles and appeals: 'Jack is more busy than
words can say . . . he is simply snowed under with appeals, demands,
almost threats, 6 appeals for public appeals from his pen in the last

3 days.'[15] The Galsworthys were well accustomed to packing up for long journeys, but this time they were, as Ada wrote with some relish, 'entirely under the orders of our Hosp. Chief'.[16] They also had to undergo a series of innoculations, which suited neither of their somewhat delicate constitutions. However at last, after several delays, they left England on 13 November, crossing the channel to Le Havre.

Their crossing was peaceful, and romantic, reaching Le Havre in the moonlight: 'A night approach to a city by water has the quality of other-worldliness. I remember the same sensation twice before: coming in to San Francisco from the East by the steam ferry, and stealing into Abingdon-on-Thames in a rowing boat . . .'[17] They spent a few days in Paris before going on to Valence, where they noticed 'v. little difference from times of peace. Far less than in London.'[18] While in Paris they renewed their friendship with the Chevrillons, and Ralph Mottram 'turned up at 9.0 p.m. Long and voluble chatter on his experiences at front etc.'[19] (Mottram was now serving in the forces.)

At last they reached their destination, arriving at Die on 18 November. On the train journey they had had the opportunity to observe the French *poilus* whom they were to work among, and were much impressed by the appearance of the men they saw, finding them much superior to the English 'Tommy'. '. . . every face has character, no face looks empty or as if its thought were being done by others . . . Alongside their faces the English face looks stupid, the English body angular and – neat.' On their arrival at Dauphine 'A tall, strong young soldier, all white teeth and smiles, hurries our luggage out, a car hurries us up in the rainy wind through the little town, down again across the river, up a long avenue of pines, and we are at the hospital.'[20]

The Hôpital Bénévole, Martouret, Die, was set in a 'charming spot circled by low mountains'. Here they were welcomed by the small staff of four women and settled into their 'cosy dark quarters with a big hearth and wood fire'.[21] In two days Galsworthy started on his massage, and found it interesting. By 21 November he had an established routine, and in characteristic fashion had drawn up a timetable of his day's work, beginning with breakfast at 8.15, and consisting of three sessions of massage and one of Muller exercises. His day ended with his last massage period at ten o'clock at night. A photograph of Ada and John with some of the *poilus* shows John in the uniform of a British army officer. The enterprise, undertaken with the authority of the War Office and at the same time carried out on a completely amateurish level, would be unimaginable today.

'My massage seems – oddly enough – to be of some use,' John wrote to his sister, Mabel Reynolds. 'I do about ten patients a day, about five hours in all, and half an hour's Muller exercises with some of the men, and help to serve the dinners. Ada does linen, and sews pretty well all day long except from one till four-thirty.'[22] The whole Martouret adventure will seem a little less strange when one considers what an important part of Galsworthy's character caring for people was. Rudolf Sauter has emphasized what a gift his uncle had for nursing, and, as his diary shows, much of John's life with Ada was spent in caring for her during her numerous illnesses. The months they spent at the Hôpital Bénévole were to be almost certainly the happiest time of the war for Galsworthy. At last he was able to do something for those who had suffered through the fighting. His days were incredibly busy, leaving no time for the brooding distress that had dogged him during the last eighteen months.

Galsworthy threw himself into the new work with characteristic enthusiasm and dedication; thus when they left Martouret at the beginning of March 1917 he could record in his diary that he had not missed a day's work during his stay at the convalescent home. Ada too seems to have enjoyed her war work; mainly in charge of the linen, she was nevertheless sufficiently important to be left in charge of the hospital when Mrs Allhusen went to England for a brief visit at the end of December. She also seems to have been physically in much better health than usual; judging from a letter written to Ralph Mottram from Wales shortly before they left England rebuking him for complaining about his gastritis, she admitted that this was so: 'Look at me! from 15 to over 30 a martyr really in continual misery, living on Bengers and dry toast; now I can nibble at pickles, melon, cucumber and avoid destruction.'[23]

Their work was not limited to the practical things of massaging and caring for the linen; they both became personally involved with their French patients, and the story 'Flotsam and Jetsam' is an affectionate and delightful description of two of these *poilus*. A car was provided in which the invalids could be taken out, and also a gramophone, which Ada found 'a doubtful joy to me, but first rate for the men'.[24] She also accompanied the men as they sang their traditional *Petits*

Chansons. The Christmas of 1916 must have been one of the happiest the Galsworthys ever experienced: 'Our Xmas dinner table at the hospital under the green hanging wreaths and the gay chinese lanterns: the hum, the chatter and the laughter of the free and easy souls in their red hospital jackets. The French are so easily, so incorrigibly gay.'[25] Ada and John were completely enchanted by the French and their way of life: 'We got terribly fond of our *poilus*. English ones could never be so interesting. We are both violently in love with France.'[26]

Throughout these months in France, despite, or perhaps because of, the break from writing, Galsworthy seemed to be unusually aware of himself; he was introspective, even openly, in a way that was uncharacteristic in a man who despised and regarded as self-indulgent any consideration of his own personal feelings. The war, and before that what he saw as his betrayal of Ada in his infatuation with Margaret Morris, had made him more aware of himself and unsure of his motives. Once life had seemed straightforward and his motives clear; now, in his writing and in his personal life, he was confused and uncertain. Seen in this light it is less surprising that when writing to Mrs Allhusen about the date of their leaving the hospital he should have suggested that she might in any case 'have become "fed-up" with my very peculiar nature, and be glad for us to go'.[27] Nobody but Galsworthy himself was fed up with his peculiarities; he, one must suspect, was growing increasingly dissatisfied with himself. He could no longer hide his hideous anxiety that he was, as a man and a writer, a failure. Moreover he was still tormented by fears that he was not doing enough for the war effort: 'I'm beginning to feel I'm not pulling my weight,' he continued his letter to Mrs Allhusen. 'I expect the National Service Bill will pass early in February, and I'd like to be back before it gets into action, unless I'm doing much more good than I am at present.'[28]

In fact the Galsworthys did not return to England until the end of March 1917. They spent the first fortnight of the month at Cassis in the south of France, and from there Galsworthy was able to take the opportunity of visiting the Ecole Joffre, at Tourvielle, an establishment for training disabled soldiers. They returned to England via Paris, and there again he visited institutions for disabled soldiers. His experiences at the Hôpital Bénévole had intensified his interest in the problems of the disabled serviceman. What was his future, how could he be trained and fitted for some sort of life in the post-war world? Or was there a grave danger that the country he had served would forget him once there was peace again?

So ended their four and a half months' stay in France: 'On the whole I think the most tolerable time since the war started,' he noted in his diary.[29]

Chapter 28

Last Years of the War

Back in England Galsworthy immediately started writing again, working on a long short story entitled 'The Indian Summer of a Forsyte'. It is significant that this tranquil and accomplished piece of writing, that was to be, at a later date, the forerunner of so much more about the Forsyte family, should have been the first thing he wrote on his return to England. It suggests that during those months at Martouret Galsworthy did find some sort of peace within himself. Perhaps he was able to come to terms with his own achievement as a writer, to an acceptance that it might not be in his power to write a book as accomplished as *The Man of Property* and yet having the profundity that he had striven for in *Fraternity*. It was not in his nature to explore the complexities of his own character, and then to lie it exposed, on the pages of his books. Basically such a personal approach offended his sensibilities; he was too much of a 'gentleman' to attempt it, and yet as a writer he saw it could be necessary for his development.

'On the last day of May in the early 'nineties, about six o'clock of the evening, old Jolyon Forsyte sat under the oak tree before the terrace of his house at Robin Hill . . .' This story of old Jolyon picks up the threads of *The Man of Property*: Jolyon Forsyte is now living in the mansion at Robin Hill built with such unhappy consequences by Soames Forsyte for his wife Irene. Jolyon, now a very old man, faces philosophically the fact that time for him is fast running out. Now, in his old age, of the Forsyte values, beauty, upright conduct and the sense of property, only the first, beauty, is still meaningful to him. 'He had always been responsive to what they had begun to call "Nature", genuinely, almost religiously responsive . . . But nowadays Nature actually made him ache, he appreciated it so.' It is easy to recognize the portrait of Galsworthy's father.

John Galsworthy in 1917 was still only fifty years old, but for him, as for old Jolyon, his love of natural beauty was perhaps the only thing that had never failed him. The months at Martouret, massaging the wounded bodies of French soldiers, had undoubtedly soothed the aching wound in his own spirit, and he was now better fitted to bear the mental burden of the war. So, like Jolyon Forsyte, he saw again that the world was still a beautiful place, that the birds still sang, that the Alderney cows still chewed the cud, 'flicking slow their tufted tails: and every one of these fine days he ached a little from the sheer love of it all . . .' Galsworthy's writing found new life in his most viable family, the Forsytes. The family had frequently before demanded a renaissance. Young Jolyon appears in *Danae* (the first draft of *The Country House*) and was also seen as possibly the commentator in the series of social novels that were to follow *The Man of Property*. Now they all began to live again in his new story; old Jolyon, young Jo, his children, Jolly and Holly, and the beautiful, but still enigmatic, Irene, living independently apart from Soames in restricted financial circumstances. It is Irene, revisiting the scene of her now long past love affair with Bosinney, who forms a close and tender relationship with the old man, Jolyon. This is his 'Indian Summer', that brings him not only the beauty of nature, but that of a lovely woman.

So the Forsytes were born again, though it was not until a year later that Galsworthy conceived the idea of continuing their family chronicles into a trilogy of novels, *The Forsyte Saga*. This was fortunate, for though Galsworthy was happier he was still writing under considerable pressure and strain, and his next novel, begun in August and written in about six months, *Saint's Progress*, is a mediocre and unsatisfactory piece of writing.

Nineteen seventeen, despite the war, was altogether a happier time for the Galsworthys than the earlier war years; the experience of Martouret was still having its therapeutic effect. And much more was happening on the literary scene: his new play *Foundations*, rejected in December by Harrison of the Haymarket Theatre, was now to be produced in the summer at the Royalty Theatre in a triple bill; there were also other provincial productions of his plays. A completely new outlet for his writing was the cinema; *Justice* was adapted and made into a film by the Ideal Film Company, with Gerald du Maurier playing Falder: 'saw the whole film reeled off. Of its kind it is good, but the whole process most repellent.'[1]

During the summer of 1917 the Galsworthys' lives returned much more to the pattern of pre-war days; they travelled more, though after the French interlude entirely in England, and saw more people. At Tintern on the Welsh borders, Galsworthy 'Walked past Coed Ithel, where I used to stay as a boy with Col. and Mrs. Randall, and had my calf love that lasted so long – off and on, *bien entendu* – for S[ybil] C[arlisle].'[2] Then they went on to Oxford, where they stayed for some time, seeing the Masefields, but finding the town 'a melancholy place, the Colleges full of cadets . . .'[3] At Littlehampton, where they had some idea of finding a permanent home – 'As always we mentally envisage the settling down here when we are too decrepit for the hard life on the moor'[4] – they failed to find a house but spent the 'two happiest days since the war began'.

The Galsworthys were house-hunting in earnest, both in London, where the flat at Adelphi Terrace was proving too small for their needs, and in the country for a possible replacement for Wingstone. They actually looked at a house in the village of Bury, where they were ultimately to settle, but rejected it as being 'too near a church, and close to floods of water. No go.'[5] In London their search for a house was more successful: in Hampstead they 'found Grove Lodge, the very house we had coveted to settle in at the end of 1904. Now it is very charming and we covet it again. We look no further.'[6] Nevertheless, though the decision to buy the house was made in November, it was to be nearly a year before they moved into the new house, at the end of September 1918.

In London the physical hardships of the war were much more apparent than in the quiet of the Devonshire countryside; despite the dinner parties that Ada still records in her notebook and the almost unabated stream of social life, they 'both feel rather hungry all the time – thoroughly interested in rather inferior food! We occasionally have a tremendous orgy of oysters, which is pardonable, we think.'[7] Bombs fell in the vicinity of Adelphi Terrace – '10 within a quarter of a mile' of the building – and one evening, when they were dining with the Arnold Bennetts, Ada wrote to Mottram that they 'passed some hours in a warmed and lighted basement'.[8] Bennett records the same incident: 'We went down into the basement . . . I noticed that John was just as chivalrous to the cook as to any of the other women. He even gave her a chocolate.'[9]

It was during this winter that Galsworthy met for the first time the young writer, D. H. Lawrence. Lawrence had already published some of his most important novels, among them *Sons and Lovers* (1913) and *The Rainbow* (1915). Galsworthy found Lawrence: 'Interesting, but a type I could not get on with. Obsessed with self. Dead eyes, and a red beard, long narrow pale face. A strange bird.'[10] The feeling of distrust was mutual, as can be judged by the bitingly vicious essay Lawrence wrote on Galsworthy: 'we see Mr. Galsworthy, after *The Country House*, very safe on the old highway, very secure in comfort, wealth, and renown . . . He at least has gone down in no bog, nor lost himself striking new paths . . .'[11]*

Galsworthy was also seeing much more of his old friends of the writing world, the Conrads, Massingham, E. V. Lucas and James Barrie among others. Incongruously the Galsworthys gave dinner parties at the Automobile Club, 'to which in a misguided moment J. has belonged' Ada wrote in her notebook.

The year ended with one of the strangest incidents of Galsworthy's life, the offer of an unwanted knighthood. The Galsworthys spent Christmas 1917 at Littlehampton, John working on his new novel *Saint's Progress* and also writing a series of essays entitled 'Grotesques'. On New Year's Eve they had friends in and were discussing 'the affairs of the Nation', when Galsworthy received a telegram from the Prime Minister, Lloyd George, ' "Please wire by return whether you accept offer of knighthood." I wired: "Most profoundly grateful but feel I must not accept." Told A. when our visitors had gone and we went to bed considerably disturbed by the thought might be too late [*sic*]; but confident that they would not take silence for consent.'[12] His diary of 1 January continues the story:

* When Galsworthy read *Sons and Lovers* he found it 'a book that in parts excites my genuine admiration and in other parts my genuine irritation and dislike. The Mother and all about her is fine; the love episodes are worrying to a degree. And the general impression left by the book is that the man has some genius, but not the best sort.' Letter to Hugh Walpole, 15 April 1914.

'. . . that kind of revelling in the shades of sex emotions seems to me anaemic. Contrasted with Maupassant's – a frank sensualist – dealing with such emotions, it has a queer indecency; . . . It's not good enough to spend time and ink in describing the penultimate sensations and physical movements of people. There's genius in the book, but not in that part of the book. The body's never worth while, and the sooner Lawrence recognizes that the better –' Letter to E. Garnett, 13 April 1914.

They did take silence for consent. To my horror my name was among the New Year's knights. Instantly wired to Lloyd George 'that I must persist in my refusal to accept, and asked for his contradiction in the Press.' A very unhappy twenty-four hours. I've always thought and said that no artist of Letters ought to dally with titles and rewards of that nature. He should keep quite clear and independent. Wrote and Ada wrote innumerable letters to our friends telling of the mistake.

It seemed to John that to accept such an honour would be a betrayal of his principles, and he felt too that his friends would share his feelings: 'We spend an unpleasant day, thinking of all our friends weeping and gnashing their teeth.'[13] They spent the next few days answering the 175 letters and forty telegrams that arrived. 'We have had a most jolly stay here by the sea, in spite of the hurricane of letters, first of congratulation moderato, and second of congratulation con molto brio,' Ada wrote to Mottram.[14] 'Oh yes! A lot of people did write to Lady Galsworthy but *I* also wrote about 200 letters to disabuse them, so now they know.'[15] (It has been suggested that Ada would for herself have very much liked to be Lady Galsworthy, and was disappointed at John's refusal – though she loyally endorsed his view at the time.)

Though Galsworthy insisted that it was quite different, it is a little hard to see why the Order of Merit was so acceptable eleven years later: it was certainly a more suitable award for a man of letters, but it still belied the principle that 'Literature is its own reward'. Would he, one wonders, have accepted the O.M. in 1918, or the knighthood in 1929?

The satirical series of essays, 'Grotesques', which Galsworthy originally intended to publish under a pseudonym, eventually appeared as the last section of the collection *Another Sheaf*. There is an underlying bitterness to these essays. Galsworthy already felt out of tune with the world of his contemporaries, that he, as a writer and thinker, had been discarded in favour of new gods. The scene is supposedly set thirty years on, and the Angel Aethereal, on his official visit to the earth in 1947, is conducted on his tour by his dragoman. They visit the Stock Exchange, the country, the divorce courts, the world of the arts, etc., and in everything they see they are disillusioned:

'Are there no plays, no operas?' asked the Angel . . .

'Not in the old and proper sense of these words. They disappeared towards the end of the Great Skirmish.'

'What food for the mind is there, then?'

'. . . The mission of art – now truly democratic – is to level – in principle up, in practice down . . .'

This quotation serves to illustrate Galsworthy's growing apprehension that the sort of work he was able to do was becoming increasingly unacceptable. He wrote a second, somewhat similar piece only a few months later, this time a short novel entitled *The Burning Spear*. The hero, John Lavender, was envisaged as a modern Don Quixote, whose idealistic adventures always ended in misfortune and ridicule. Galsworthy had the greatest admiration for the novel by Cervantes, regarding it as the 'first great Western novel', and in April 1918, when he was working on his own *Burning Spear*, he was urging his nephew to read *Don Quixote*, 'a great book'. His novel was first published in 1919 under the pseudonym A.R.P. – M., and in 1923 was reprinted under Galsworthy's own name.

Galsworthy wrote to Walpole on 3 March 1918: 'We stick down here [Wingstone] till my novel is finished. I tried London for ten days and didn't write a word – what with lunching, and people taking me to see babies, and land committees, and talk and talk and talk one feels like a shredded shrimp.' His main undertaking at this time was his novel *Saint's Progress*, 'written in 1917 and the first months of 1918 at a time when the hearts of all of us at home were very sore. If . . . its atmosphere concretes that long and grinding ache, the book has achieved the other half of its purpose . . . and I think it does.'[16] The war at this time had reached a period of renewed horror and despair: the Galsworthys were at Littlehampton when they heard the 'gruesome news of the last German advance, which so nearly broke up the British line [Easter Sunday]. We went that day to the "Green Hill Far Away" [a favourite spot near Littlehampton]. All the remaining days of our stay were spent in very depressed mood.'[17]

This was the background of his novel, whose chief character was a clergyman, Edward Pierson, who was 'not a typical priest of today, but rather a symbol of the English Church, left somewhat high and dry by the receding waters of orthodox faith'.[18] Pierson is a good man, but he cannot escape from the bonds of the orthodoxy in which he has been brought up; when his favourite child Noel falls in love with a soldier and wants to marry him hurriedly before he departs for the front, he refuses to give his consent. In consequence Noel gives herself to her lover the night before he leaves England, and after he is killed is happy to bear his child. All this is incomprehensible to Pierson, who becomes more and more estranged from Noel. Ultimately she falls in love again, this time with an older man, Jimmy Fort, who is known to have been having a casual love affair. Once again Pierson cannot approve of his daughter's choice, and out of his depth he leaves England and his parish to serve as an army chaplain.

The war, the hurried writing (it was finished and revised by 10 April 1918, and it was a long novel of between eighty and ninety thousand words) and the unfamiliar background make it an unsatisfactory piece of work. 'A curious book,' Galsworthy noted in his diary.[19] Like *Fraternity* it was a novel in which he needed to go a great deal deeper than he dared. Pierson's religious and personal difficulties needed far more profound exploration than he was at this time capable of; he was writing with only half himself, and concurrently working on those strange satires, 'Grotesques', and *The Burning Spear*. A romance, such as *Beyond*, could possibly have been attempted as a purely professional exercise; a novel with a subject such as *Saint's Progress* could not.

Was he doing the right thing in this selling of his talent to make money for the war effort? There must have been considerable doubts, and certainly there was criticism from his public. 'You know why he's sown broadcast in paying magazines? So that the proceeds may be fat and all go to the country's needs. We've had some wonderfully abusive letters from America commenting on his "filthy greed" in descending to this level etc. but naturally it's not a matter one can explain. Isn't it beastly? He doesn't care, but I do!' Ada wrote indignantly to Ralph Mottram.[20]

But writing was not Galsworthy's only contribution to the war effort; his work at Martouret gave him a permanent and semi-professional interest in disabled soldiers, in their future and in the possibilities of their being trained to lead some sort of useful and ful-filling life. This concern already had a practical outlet in England: the Galsworthy home, 8 Cambridge Gate, which had been given to the Red Cross at the end of 1916, was opened in February 1917 as a club for wounded soldiers called Kitchener House. This club aimed to provide the wounded with recreational facilities and also instruction and training in a wide variety of subjects; men were taught singing, piano, violin, mechanics and cobbling, as well as languages, book-keeping and stenography. 'I've been marked down by the Red Cross and other Authorities for work in connection with the re-education of the disabled soldier . . .' Galsworthy had written to Chevrillon on 12 March 1917, before his return from France. Now his work was to take a new form, and one especially suited to a writer with many connections in the literary world.

A magazine called *Recalled to Life*, devoted entirely to the needs and interests of disabled soldiers, already existed under the editorship of Lord Charnwood. It was now suggested that Galsworthy should take over the work of editing the magazine; this he agreed to do on condition that he had a completely free hand in reconstructing the magazine as he thought fit. So on 17 April 1918 he was appointed editor of the periodical, which he immediately renamed *Reveille*. The new magazine was to be a mixture of contributions by distinguished authors and artists, who would give their work without payment, and articles on technical and general subjects relating to rehabilitation and retraining.

Galsworthy, with his almost over-sensitive imagination, was perhaps one of the few who saw ahead to a time when the post-war world might forget those who had given so much in the service of their country. These men had to be trained, wherever possible, so that they would be able to live useful lives in some capacity. If they were not prepared for their future, he wrote in his introduction to the first edition of *Reveille* (August 1918),

> we are in for the most horrible tragedy and disgrace a few years hence . . . special permanent niches . . . will be usurped by the flood of returning labour, and thus what is at present a real opportunity will rapidly become invisible.
>
> The economic aftermath may not come on us at once, but when it comes it will be unexampled for severity. The disabled, unprovided for by special work, will be the first to suffer.

As always Galsworthy took his new undertaking with enormous seriousness. With Ada beside him as his indefatigable secretary, he wrote hundreds of letters asking for contributions, acknowledging them when they arrived. 'I labour after him as a secretary should, and try to remember where things are, and pick up the pieces generally.'[21] The three issues of *Reveille* published under Galsworthy's editorship are remarkable for the eminence of the contributors: they included such names as Rudyard Kipling, Max Beerbohm, J. M. Barrie, Joseph Conrad, E. V. Lucas, Jerome K. Jerome, Thomas Hardy, and Robert Bridges. Each copy was sold at the modest price of half-a-crown, and the first edition sold about thirty thousand copies and attracted considerable notice in the Press. The magazine under Galsworthy's editorship only ran into three editions, and all were of the same very high standard. The editorship was given up because of a question of censorship over the articles, and Galsworthy felt it was essential that as editor he should retain a critical independence.

During the summer of 1918 the war news began to improve: 'News better and better,' Galsworthy wrote in his diary on 26 August, and with the hope of peace there were signs that Galsworthy's own life was moving into new and more hopeful channels. His final rejection in July by the National Service Medical Board as being unfit for any form of military service was a weight off his mind; now he need no longer accuse himself of shirking the full horror of war. His collection of long short stories, *Five Tales*, was published on 25 July; this was work of a quite different standard from the very second-rate *Beyond* or *Saint's Progress*. 'The Apple Tree' or 'The Indian Summer of a Forsyte' could take their place without shame beside the best of his work, and Galsworthy was well aware of the fact. The new volume carried the telling sub-title 'Life Calls the Tune – We Dance'. But now at last the 'Dance' was going to be better: already he had the germ of the idea for his most ambitious work, *The Forsyte Saga*; he and Ada were moving out of the cramped flat in Adelphi Terrace, in which they had never been happy; and, above all, at the beginning of the winter the war ended. 'November 11. *Armistice signed. Peace at last. Thank all the gods there be.*'

Those four agonizing years were over; for Galsworthy, a non-participant, they had meant much mental anguish and heart-searching. It is strange, but characteristic of the man, that once over the event was seldom discussed by him; to Ralph Mottram, newly back from the front, he observed: 'The war was a jolt, Ralph.' Surely a classic understatement?[22]

Chapter 29

A Literary Figure

In the late summer of 1918 Grove Lodge began to loom like a promised land for the Galsworthys – or at least for Ada. Since their departure from Addison Road over five years ago after the unhappy winter of 1911–12, they had never really had a London home. The flat in Adelphi Terrace had always been too small for their needs – 'too small for two, but just large enough for one. Bedroom, dressing-room, bath-room, kitchen, two sitting rooms.'[1] The early years of the war they had spent at Wingstone, but latterly that house had been largely occupied by Galsworthy's sister Lilian and her household, and anyhow the Dartmoor winters had proved too severe for Ada. Consequently much of their time had been spent in hotels and boarding houses, at Littlehampton, Tunbridge Wells and Oxford. Now this beautiful fair-sized house, set in its own large garden in a most attractive part of Hampstead, was to be theirs. From August until November when they finally moved in, Ada's letters to Rudolf Sauter are full of their preparations for setting up their new home in London. She describes, blow by blow, the progress of their arrangements to move.

August 12; We shall be coming up in about a week to try and settle a few things about the new little house at Hampstead. I am quaking for my poor taste and the poor choice of colourings and materials combine to make a terrifying prospect. [It should be remembered that Ada was renowned among her friends for her exquisite taste!]

September 24; We trek to our Hampstead happy home (I hope) on Friday, or so we think . . . It is so long since I even pretended to like living in Central London; the streets are always amusing, but to live in the thick of things is not amusing . . . Pray for me on Friday when the grand piano of my heart has to go down this peculiarly narrow staircase; perhaps the workmen involved ought still more to be prayed for. I am glad to say it is a ground floor affair in the house to come, though it will certainly spoil the look of rather a pretty shaped drawing room.

September 30: Unc is fearfully busy with his editorial work [*Reveille*], and pursues it though painters chase him from room to room, and furniture people shout and bang. Tomorrow carpet layers will hammer violently, but will still edit.

October 29: Chaos reigns still at Grove Lodge. I must tackle it in earnest now. Minnie [the maid who was with the Galsworthy family for her whole working life] writes despairingly about furniture that doesn't arrive. I can't think what she is expecting – something far beyond my wildest aspirations, I fear. As to Unc – he is under the impression that a bed and a chest of drawers with a mirror the size of a man's hand, is handsome furnishing for any room. Between these two extremes I hover sadly, anxiously.

On 1 November the Galsworthys spent their first night at Grove Lodge, though it would seem from Ada's letters that Galsworthy had carried on with his work in the house during most of the lengthy move. Even now Ada was 'extremely busy for many weeks after, getting straight in the new house'.[2]

R. H. Mottram, in his book on the Galsworthys, admits that this elegant and expensive house was bought mainly to give pleasure to Ada, and that for John, even with his family wealth, it was expensive. 'Grove Lodge wasn't cheap, I can tell you!' he told Mottram with a touch of bitterness.[3] In the new house there was a downstairs study, mainly for business affairs and papers, and an 'upper study', secluded and private for writing, and also an open-air 'writing room' in the garden. Despite these facilities, by the New Year Galsworthy was still finding it difficult to establish a pattern of work in the new home: 'Grove Lodge does not at present reveal itself as a good writing place, but when we get the very top room in order, I think he will have a very good crows' nest and be happy there. It has something of an outlook, just over treetops, and he can tramp up and down in as empty a room as we can manage,' Ada wrote from her bed to Mottram, having the hefty 'beginnings of a cold'. But downstairs life was in full swing: 'Myra Hess playing like a whole band of angels just below me, and for a few minutes standing in white fur (or angels feathers) by my bed in the dim firelight, looking like a strong dark capable angel.'[4]

The house at Grove Lodge made the ideal background for the social and cultural life that the Galsworthys were to lead in the post-war years. John Galsworthy was no longer an *enfant terrible* of the writing world; far from it, his position was that of one of the most established and respected writers in the country, and he was already becoming the target for sneers from the avant garde of literature. At Grove Lodge, waited on by their devoted retainers Minnie and Rhoda, they lived a life almost incomprehensible forty years later. Minnie Green, who only died in 1975, remained faithfully nursing Ada until her death in 1957, and speaks with enormous devotion of Ada and John. She recalls how John rose every morning at seven to go riding on Hampstead Heath; he would then work in the room at the top of the house, where he was never permitted to be disturbed. Ada, she admits, 'was more difficult than he was . . .' But, said Mrs Green, 'he never left us out': the staff were given tickets to go to his plays, and signed copies of his books; moreover, what is more important, he was anxious to know 'what we thought of it'. Gazing at a signed studio portrait she sighed: 'it's so wonderful to look back at.'

The Galsworthys gave many dinner parties, that are often mentioned in memoirs and biographies. The young Siegfried Sassoon must have been one of the first guests at Grove Lodge, as he visited Galsworthy to discuss his contribution to the magazine *Reveille*:

Memorable it was but mainly through an atmosphere of achieved serenity. The only other guest was a shyly uncommunicative young lady writer [Dorothy Easton, Galsworthy's goddaughter], and the whole evening appeared designed for the promotion of comfort and kindliness. Even when I got to know him, Galsworthy produced an impression of being a reticent revealer of himself, for he was essentially modest and unegotistical. At our first meeting his reserved but shiningly sympathetic manner made me – partly owing to politeness – so talkative that I felt more like an impulsively informative nephew than a contributor to the next number of *Reveille*. As he sat at the dark polished table his strikingly handsome face and unassuming dignity seemed somehow avuncular, suggesting that, when we had finished our discussion of Turgenev and Thomas Hardy and I was sipping a second glass of the '87 port, he would enquire with a subdued smile whether a slight increase in my college allowance would meet with my approval. By the end of the evening I almost felt that I ought to call him 'Uncle Jack'. Mrs. Galsworthy, too, seemed well qualified to become 'Aunt Ada' for she was full of charm and lively intelligence.[5]

'I am dining with John Galsworthy in the True House of Seriousness, The Grove, Hampstead', wrote the more frivolous Arnold Bennett to his nephew in 1922, nevertheless capturing the atmosphere of the Galsworthy household.

But of even greater importance than the move to Grove Lodge was the fresh infusion of life that came into Galsworthy's writing in the summer of 1918. 'The Indian Summer of a Forsyte', written a year earlier, was now published in the collection *Five Tales*. During August, which was spent at Wingstone, Galsworthy recorded that he began a 'Second Part of *The Forsyte Saga*, to be called *The Second Flowering*'. In a general note he explains his intention:

> The idea of making *The Man of Property* the first volume of a trilogy cemented by *Indian Summer of a Forsyte* and another short episode came to me on Sunday July 28th, and I started the same day. This idea, if I can ever bring it to fruition, will make *The Forsyte Saga* a volume of half a million words nearly; and the most sustained and considerable piece of fiction of our generation at least. For if I can do it, it will have a much greater coherence than ———'s slop-sided trilogy.* But shall I ever bring it off?[6]

It might have seemed that the end of the war, the new life at Grove Lodge and the decision to continue his Forsyte family into two more novels would have heralded a new, more vigorous phase in Galsworthy's career as a writer, and one in which his writing could develop without the endless interruptions to which it had hitherto been subject. There certainly was a change in Galsworthy's life, but not the change one might have hoped for. Peace meant the resumption of foreign travel, a return to the itinerant pre-war years – but with a difference. Galsworthy, now a knight *manqué* and a distinguished man of letters, was in demand. When he travelled, he travelled as a 'great writer'; everywhere, especially in the United States, there were receptions, formal dinners and requests for lectures and addresses. 'I get awfully little time for any creative work nowadays,' he ended a letter to Dorothy Easton on a note of despair.[7]

Galsworthy's enormous affection for the writer and naturalist

* Galsworthy probably meant Hugh Walpole's Jeremy trilogy.

W. H. Hudson perhaps reflected his own yearning to be such a person, a man who seldom mixed in society or travelled abroad. 'He reminded me of an embodiment of Nature which by accident had got entangled in our civilization . . . As a rule I do not worship heroes – no rule but has its exception.'[8] He was to Galsworthy the one man who seemed able to retain his integrity and resist the pressures of the twentieth century. 'He is to me the great writer and liver in an age which has lost nature,' he wrote to Dorothy Easton, recommending her to read his works.[9]

For Galsworthy the future held no such promise of peace or retirement; America, more than his own country had ever been, was ready to lionize and make much of the writer whose plays and writings had become so popular during the war.

Early in the New Year of 1919 an invitation came for Galsworthy from the American Academy of Arts and Letters to go to America as a representative of English literature at the Lowell Centenary celebrations. The invitation was accepted, and on 1 February he and Ada left England on the S.S. *Carmania*. On the voyage Ada was ill and spent most of the time in her cabin, and both of them settled down to do their homework for the forthcoming Lowell Centenary. 'We have both been diligently reading Lowell, Emerson, Thoreau and the New England Group generally. Emerson is much the most trenchant and interesting as a writer, we think, or rather, *he* thinks, for *I* am quite incapable of thought on board ship.'[10]

In terms of what was achieved, this American tour was an enormous success. Ada and John were fêted everywhere they went; the many lectures that Galsworthy gave struck exactly the right note and were delivered to large enthusiastic audiences – 'there was, nineteen times in twenty, an immense overflow audience to whatever sized hall had been taken for him.'[11]

By the end of the tour, when all expenses had been paid, a reasonable profit had been made, 400 dollars, which Galsworthy immediately donated to the Armenian and Syrian Relief Commission.

One cannot help feeling enormous compassion for a man to whom 'success' so constantly brought the wrong reward. Here was a man who longed to write, to live privately in the country, who was diffident and shy in the face of publicity, who, we are told by his nephew, was bathed in sweat from nerves after giving any public address, but who was driven by circumstances to live increasingly in the public eye. In 1911 Galsworthy is first recorded making a speech following a performance of *Strife*: 'J.G. made 2 speeches, an unheard of innovation, for he loathes speaking.'[12]

Writing to Hugh Walpole on his return from America he strongly urges the young writer not to go to his American agent, Pond: '*if* I lecture again in America it'll probably be in a gentlemanly way to Universities. Which doesn't need much rushing round. Pond is a bit of a whipper snapper . . .'[13] From the moment they arrived in New York on 11 February, with the exception of a short holiday at Charleston, in South Carolina, the Galsworthys' American tour, which lasted until 28 April, had meant 'rushing round' all the time. They were met at the wharf by a representative of Scribner's, the publishers, but Ada retired to bed with influenza for the first nine days. 'All those days were a perpetual rush round of interviewing and such-like, from the moment of being snapped for the cinema, both of us, on the boat. One of those experiences one doesn't know how one lived through afterwards . . .'[14]

The first function was of course the Lowell Centenary Dinner, at which Galsworthy delivered his first address. This lecture took as its subject the bond that is between the peoples of America and England, their common language; on this can be built a common brotherhood, an ideal of 'Truth' and ultimately a world that will 'further the happiness of mankind and keep immortal the priceless comradeship between us'.[15] These American lectures are all on closely allied themes, similar in subject to the numerous papers he wrote during the war for periodicals and newspapers. Galsworthy was not only a writer, but also a preacher, a humanist preacher. Despite the lesson of the war he still believed that there could one day be an ideal world, or at least a world that was more ideal; and it was the communication of these ideas that made the terrible toil of these long lecture tours worth while.

Even Ada's notebook is unable to cope with the sheer quantity of engagements that were laid on for the Galsworthys. 'Annexed is a list of engagements, showing the sort of life we led.' 'A list of eighty-seven follows,' Marrot notes. The tour ended in New York. 'Then began 8 days with 16 functions.' And at last they boarded the *Adriatic* and sailed for England on 28 April. 'We read next morning that our *Adriatic* had been on fire for several days during our passage, which was the best we have had, agreeably warm on the whole . . .' Ada wrote in her notebook.

Despite an astonishing itinerary, Ada wrote of that journey in 1919 that Galsworthy 'stoutly resisted being hustled, and would never consent to dates and places that did not fall into a convenient sequence, geographically and chronologically. He would not cover the ground twice, and he would not undertake immensely long journeys if they could anyhow be avoided . . . A lecture, in general, was not a pleasure to him. He took it seriously, prepared it with great care, whatever the subject, was nervous beforehand, and usually fatigued afterwards.'[16]

This American tour was to be followed by three other long winter journeys in the United States. Ada found that the climate suited her; there were places like Santa Barbara in California where the winter months were much more endurable than anywhere in England. They were in America for the winter of 1920–21, and then again from December 1925 to April 1926, and finally, on their last visit, in December 1930, returning in the spring of the following year. They were accompanied on their two last visits by Rudolf and his wife Vi, who from 1924 onwards almost invariably went with the Galsworthys on their foreign journeys. Vi proved a most congenial companion to Ada when John was working, and Rudolf saw to all the practical matters concerning their tours. The arrangement proved thoroughly satisfactory for both the couples.

One has only to examine Ada's long list of some seventy-two items 'For Travel', which included such varied things as Shakespeare's sonnets, manilla rope, toilet paper, a rubber tub, mustard leaves and an Etna stove, to realize that the Galsworthys' journeys were considerable and carefully planned undertakings. When they travelled into the desert before the war they took with them almost the complete paraphernalia of living – furniture, tents, cooking equipment, medical supplies; when they travelled into more civilized parts they took almost as much. 'On arrival at a new place we quickly settled in. Ten minutes later Ada had transformed her room into the nearest thing to a home-from-home, and changed its atmosphere completely. Our rooms became centres for work as well as relaxation . . .'[17] Even on the long train journeys through America, which they found incredibly tedious – 'Oh! the tedium – the tedium!' Ada exclaims in her book *Over the Hills and Far Away* – they travelled in 'the little so-called drawing rooms – small private dens at the end of each car, with which we always provided ourselves.' As the list shows, Ada still carried with her a rubber bath, and on one occasion, on being told that there was no hot water in the taps, was immediately able to set up her own bathroom.

On their journey to Africa in 1924 they travelled largely by hired car with a chauffeur, as at that time none of the party drove. This vehicle had to be large enough to carry 'luggage suitable for all kinds of prospective occasions and for perhaps as much as five months at a time . . . In addition there was always the typewriter, which sometimes caused so much trouble at the customs, and my own [Rudolf Sauter's] easel, canvases and oils, squeezed into a heavy iron-bound case . . .'[18]

During the last ten years of his life Galsworthy was out of England for nearly as much time as he was in it. Writing to Ralph Mottram in January 1924 Ada told him, 'My poor dear, you won't come to Wing-stone again. Now that I have to be out of England a whole six months of a year, we don't feel justified in keeping two homes going.' (Wing-stone had already been given up at the end of the summer of 1923.) But though this way of life continued, Galsworthy's love of the country was too great for him to face permanent exile from it, and within two years he was searching for another home in the country.

Chapter 30

The 'Shores of Permanence'

In these early years of peace, 1919–21, Galsworthy wrote some of his most 'successful' work, his play *The Skin Game*, and his novels *In Chancery* and *To Let*, which with *The Man of Property*, and two linking stories, were to form the best selling trilogy, *The Forsyte Saga*. These two novels were not distinguished works, nor were they ambitious pieces of writing, but they gauged exactly the mood of the day. They harked back to the pre-war world, to a world untroubled by the frightful conflict of 1914; they were nostalgic, but at the same time, though well written, undemanding and easy to read. In the past Galsworthy had frequently had cause to write to his publishers complaining that his sales increased so little,* and to theatrical managers because his plays had short runs, and were not, in terms of box-office takings, successful. Now, in his middle fifties, his work was welcomed by a fantastically enthusiastic public; the sales of *The Forsyte Saga* rapidly topped the million mark in both England and America. Success was his, and yet, inwardly, there was a gnawing ever-growing sense of failure. In September 1920 he wrote to Dorothy Easton, 'I feel absolutely without hope of ever writing anything worth reading again.' And yet he had just completed the trilogy that was going to bring him fame and 'success' beyond his wildest dreams.

It is a sobering thought, but how often does the public applaud the right things? How frequently it is the second-rate that it takes to its heart, the masterpiece that it neglects. How tragic are the Van Goghs, the Keatses and the Emily Brontës, who die without the world's acknowledging the greatness of their work. And perhaps equally tragic are those who know in their deepest hearts that they have failed, and

* John Detmor of Heinemann's recalls that Galsworthy was convinced that if his novels could be priced at 7/– instead of 7/6d. a great many more copies would be sold.

yet their cries of despair are ignored, and the rewards of greatness piled on them, the O.M.s and the Nobel Prizes, as they were on the dying Galsworthy.

Galsworthy was not a happy man during the last ten years of his life; those who knew him have commented on the impression of sadness he gave, at least in public. Rudolf Sauter has said his uncle was often amusing and gay, and that within the family group – John and Ada, Rudolf and his wife – there was a constant banter of family jokes, but outside the family this was not so. Galsworthy had always been a grave and solemn person and as the years passed he became more so. Hugh Walpole describes a dinner with Galsworthy, E. V. Lucas and Granville Barker, in December 1917, which he said 'was quite fun although J.G. never sees a joke – and especially not E.V.'s'.[1] His writing too is very seldom humorous, though long ago, in *Jocelyn*, he had created a really witty character in Mrs Travis.

After their return from America in May 1919 the Galsworthys spent the first part of the summer between Grove Lodge and Wingstone. During the American tour there had been no time for anything but the preparation of speeches and lectures, and it must have been with difficulty that Galsworthy resumed work on the novel (*Saint's Progress*) he had begun nearly a year ago. It is perhaps not surprising that another much more compelling idea attracted his attention, that for his play *The Skin Game*, which he began in July and wrote with uncharacteristic speed: 'written straight on end and finished in London on July 17th,' he recorded in his diary.

But as usual Galsworthy was writing against the clock: a summer holiday in Ireland with the Masefields at Cushendun House was planned for the latter part of July. At least it gave him time to revise his new four-act play and the opportunity to read it out loud to an appreciative audience: 'I read it out last night to Ada and the Masefields, and the verdict was favourable, though – as usual – it's pretty grim.'[2] Their visit appears to have been a most enjoyable one: 'Spent the time for the most part in eating salmon, and black currants, and seeing circuses ... A. did up the garden, which was in a rank condition, working like a troop of horses. I bathed with the others.'[3]

A week later, on Galsworthy's fifty-second birthday, Rudolf Sauter was released from his internment camp at Alexandra Palace, 'looking fearfully well' despite his long detention of sixteen months. After the celebration of the double event the Sauters departed for Wingstone and were followed there by Ada and John ten days later. By now the dog population at the farmhouse was quite considerable. Ada listed them lovingly in her diary: 'Bounce, Joey a white sheepdog, dear Biz, blue sheepdog, Chloe, a brown and white spaniel, and Truwell, a foxhound lady pup, an overwhelming and delightful lot.' And of course this menagerie bred: 'We are here now,' Galsworthy wrote to Dorothy Easton from Grove Lodge in October, 'and seem to spend all our time over the puppies.'

During 1919 two books were published which were a hangover from that period of the war when Galsworthy's writing sank to its lowest level, *The Burning Spear* in April (fortunately under a pseudonym) and *Saint's Progress* in October. The appearance of these books must have been a depressing event for their author. 'The Press say it's [*The Burning Spear*] very bad,' he wrote to Gilbert Murray. 'I have some sympathy with it and its author.'[4] Of *Saint's Progress* he wrote, 'I don't set much store by the book.'[5] But it must have been a considerable consolation to find that Hardy had become an avid reader of his work. Mrs Hardy writing to Ada tells her: 'I have meant for so long to write and tell you how much pleasure *Saint's Progress* gave us both. I read aloud every word to my husband, and I think he really prefers it to any other of Mr. Galsworthy's works . . . Mr Galsworthy's novels are about the only ones he will listen to straight through (though I feel I should only write that in a whisper). He listens to parts of others, and then says, "That's enough." '[6]

The autumn of 1919 was an uneventful one, spent largely at Grove Lodge, with a short visit to Littlehampton. During this visit Galsworthy spent a few days on his brother Hubert's boat: 'Hubert had bad lumbago, and though it was pleasant enough on the one fine Sunday, especially the look of the river at dawn, very green, broad, and other worldly and peaceful under high woods, he would soon have got tired of so cramped a life,' was Ada's slightly caustic comment.[7] (She loathed her one visit to the boat.) But John was completely absorbed in his new Forsyte novel *In Chancery*; he was like a man coming home after years of travel. He had experimented with other types of people, with other backgrounds, with the intellectual, middle-class Dallisons of *Fraternity*, with the aristocratic politicians of *The Patrician*, and lastly with the clerical world in *Saint's Progress*, but none of them had been completely successful. Now, with his Forsytes, he was back with his own people, in the world in which he had grown up, in the houses which he had known as a boy. 'One Sunday we motored down to Coombe, and had a look over Coombe Leigh where J's family lived from 1875 to 1886, a hideously destroyed house, worse decorated and furnished than anything ever seen, and only the view unspoiled.'[8] Coombe Leigh was, of course, Robin Hill, the house built by Soames for Irene, now inhabited by young Jolyon and his two children Jolly and Holly.

In the year 1899, when the novel opens, the old generation of Forsytes, though decimated by death (five now remain of the ten brothers and sisters), still by their very presence give the family its strength, its sense of permanence in a changing world. In a lecture to PEN Galsworthy once said: 'When I was a boy I had a lot of old uncles. Out of one of them I got a bible covered with mother of pearl; out of another his double-barrelled pin-fire shot-gun; out of a third a scorpion bottled in gin; covering between them you see the whole produce of the British Empire. When I had got that out of them they died.'[9] Of course he was wrong. What he really got out of those uncles was the material to write his most successful series of novels.

In Chancery is set in a world in which the Great War, the years 1914 to 1918, might never have been, and in writing it Galsworthy must have cleared from his mind the bitter agonies of those years. Certainly the characters have their problems: Soames Forsyte is 'In Chancery'; he is tied by legal bonds to his separated wife Irene, and yet, with his love of property, he longs for a son and heir. Irene refuses to consider returning to their marriage; instead she flees to France, where she grows to know and love her trustee and cousin by marriage,* young Jolyon, son of old Jolyon, who has left her a small dependency following their encounter in 'The Indian Summer of a Forsyte'. It is this relationship that enables Soames to get his divorce and marry instead a young French girl, Annette, the daughter of a Soho restaurateur, who bears him, not a son, but a daughter, Fleur. In the meantime Soames's father, James, is dying; he too longs to see his line continued, his name perpetuated in a son for Soames. It is an ironical and humane touch that as he dies Soames lies to him: 'Good news, dear, good – Annette, a son.'

* This was exactly the situation of Ada and John, who became one of Ada's trustees in 1904. The idea of a woman having an income settled on her in trust was of course familiar to Galsworthy and old Jolyon in this played the role that Dr Emanuel Cooper had played in Ada's life.

So an era passes away, historically as well as fictionally. In their different ways the characters of the novel – Soames, Irene and the octogenarian James – witness the funeral procession of Queen Victoria. James sees with sadness the passing of his world: 'what James heard was the groaning in his own heart at the sight of his Age passing. "Don't you ever tell me where I'm buried," he said suddenly, "I shan't want to know."'

Death is something outside the Forsyte landscape, something they fear inordinately; it is the loss of property, and what is there instead? Galsworthy too had nothing in his philosophy that could help him to understand or accept this one certain event: 'I remember my uncle telling me how different his whole outlook on life would have been if only he could have been certain that he would not be parted from Ada in death. But, for all that he hoped it might be so, it seemed to him to strike at the very roots of probability that they should ever meet hereafter . . .'[10]

In these two novels of the trilogy the subject of death, of the impermanence of earthly possessions, comes constantly to the fore. Jolly, the son of young Jolyon, who, Ralph Mottram says, was based on Galsworthy's own youth, dies in the Boer War, in a moving chapter entitled 'Over the River', the same title that Galsworthy gave to his last novel, when he knew that he himself was a dying man.

To Let ends with Soames's long meditation on the vagaries of life and death in Highgate Cemetery, where the Forsytes lie buried in their ostentatious family vault: '"To Let" – the Forsyte age and way of life, when a man owned his soul, his investments, and his woman, without check or question. And now the State had, or would have, his investments, his woman had herself, and God knew who had his soul . . .'

These two novels, *In Chancery* and *To Let*, have to be considered together; in fact there was only a break of weeks between the finishing of *In Chancery* in November and the beginning of *Awakening*, the long, rather sentimental story of the childhood of Jon Forsyte, son of Irene and young Jolyon, that links the two novels. *To Let*, the last novel of the trilogy, was started in Malaga, then having the title *For Ever*.

The hero of all three novels is, of course, Soames Forsyte, undoubtedly the most powerful character that Galsworthy ever created. So powerful, indeed, that although he is cast originally as the villain in *The Man of*

Property, identified completely with the wicked Major Galsworthy who so maltreated Ada, he becomes increasingly the true hero, with whom the reader can most easily identify, and who attracts all our sympathy. Dorothy Easton, Galsworthy's hero-worshipping goddaughter, presumably complained of this development, as he told her that 'he [Soames] came to life, and started changing in his hands'. 'I had to follow him,' Galsworthy said.[11] So the 'wicked' Soames becomes the 'good' Soames, and the 'good' Irene, who had never been very securely good, becomes the 'at least not-very-good' Irene.

To Let is concerned with the love affair of the children of Soames and Irene by their new partners, Annette and young Jolyon. As infants Fleur and Jon make their appearance in the closing chapters of *In Chancery*, and now as young adults they meet, by one of those extraordinary coincidences on which literature depends, in the art gallery of June Forsyte, young Jolyon's eldest child by his first marriage, and promptly fall in love. Soames and Irene are appalled by this ill-chance, which resurrects in a distressing way their own unhappy marriage. Both regard it as essential to keep the young people in ignorance of their early relationship, but when Jon and Fleur announce their intention of getting married Soames, who really loves his daughter, is prepared to plead with Irene for her happiness. But Irene regards it as a personal affront that *her* son should love the daughter of the revolting Soames. Fortunately for her, young Jolyon dies of a heart attack just as the young couple are about to take life into their own hands, leaving a long letter in which he tells Jon the whole story of Irene and Soames, and that he, Jon, is 'blindly moving towards what must utterly destroy your mother's happiness . . . what I want you to realize is that feelings of horror and aversion such as those can never be buried or forgotten . . . The idea that you should marry his daughter is a nightmare to her . . .' It is the worst possible form of emotional blackmail but, coupled with his father's death, Jon cannot bring himself to inflict yet another blow on his mother. He gives up Fleur, which ultimately, as we read in the trilogy *The Modern Comedy*, destroys her life and happiness.

It is difficult to see how Galsworthy can have seen Irene's behaviour as being anything but selfish, and appallingly possessive – and possessiveness was the very vice he most abhorred. One can only conclude that even thirty years after the event he was still blinded in his judgement by the horror he had felt over Ada's account of her married life with Major Galsworthy.

So the novel ends with Fleur, broken-hearted, marrying without love her worthy suitor, Michael Mont, and Soames distraught by his daughter's distress: 'Why could one not put happiness into Local Loans, gild its edges, insure it against going down?' Soames, the man of business, the man of property, trying to fit his daughter's happiness into his world of financial dealings is, somehow, deeply touching.

That so much writing was achieved over the winter of 1919–20 is surprising, for Ada had been having, even for her, an exceptionally miserable time with her health. After *In Chancery* was finished at the beginning of November the Galsworthys travelled about England visiting their friends: they took Rudolf to Canterbury for two nights and were joined there by Dorothy Easton; they visited Conrad in his new house, Oswalds, at Bishopsbourne, and finally they spent a day in Oxford, seeing the Masefields and the Gilbert Murrays, a typically foggy November day, 'which gave poor A. a cold, whence many tears'.[12] This cold started off a chain of illnesses which lasted more or less the entire winter. They left England for Paris on 8 December and after 'a desultory five days . . . A. fell ill of neuritis in the jaws and ears. Most painful; till the end of the month great pain for A., strenuous nursing for J.'[13] Marrot, presumably informed by Ada herself, goes into further detail about this unpleasant illness. 'For two days the pain was so extreme that Mrs. Galsworthy had to sit upright continuously; even to put her head on the pillow being impracticable . . . And as if this were not enough, for a fortnight total deafness supervened.'[14] By 27 December Galsworthy could write to Dorothy Easton: 'My dear has been out of pain for some days now, but only got up yesterday, and to-day dresses for the first time in a fortnight. A young English doctor whom we called in yesterday for her deafness, tells us that the attack was undoubtedly neuritis of nerves . . . It's been a horrid experience. I expect we shall move South about Wednesday.' In fact they were able to leave for Biarritz on New Year's Eve. Here Ada found the 'ozone-laden air' highly recuperative, though she thought the town itself greatly changed for the worse since she had visited it with her mother as a young girl. It was also 'a good place for writing, and Himself could be seen any morning seated at our south-facing sitting room window quietly working till lunch time, when we made our way to the grill room of the Bar Basque, and found excellent cooking'.[15] 'At this little junction La Nepresse it smelled as the world hasn't smelled since we left Wingstone,' Galsworthy wrote to Rudolf Sauter.

'I find it difficult to live in towns nowadays – they don't smell good . . . I'm beginning to write again.'[16]

They continued their journey into Spain, stopping briefly at Madrid to look at the Goyas in the Prado, and then travelling on to Seville and Malaga (where Galsworthy began *To Let*). At Granada misfortune struck again, and Ada 'succumbed to Spanish influenza, followed by pneumonia in due course. This was both unwise and unkind, for though Himself was most divinely gifted as a nurse, anxiety at my wretched condition was added to the uneasiness we both felt at my being in the hands of a Spanish doctor of decidedly medieval training . . . He kept us continually amazed by the strangeness of his advice and procedure, not to speak of his rudimentary English.'[17] This doctor Galsworthy always referred to as 'the horse-doctor of Granada'.

Even the journey home was dogged by disaster: a train strike meant that they travelled 'by backways, during which A. nearly suffocated, reached Madrid, and promptly went to the Prado, a great instance of spirit, on the part of A. after 24 hours of travel. The same enthusiasm for Goya as on the way out . . .'[18] It took Ada 'six weeks' internment at Grove Lodge' to recover from the rigours of this ill-fated winter's holiday.[19]

April 1920, following his return from Spain, must have been for Galsworthy reminiscent of that other period of outstanding achievement, 1906. His new play *The Skin Game* opened that month at the St Martin's Theatre, and was immediately an enormous success: 'The reception of the play on Wednesday was tumultuous, for the audience recognized that it had witnessed a play quite out of the common run, and demanded a speech from the author – a demand with which Mr. Galsworthy very wittily and gracefully complied.'[20] Hardy wrote to Galsworthy quoting the opinion of a friend of his, Sir George Douglas, who told him, 'I have seen *three times* one really fine and finely acted play; Galsworthy's Skin Game.'[21] So congratulations poured in, this time for a play that was to make money for its managers as well as for its author, unlike his earlier plays which had often been acclaimed by the critics but had never been commercially viable. *The Skin Game* was also published later in the month in book form in the collection *Plays: Fourth Series*. In March another collection of essays had appeared, *Tatterdemalion*, which, though it received a fairly neutral press, was reprinted the following month.

The Skin Game is a play which, though dated in language and sentiment, has stood the test of time. In fact the problem it deals with has an almost contemporary interest. The question is whether a factory should be built by the up and coming, newly rich Hornblower family in such a position as to spoil completely the view from the house of the Hillcrist family, landed gentry who have for generations enjoyed their property in unspoilt surroundings. Bitterness is added to the conflict by the fact that Hornblower feels that his wife has been ostracized by the snobbish Mrs Hillcrist. Mrs Hillcrist, in a thoroughly discreditable fashion, discovers unsavoury details about the Hornblower family which she threatens to disclose if they do not undertake not to build their factory. The only character who comes really well out of the play is the youthful and naïve daughter of the Hillcrists, Jill, who sees how badly both families have behaved. This part was played originally by the young actress, Maggie Albanesi, who died tragically young, and to whom Galsworthy wrote a moving tribute which ended, 'Not often does Death so wastefully spill.'[22]

But of even greater importance than the success of his play was the growing confidence he felt in his new Forsyte books. In April Conrad, having read the manuscript of *In Chancery*, was writing to him, 'I am very much impressed by the ampleness of the scheme, the masterly ease in handling the subject, and (in sober truth) the *sheer* beauty of these pages. Oh! my dear fellow, it *is* good! A great Saga . . .'[23] How much this project meant to Galsworthy can be judged by a passage in a letter to Granville Barker:

> I think the July Sunday at Wingstone in 1918, when it suddenly came to me that I could go on with my Forsytes, and complete their history in two more volumes with a link between, was the happiest day of my writing life. And on the whole *The Forsyte Saga*, when published in one volume containing *The Man of Property*, *Indian Summer of a Forsyte*, *In Chancery*, *Awakening*, and *To Let*, will be my passport, however difficult it may be to get it vised [sic] for the shores of permanence.[24]

The writing of the two books that completed the Saga was carried through with a sense of determination that refused to be eroded by outside events or catastrophes; through Ada's illness, through the rehearsals of *The Skin Game*, the writing of *To Let* forged ahead. After twenty-five years of work on books and plays that had established him in the world of writing, that had brought him a certain 'success d'estime', he now knew that this was different. The 'shores of perman-ence' were in sight; perhaps not the 'shores' he might have hoped for, not a book of tremendous depth or intellectual insight, but the story of his own Forsytes, the progeny of those not over-generous 'old uncles'.

Chapter 31

Family and Community

There was once again a sense of urgency about completing this important piece of writing that was to complete *The Forsyte Saga*: the Galsworthys were scheduled to leave England for America on 20 October. This time, apart from productions of *The Pigeon* in Canada and *The Skin Game* in New York, the trip was intended as a winter holiday rather than a business trip. Galsworthy had learnt by bitter experience how demanding the American public could be, how insatiable for lectures, receptions and addresses.

Fortunately the summer of 1920 at Wingstone was an uneventful one. *To Let* was finished 'in rough' early in September, and 'polished' at Grove Lodge before their departure in the middle of October. Even for Galsworthy, who eschewed press cuttings and at least affected a certain indifference to the public reception of his work, to have to leave England two days before the publication of *In Chancery* on 22 October must have been exceedingly disappointing. For the fate of this book was all-important to the ultimate success of the trilogy. In fact the critical success in both England and in America was disappointing. C. E. Montague in the *Manchester Guardian* comments that the war had not interrupted (or, it is implied, changed the course) of Galsworthy's writing plans for his *Forsyte Saga*, and he regrets that it does not have 'a higher pressure of something like animal spirits . . .' which 'would somehow set a redder blood running through the book'.

The Galsworthys remained in America and Canada from the end of October until April 1921. For ten weeks they were at Santa Barbara, at the San Ysidro ranch, four miles out of the town. 'This ranch, which consists of many little bungalows grouped among orange and other trees, round a stone-built dining-room, is kept by an English lady, Mrs Harleigh Johnston, and is full of homeliness and charm . . . The only handicap to a very delightful stay was the bronchial trouble which made poor A's nights a very bleak business. Having faces set against social gaieties, we went out very little, but enjoyed ourselves all the more.' Here Galsworthy played tennis, and did a fair amount of writing, though none of it of great distinction, a number of short stories, and the play *A Family Man*. They also experienced a small earthquake, 'which seemed to blow our first floor cottage bedroom nearly over.'[1]

After two months in Arizona, the long winter ended with another short visit to New York during which Galsworthy gave two lectures, and they received 'odds and ends of hospitality'. The voyage back to England on the liner *Adriatic* was extremely social: a select dinner table was made up which included the Drinkwaters and, by chance, John's cousin, Frank Galsworthy. They landed in England on 15 April, and on their arrival were 'Vociferously greeted by dogs and others'.[2]

It has some significance that in the notebook written in Ada's handwriting, and apparently dictated by John, it should have been recorded that 'the feature of that summer [1921] was the introduction of village cricket. J. the veteran member of the team, and President. Mostly responsible for scores of 1 & 3, but made 20 against Moretonhampstead, to the considerable astonishment of all present . . .' Galsworthy, during this last period of his life, had become in many ways an isolated figure in the literary world, and his involvement was much more with his family and the local village community. He had drifted apart from the close friends of his early years, Conrad, Edward Garnett, and Granville Barker, and though he had many acquaintances in the writing world, such as the Masefields and the Gilbert Murrays, they were of an absolutely different ilk from those friends of the pre-war years. Though he and Ada were childless, the family – his nephews and nieces, the children of Lilian, Mabel and Hubert – were becoming the people for whom he cared most. Rudolf Sauter, since his father's return to Germany following his internment, had become almost a son to Ada and John and after the death of his mother in 1924 he and his wife Vi were to become completely involved in the lives of the Galsworthys. His goddaughter and cousin, Dorothy Easton, was another protégé who for a time had been partly dependent on him, not only for advice and guidance but also financially, for he made her a regular allowance, called jokingly between them her 'wings', because it gave her some freedom in which she could develop her talent as a writer. There is almost no member of the Galsworthy family who was not, at some time or other, helped substantially by John's enormous generosity: the Sauter household, his nephew Hubert and his sister

Muriel, and Dorothy Easton, after her marriage to Ralph Ivens, were all provided with the means to buy or build their homes. It is worth quoting a letter from Galsworthy to Rudolf, written in 1920 from Spain, as it shows the enormous sense of responsibility that Galsworthy felt towards his family:

> And there's one thing especially you and your mother should remember. Your Grandfather intended his children and their offspring to share his money *equally*. If the Government is so un-English as to deprive or sequestrate the English property of an English-blooded person, [Lilian], to pay the claims of another English-blooded person, it behoves me, who am blessed by Providence, to see that my Father's sacred wishes for which he laboured all his life are not upset to any material extent. Your mother is not fit to rough it, and it will only handicap you all to try the experiment ... And no high horses should be stabled. Having no children, you see, we are bound to look on you with a special eye; and it would be in the nature of the ridiculous for you to stand on ceremony with us in material matters, don't you see?[3]

Alongside this 'paternal' attitude towards his family was a similar sense of responsibility and commitment towards the community in which he lived. During the last years of their time at Wingstone, this feeling, which undoubtedly had its roots in the early days of the war and in the village rifle range started long before 1914, found further expression in the establishment of the Manaton village cricket team. Not only was cricket the game he loved above all others, but the existence of the team was a way of making his village 'family' aware of its identity as a community. At Bury this paternalistic attitude was to go a great deal further: here the village cricket team continued to be a focal point, but far more than that was the sense of responsibility that Galsworthy, by then a comparatively rich man, felt towards the community in which he lived.

'Prepare for cricket and bring flannels and shoes,' he wrote to Rudolf on 21 August. 'There's a match on Saturday in which I've engaged you to play, and probably a practice on Friday evening. No need for anxiety you cannot be worse than most of us. Yesterday we played Moreton and thumped them. We made 119 to their 63.' A year later Dorothy Easton watched 'Uncle Jack' and C. S. Evans of Heinemann practising on the lawn, while Ada kept wicket, and she herself fielded. Galsworthy's enthusiasm for the game was soon shared by his goddaughter; it was, she said, the ideal game for a man of his temperament, quiet, civilized. It was a game he played and enjoyed until the end of his life. Jack Detmor, then an office boy at Heinemann's, recalls the annual match between the publishing firm and the Bury cricket team, and how one member of the staff was almost sacked for bowling out Galsworthy: instructions were that the office team were to practise extreme restraint when their writing host was in to bat. Nevertheless Detmor's admiration for the author was unbounded and he remembers how every time Galsworthy visited the publisher's office he saw many of the members of the staff, interested himself in their problems, and gave them signed copies of his books as they appeared.

But cricket was not the only activity of that summer at Wingstone: during the holiday at Santa Barbara Galsworthy had had the idea for a play in which he felt for him most unusual confidence. 'This was the only play of J's of which he was able to say when he finished it, "No manager will refuse this."'⁴ The play was *Loyalties*, and the writing of it was the main work of the summer months. The play describes how in the course of a house party, one of the guests De Levis (a social climber and a Jew) accuses the popular ex-army hero Dancy of stealing a thousand pounds from his room. Opinion is entirely on Dancy's side against the outsider De Levis; he is blackballed from his club and Dancy issues a writ against him for libel. In the event Dancy is proved guilty and shoots himself in shame.

The play was as successful as its author had predicted. It was produced in March the following year (1922) and was immediately acclaimed by the critics as possibly Galsworthy's best play. 'Galsworthy's finest effort to date . . . the work is almost entitled to rank as a classic of its kind,' said the *Sunday Times*.

Galsworthy was fifty-five when the publication of *The Forsyte Saga* brought him world fame, still a man comparatively young with, one would expect, years of development before him as a writer. His ambition was outwardly fulfilled but he was not a happy man; Ada's notebook stops at the end of 1922 and it ends on a note of despair, a despair that is often echoed in the years that followed: 'Rest of the year under the cloud of A's misery . . . Ghastly Christmas; both A. and Rhoda [the house-maid] ill.' Mottram has also commented on the change in Ada and John, particularly after they left Wingstone. 'Slowly as I then realized it, both of them had begun to age, however well they concealed it, and they were both adepts, never wishing to lessen the service they could render their friends. Neither of them really recovered from the war and its injury to the spirit.'[5]

Chapter 32

A Sense of Failure

For two years, from the end of 1923 to 1926, the Galsworthys were content to be without a country house. Wingstone at first seemed irreplaceable to John, to whom no other place would ever mean so much, but for Ada it was undoubtedly a relief to have left it. As she had so often confided to Ralph Mottram, she seldom felt well or happy in the remote damp world of Dartmoor, and Grove Lodge, that beautiful and elegant house in Hampstead, suited her perfectly. Partly no doubt because they no longer had a country retreat, during the years that followed the publication of *The Forsyte Saga* the Galsworthys travelled abroad even more than before; the list at the end of Rudolf Sauter's book on his uncle of the journeys they made during this period is terrifying in its length. Were they ever settled in one place for more than weeks at a time, and how under such circumstances could Galsworthy have hoped to achieve any sustained piece of writing, are questions one must inevitably ask.

In the autumn of 1921, a new interest came into Galsworthy's life, PEN, the international writers' club. PEN was the brain-child of Mrs Dawson Scott, and it officially came into being on 6 October 1921 at the Florence Restaurant with Galsworthy as its first president. The aims of the new club were to 'promote friendship and understanding between writers and defend freedom of expression within and between all nations'. It is not difficult to see why such an organization should have appealed so much to Galsworthy: he had long believed that if only writers and thinkers from all countries could get together, could share their ideas and hopes, it might promote such understanding that another world catastrophe such as the recent war would become much less likely. He was ready as always to throw himself wholeheartedly into the work of the new society; ironically as PEN began to spread its centres throughout the world, as there were more and more meetings to attend, it became a major factor in drawing Galsworthy even further from his main purpose, that of his own writing.

The publication of *The Forsyte Saga* as one volume in May 1922 was an even greater success than Galsworthy could possibly have hoped for. As recorded by his biographer, H. V. Marrot, in his astonishing language, 'the public took mightily thereto, and in an incredibly short time the sales had passed the 6 figure mark on both sides of the Atlantic.'[1] He also comments that 'the stream of his life broadens out like some river'.[2] It is to be remembered that H. V. Marrot wrote his life of Galsworthy under the guidance of the recently widowed Ada; for Galsworthy himself the change from stream to river could be nothing but loss, even though his ambition to be a best-selling author was at last fulfilled.

It is perhaps symbolical that the new era was marked by the end of Wingstone, that place that was so infinitely important to Galsworthy, that stood for all that was most personal in his life. As he wrote to Granville Barker in June 1923, 'alas, for us! – or for me, rather, because I think Ada is almost glad to be quit of Devonshire damp – Wingstone will be reft from us next month . . . to me it's a blow. *I don't say so however.*' It was not until three years later that Wingstone was replaced by the much grander and more formal Bury House in Sussex.

Galsworthy's commitment as president of the newly formed PEN club inevitably added to their huge programme of travelling: during the ten years of his presidency Galsworthy attended no less than eight international congresses – though it would be tedious to detail each one of these journeys, which followed always the pattern of their earlier travels. Ada had by now made an art of travelling, and they carried with them an enormous quantity of luggage, clothes and equipment, sufficient to meet every possible contingency. On reaching their destination they rented wherever possible a suite of rooms or a private chalet where they could live and eat apart from the other tourists; during the mornings John wrote and in the afternoon he and Ada walked or went on sightseeing expeditions. From 1924 onwards, as we have seen, they were very often accompanied by the young Sauters.

The close involvement of the Sauters with Ada and John Galsworthy began soon after the death of Rudolf's mother and continued until Galsworthy's death some eight years later. Lilian Sauter died suddenly in October 1924. Always delicate in health, the burden of Georg and Rudolf's internment during the war, and her husband's decision that he could no longer make his home in England or even live happily with his English family, had left her a broken and deeply saddened woman, and when illness struck she had neither the will nor the strength to combat it.

To John the death of his sister was a great blow; of his brother and sisters Lilian had always been closest to him, and by all accounts she was a most exceptional and gifted woman, and someone with an unusual gift for friendship and understanding. And this loss had followed close on the heels of another death: on 3 August that year Joseph Conrad had died after a long-drawn-out illness. These two, Lilian and Conrad, had been among the first to encourage Galsworthy's early aspirations to become a writer. With Lilian long ago on the family holidays in Scotland he had discussed writing and philosophy, and then in 1892, on the sailing ship *Torrens*, he had fallen in with the merchant seaman, Joseph Conrad, had listened to his talk of writing, and later at the home of the Sandersons at Elstree had most probably read the first draft of his novel *Almayer's Folly*. Now, within two months of each other, they were dead. It was a painful wrenching away of his past. It was natural that he should turn to his links with the younger generation, and shortly after Lilian's death he took Ada and the young Sauters on a lengthy holiday.

As far as work was concerned 1924 was also a depressing year for Galsworthy: two plays, *The Forest*, produced in March at the St Martin's Theatre, and *Old English*, produced in October, had an unenthusiastic reception from the critics. The former, an unusual play about Africa, which Hermann Ould described as symbolizing 'the great Imperialist jungle which takes its toll of men – the jungle law which prevails in the politico-commercial world'[3] was, as one critic said, 'curious fare to come from the pen of John Galsworthy'.[4] It was to do with this play that Marrot commented that it was the only occasion on which he had seen Galsworthy show any bitterness: 'I give them something new – a play with only one woman in it, and practically no love interest – and they won't have it.'[5] *Old English*, a dramatization of his story *The Stoic*, was unanimously condemned as being very dull.

There can be no doubt that Galsworthy was worried about his writing. Of *Captures*, yet another book of essays that had been published the year before (13 September 1923), he had commented: '*Captures* has a notice too in *The Times Literary Supplement*, which seems to me very just and kind. I *have* lost fervour.'[6] He tried to protect himself by refusing to take on work which would interfere with his novel-writing. When

Cambridge University offered him the appointment of Rede Lecturer, he declined: 'I find the writing of a lecture or address terribly difficult, and I'm afraid that it would completely spoil my power of concentration on the novel.'[7] But from the endless restlessness of Ada's passion for travelling there was no respite.

On 30 October 1924 *The White Monkey* was published, the first volume of the new Forsyte trilogy *The Modern Comedy*. In a letter to a Mrs Chichester Galsworthy describes the writing of this book, in different places, even different parts of the world. The final result is a rather confused novel, with too many disconnected plots and ideas.

> You will perhaps like to hear exactly where *The White Monkey* was written. It was begun in my house at the top of Hampstead on the very border of London in November 1922. Rather more than the first part was written there by the end of May 1923; the second part was finished at Cortina in the Italian Tyrol in June and early July; and the third part was written in Madeira, in November, and at Mont Estoril, Portugal, in December 1923. You see, a writer has only to take pen and ink and his head about with him.[8]

The White Monkey is principally concerned with Soames Forsyte's daughter, Fleur, now married half-heartedly to Michael Mont. She comes near to having an affair with a poet, Wilfred Desert, but withdraws at the last minute. In the meantime Soames is engaged in averting a major scandal in the business world, for a fraud is discovered in the dealings of an assurance company of which he is a director. In these scenes Galsworthy shows his intimate knowledge of the world of big business and high finance, the world of his Forsyte father and uncles. Yet another sub-plot deals with two minor characters, Bicket and his wife Vic, who, struggling against their poverty, are trying to save up to go to Australia. The novel ends and is drawn together by the birth of a child, a son of Fleur and Michael; as at the end of *In Chancery*, a birth brings hope and a future for the family.

Though messy and without direction as a novel, this book tells one much about Galsworthy's state of mind when he wrote it. Again and again passages reveal his sense of despair about the futility of life, the inevitable snuffing out of death; where was there hope or meaning in the pattern? In the mouth of Soames:

> That was life – gardener rolling lawn! . . . Rolling lawn to keep

it lawn! What point in lawn? Conscious of pessimism, he rose. He had better be getting back to Fleur's – they dressed for dinner! He supposed there was something in dressing for dinner, but it was like lawn – you came unrolled – undressed again, and so it went on! Over and over and over to keep up to a pitch, that was – ah! what *was* the pitch for?

Or the thoughts of Michael Mont:

Gosh! what sealed books faces were! Each with pages and pages of private thoughts, interests, schemes, fancies, passions, hopes and fears; and down came death – splosh! – and a creature wiped out, like a fly on a wall . . .

At least one of Galsworthy's admirers found the new novel totally absorbing: Mrs Thomas Hardy wrote to Ada, 'He [Thomas Hardy] took the book to bed so that he might read some of it himself, if he were wakeful – the first time I have ever known him to have a novel by his bed . . .'[9]

Within days of the publication of *The White Monkey* Lilian Sauter's death had caused John and Ada to take refuge once more in travelling. They were joined by the young Sauters at Merano in Italy on 19 November. Rudolf kept a diary of this journey which describes the endless ministration of John to Ada's needs; on the night train south to Sicily, 'J.G. made us all very comfortable. It is perfectly wonderful to see him take care of A. on a journey – everything is made right, and each and every want attended to.' Or at Syracuse: 'J.G. is full of plans to get away to the sun, Africa, S. Africa and Egypt on the way, as the weather will not lift and clear. Always thinking of A. and what will suit her.'[10]

It is interesting to read how Galsworthy's attentiveness appeared to an outside observer; in her *Portrait of Barrie*, Cynthia Asquith writes:

Galsworthy, whom I like more and more, was looking specially like the ideal stage schoolmaster, and his manners were as sedulous as ever. The way he springs to his feet at breakfast the instant his wife enters the room, and darts to the sideboard to help her to food had a highly disturbing effect on other husbands. Feeling they ought to follow his example, they pretended – unconvincingly – that this was quite usual behaviour. Result of their unpractised zeal; much clattering of dish covers and upsetting of coffee cups . . .

On their travels John often read aloud to his travelling companions. In Tunis he returned to his old favourite *The Pickwick Papers*, and in Arizona in 1926 to *Treasure Island*. Later on the same trip, reading aloud from *Pride and Prejudice*, he commented, 'How lengthy and stupid this all is! as if people ever *talked* like this . . .' Jane Austen appears to have been a blind spot in his literary taste. One notices how loyal he is to his early favourites, among whom Stevenson still ranks high. Turning aside from Jane Austen he read to them from *Catriona*, making the comment: 'When you come to compare Stevenson and Hardy, there really isn't any comparison at all. Stevenson's all life and Hardy's all death . . .'[11] Among the younger writers of his own period he found Henry Williamson very sympathetic, and did much to forward his early work; Margaret Kennedy's *Constant Nymph* he saw as 'the best novel by a woman for a long time',[12] and he wrote a preface to the novel *The Spanish Farm* by his old protégé Ralph Mottram. He also read aloud from whatever piece of writing he was currently working at; during the Italian-North African journey this was *The Silver Spoon*.

It was almost six months before the Galsworthys returned to England in the first days of May 1925. It was to be another year in which Galsworthy's work completely failed to find favour with the critics: his new play *The Show* ran for only a short time at the St Martin's Theatre in July. 'The Press, whose knuckles have been rapped (as was unavoidable) have done their best to "do it in",' he wrote in a letter to André Chevrillon.[13] And the following year *The Silver Spoon*, though a best-seller in America and England, again had an unsympathetic reception from the critics.

No doubt disheartened by these failures, Galsworthy declared that his next play *Escape* was to be the last play he would ever write. *Escape* was written during February 1926 in America: 'I suddenly burst into drama and wrote a play in a fortnight (forgive me – such a thing I have never done before). It's a queer play – just episodic . . .'[14] he wrote to Granville Barker. But his 'episodic' play about a young man who accidentally kills a policeman, because he unjustly accused a prostitute of soliciting, and escapes from the injustice of the law, was in fact a great success. It ran for a year at the Ambassadors Theatre, produced by Leon M. Lion.

Chapter 33

Bury House

The Sauters had by now become an essential part of the Galsworthys' life, and it was a logical decision that they should share some sort of a permanent home with their uncle and aunt. Freelands, the house that Galsworthy had bought for his sister and nephew, was to be sold, and a 'small' country house found for Rudolf and Vi where Ada and John could have a country *pied à terre*, as they had done at Wingstone. In August 1926, after some fruitless house-hunting in the area of Pulborough in Sussex, they chanced to hear that Bury House had just come on the market. Though its size made it obviously unsuitable John insisted on going to look at it; it was described as a 'Tudor style' mansion and had fifteen bedrooms.

> The picture of my Uncle turning the corner and looking over the descending terraces to the Downs beyond is characteristic. One quick glance at the outside:– 'This is the place,' he said, without even going inside. 'But it's much too large,' I said, horrified and with a sinking feeling at contemplation of the manorial splendour of that grey stone facade, the mullioned windows, and the great slab roof. 'Never mind, old man,' he said, '*we'll* take the house, and, if you will, Vi and you shall come and live with us instead.'[1]

So it turned out. The house was bought for £9,000 instead of the £3,000 they had intended to spend; the purchase was completed on 16 September 1926. It was the Galsworthys' house but Rudolf and Vi lived there in the capacity of caretakers, Vi doing the housekeeping. But more than that, their constant presence at Bury made the Galsworthys' life much more enjoyable than it would have been without them.

It is strange that a man normally so totally unselfish should have so decisively chosen this house, which Ada never liked very much – 'living at the bottom of a hill was to her depressing' – while the young Sauters were obviously daunted by its size and grandeur, and possibly even by being so completely swept into the lives of their older relations.

In fact Bury did dictate a grander life than any they had lived before; Dorothy Easton was appalled by it: 'it was different . . . not a tramp over Dartmoor but tennis after lunch, or croquet.'[2] Hugh Walpole found Bury 'A really lovely house, pearl-grey stone fronting lawns that run straight to the open fields. The house inside clean and shining like the inside of a nut, with the colour of his nephew's pictures which are all over the house. Everything artistic, Liberty fashion and a little beyond it. Very like a special edition of one of John's own books.'[3]

Was Bury in the end the ultimate defeat? Had Galsworthy, who as a young man had turned his back on the establishment world of the Forsytes, gone to sea on the *Torrens* and become the intimate friend of Conrad and the lively young Sandersons, and then written his hard-hitting satirical novel *The Island Pharisees*, now become, like Soames himself, the man of property? The two fine and dignified houses in which he and Ada lived were not important to him as possessions, but they were symbolic of the way of life he had accepted, a way of life not dissimilar to that which his parents had lived in their great mansions at Coombe in Surrey. He had become, too, a benevolent father figure, not only of his family, but also of the little community of Bury village. Above all he had put behind him forever any thought of mentally or spiritually moving forward into the post-war world. His writing, his thought and his way of life were anchored inescapably in pre-1914 England.

Rudolf Sauter insists that life at Bury within the family circle and with their more intimate friends could still be very merry. There was a strange game that his uncle found particularly amusing and which the whole household (with the exception of Ada) and their guests played from time to time; a cork would be fixed to the back of a chair, and the player, sitting on his hands, would then have to attempt to dislodge the cork with his mouth. The end result of the game was usually to over-balance the players, and Rudolf can remember one particular occasion in which the whole house party, including the fairly austere Oxford professor, Gilbert Murray, ended up in a giggling heap on the sitting-room floor.

More formal games such as croquet and tennis, and of course cricket matches with the village team, were part of life at Bury. Through the summer months guests poured down for the weekend, among them Lord Ponsonby, J. M. Barrie, Arnold Bennett, Hugh Walpole,

Granville Barker, Philip Guedalla and John Drinkwater. The Galsworthy life at Bury House was 'grand', but among his contemporary writers pretensions to grandeur were by no means exceptional. Arnold Bennett turned up in his Rolls Royce, commenting to Vi Sauter, 'You know I never thought I would be seen dead in a thing like that; and here I am going about in a great Rolls.'[4] He also had his yacht. J. M. Barrie had his large country house at Stanway in Gloucestershire (as well as two other houses), and here he had a regular cricketing season every summer, with large house parties. (The Galsworthys were sometimes among his guests.)

One of these weekends at Bury is described by both the guests, Arnold Bennett and Hugh Walpole. Arnold Bennett wrote:

John, always exact and quiet, always speaking with authority though saying little, always judicial, just, kindly, and broad minded, is the god of that house. The niece-in-law runs the house; Ada runs the garden (five gardeners). Ada also runs John (secretarially; he told me he could not stand a secretary) and John is God. And John deserves to be God too. He seems to do only about two or two and a half hours a day. He rides at 7.45. Breakfasts at 9.30. Then he deals with his mail, till about 11. Then writes till lunch at 1.30. Then gives the afternoon to exercise (tennis and croquet), pottering and reading. He looks quite as old as he is, sixty-one and three-quarters, but he can beat me (who looks younger) at games. I bet he can be grim at times, but always with urbanity. He is benevolence itself. But very reserved. He is now nearly bald with a forehead more terrifically domed than ever, tall, thin; not too well-dressed but well enough dressed.[5]

In a letter to his nephew Bennett wrote an even more embroidered version of the weekend: 'J.G. has 5 gardeners, 10,000,000 blossoms, 3 dogs, 3 cats, 2 horses and some really fine sherry.'

And Hugh Walpole wrote:

Delightful time only other guests Arnold Bennett and his lady . . .
The two dramatic moments were when Arnold stammering (not through modesty) related to Ada Galsworthy how for his journalism he had first 1/- a word, then 1/6, then two bob, and now half-a-crown – this 'hymn of praise' rising higher and higher in his shrill uncouth voice, ending in a scream – '*And – I like it* – journalism –

I like it!' While Ada grew paler and paler with horror at this commercial triumph and tried hard not to mind.

The other was when J.G. was beaten at croquet, which he couldn't bear. He has no sense of fun about games. They are battles for Galsworthian justice, and when he was beaten it was as though we had acted *Justice* all over again, there on the lawn in front of his eyes.

But he is a *dear* – gentle, honest, just, trying not to be self-conscious about his terrific present success. It was hard for Arnold to hear at dinner that a first *Man of Property* had just fetched £138 at Hodgson's, but he bore it well – only made a brief allusion to *The Old Wives' Tale* and told me my tie was the wrong colour for my suit.[6]

Galsworthy's charitable work continued within the local community. Mrs Dean, who with her husband had worked for the Galsworthys all the time they were at Bury, has described how every Friday she had the task of delivering envelopes to different houses in the village; these envelopes contained the small private pensions that Galsworthy paid regularly to people or families who he knew to be particularly impoverished, such sums as 5/- or 10/- weekly. As far back as 1910 he was making this sort of arrangement. 'Interview with old Mrs. Cheams. Found them in very poor straits, have arranged to pay them a 5/- pension and their rent now being paid,' he noted in his diary on 17 November that year; and again in January 1911: 'Helped a man called Drewell start in greengrocery.' As well as his pension scheme there can still be seen in Bury the many excellent cottages he built to house the people who worked for him. In fact I was told that jobs in Bury House were keenly sought after because of the excellent conditions that the people who worked for Galsworthy enjoyed; more than that they were exceedingly happy and devoted to the Bury household.

Galsworthy wrote now more from habit and as a discipline than from any wish to communicate: a pattern of a lifetime could not be abandoned, moreover the fixed framework and routine of each day was a support for a man who needed so much order and system in his life. The following 'breakdown' of his day (and night) is characteristic of his love of listing everything:

ANALYSIS OF AVERAGE DAY

Sleeping in bed	7 hours
Thinking in bed	1 hour
Trying not to fall asleep in chairs	½ hour
Eating and listening to others talking	2 hours
Playing with dogs	¼ hour
Playing without dogs (on the telephone)	¼ hour
Dressing, undressing, bathing, and Muller exercising	1¼ hours
Exercise in country (riding or walking)	2 hours at least
Exercise in London (walking)	1 hour at most
Imagining vain things, and writing them down on paper:—	
In the country	4 hours
In London	3 hours
Correspondence, and collecting scattered thoughts:—	
In the country	2 hours
In London	4 hours
Skipping newspapers	¾ hour
Reading what I don't want, or otherwise attending to business	1 hour
Reading what I do want to	½ hour
Revision of vain things; and of proofs say	1 hour
Education by life	the rest

Call it an eight to nine hour day.

    J.G.[7]

The year 1927, their first after the purchase of Bury House, was an uneventful one. In December the previous year the Galsworthys, accompanied by the Sauters, had travelled to South Africa for the winter months and returned to England at the end of March. The greater part of the year was spent at the new house and Galsworthy worked at the last volume of his trilogy, *Swan Song*. The second volume, *The Silver Spoon*, continues with the rather trivial adventures of Soames's daughter, Fleur. Her husband, Michael Mont, has abandoned publishing for politics and gone into parliament, where is he endeavouring to rally support for his own pet political theory, Foggartism, a theory dear also to Galsworthy's heart, that the future of England depended on a land policy which would enable the country to produce more of its own food. In the meantime Fleur, who has seen Michael's position as a Member of Parliament as an opportunity to become a leading society hostess, has heard someone accusing her of snobbery. Unwisely she decides to sue the offender for libel, but the case leaves her so disgraced that Soames takes his beloved daughter on a world-wide cruise to escape the gossip.

It is this cruise that is the subject of the linking story 'Passers By' published together with 'A Silent Wooing' as *Two Forsyte Interludes* in December 1927. Both these stories return to Jon Forsyte, the cousin who Fleur had loved so desperately: in the first he courts his future wife, and in the second he and Soames and Fleur only narrowly avoid meeting in an American hotel. It is Soames, feigning illness, who prevents a clash between the ex-lovers.

The return of Jon Forsyte and his wife to England is the subject of the new novel, *Swan Song*. Fleur, working in a canteen during the General Strike, meets Jon by chance and does everything she can to entice him back to her. But Jon's sense of honour and loyalty to his wife prevent him succumbing to her charms at the last moment: he will never meet her again. Fleur is distracted with grief, and throwing down a lighted cigarette causes a fire in Soames's house, Mapledurham. Soames is himself fatally injured, trying to save her from a falling picture.

To kill off Soames Forsyte was a difficult and important decision. Soames had been Galsworthy's talisman to success – the character without which *The Man of Property* and the *Saga* would have been nothing. In April 1927 he wrote to Granville Barker: 'No, Sir, Soames will survive this book. I purport killing him in a final outburst, but I expect he will outlive me yet. At present he's so young, you know – a mere seventy-two.'[8]

But on 12 August he wrote to the same correspondent: 'I've finished my novel, and after all *Le Roi est Mort* – this for your private ear, since you spoke to me about it.' And later in the same letter in a postscript: 'Sixty on Sunday. Too old!'

The decision to end Soames's life was probably a wise one; and one not unconnected with his own sixtieth birthday. Though no one, neither his family nor his public, would allow it to be so, he was losing power as a writer. The final trilogy, *The End of the Chapter*, is a poor piece of work, though here and there there are signs of the writer he had been, in the character of Dinny Cherrell and in the episode concerning Wilfred Desert. It was Galsworthy's particular tragedy that alone in himself he had to face failure, while outwardly his family and the establishment literary world continued to insist on his success.

Was *Swan Song* possibly even intended to be the last book he would write? A swan song is after all traditionally the 'last work of a poet or musician esp. one composed shortly before his death' (O.E.D.). The novel was certainly the last good book he ever wrote. His friends were enormously enthusiastic: Cunninghame-Graham called it 'the coping stone to the great edifice raised by your genius',[9] and Gilbert Murray wrote: 'Soames is a real triumph. I know nothing in English literature like his steady and convincing growth. One feels his past about him all the time – the merely possessive love that devours him in *The Man of Property* turning into the unselfish love that almost equally devours him at the end. It is really great art, that.'[10]

But it is almost impossible for a writer to stop writing, and if, when Galsworthy allowed Soames to die, he intended to put aside his pen for good, it was a resolution he was quite unable to keep. During their winter holiday in Biarritz in February 1929 he wrote of two plays on which he was working to his old collaborator, Leon M. Lion: 'I have finished the play that I took away half finished, and am at work on another. I want to know your plans and whether you are still wanting a new play, and if so what are the possibilities of production.'[11] (It may be remembered that when writing *Escape* he had resolved that would be his last play.) The two new plays referred to in his letter were *Exiled*, produced at Wyndham's Theatre in June 1929, and *The Roof*, produced at the Vaudeville Theatre after a trial run at Golder's Green in November the same year; both plays were unsuccessful and were taken off after short runs.

The death of Soames was almost immediately a matter of regret to his creator: 'it is hard to part suddenly and finally from those with whom one has lived so long,' he wrote in a short foreword to his next book, *On Forsyte Change*, 'a volume of apocryphal Forsyte tales' published on 3 October 1930. Back in the familiar world of his Forsytes Galsworthy recovered a certain ease in his writing: the stories are not brilliant but they are better than anything else he wrote at this time, and were an enormous success with his public.

On 3 June 1929 Galsworthy's name appeared in the Birthday Honours as recipient of the Order of Merit; this honour Galsworthy felt was quite different from the knighthood that he had so hotly rejected eleven years earlier, and one that a writer could suitably accept. Congratulations poured in; Max Beerbohm ended his letter 'don't answer this note . . . Just tear off the appended form and have it sent to me:

> Mr Galsworthy's seven Private Secretaries
> regret
> that they are suffering from writer's cramp.
> They hope
> to resume work shortly.[12]

Galsworthy received his O.M. at St James's Palace on 9 July. Ada very strangely left for their holiday abroad the day before.

In October 1930 Galsworthy completed the first volume of his new trilogy, *Maid in Waiting*: 'I have started on another family, the Charwells (or Cherrells as it is pronounced), representative of the older type of family with more tradition and sense of service than the Forsytes. I've finished one novel, and hope, if I have luck, to write a trilogy on them,' he wrote in a letter to André Chevrillon.[13]

'If I have luck . . .' Though only just sixty-three, there can be no doubt that Galsworthy felt that already his time was running out. He had always had exceptionally good health – he seldom visited a doctor, and never went into hospital – but nevertheless he and Ada were in their own way very health-conscious. Ada's life had of course been an almost unending series of illnesses, treatments and convalescences, and it may well have been in reaction to this that John had such an unusual dread of medical treatment. But he prided himself on keeping fit, doing his daily Muller exercises as well as riding and walking and, when occasion provided, playing tennis or cricket. He even kept an annual record of his and Ada's measurements, showing any yearly deviation! According to Rudolf Sauter it was in 1930 that a spot appeared on his nose, which worried him inordinately; he was told it was 'a rodent ulcer' and might be cured by radium treatment, but the complaint persisted.

But despite these underlying fears the year 1931 was one of unprecedented acclaim for Galsworthy. In December 1930 the family party departed as usual for their winter holiday, this year once again to the United States. They settled at Tucson, Arizona, where a routine was soon established: 'Five days a week R., V. and I ride at 7.30 – 8.30. I have a charming little mount. At 9.30 I settle down to the novel, and keep it going till nearly lunch time. If only I can keep this up I hope to bring back half the sequel to *Maid in Waiting* . . .'[14] The last three weeks of this American tour were taken up with a hectic round of lectures and a visit to Princeton to receive an honorary degree from the university. They returned to England on 15 April. In May Galsworthy was elected a Foreign Honorary Member of the American Academy of Arts and Sciences; that same month he delivered the Romanes Lecture at Oxford University, and on 24 June that university gave him an honorary D. Litt.

Galsworthy did complete his trilogy of the Cherrell family – *Maid in Waiting, Flowering Wilderness* and *Over the River*. Dinny Cherrell, the central character of the three books, is perhaps Galsworthy's final portrait of an ideal woman, combining the proud dignity of Ada with the youthful vitality and optimism he had met with in Margaret Morris. Cynthia Asquith writes of her, 'Galsworthy's courtesy has not moulted a feather. His wife embarrassed me by telling me in front of him that the description of Dinny, the girl in his latest novel, *Maid in Waiting*, had been taken from me, whereupon he made me a courtly little bow. I told Barrie I'd no idea what to say to this, or what to do with my face. "Of course you should have curtsied", he said.'[15]

The first volume, *Maid in Waiting*, is a weak and meandering book. It takes as its theme the charge against Dinny's brother, Hubert Cherrell, of shooting a man for ill-treating the mules he was in charge of while on an expedition in South America. The government of Bolivia have issued an extradition order on the charge of murder. Hubert is saved by the exertions of his sister, who is able to produce a diary of his conclusively proving that he is not guilty.

The second book in the trilogy, *Flowering Wilderness*, is far the most interesting of the three. Wilfred Desert has already appeared in *The White Monkey* as the man who Fleur loves and with whom she nearly has an affair. Now, after years abroad in the East, he returns to England and he and Dinny Cherrell fall in love. But Wilfred is a man disgraced: at the point of a gun he has abandoned the Christian faith and become a Moslem. This deed, in the eyes of Dinny's family, is seen as 'letting down the British Empire' and makes him a totally unworthy suitor for Dinny. In fact this thin and today unconvincing plot disguises a much deeper issue. Wilfred Desert is indeed a man who has lost faith, but in himself rather than in any religious creed.

This portrait of terrifying disillusion and despair is, I think, Galsworthy's last self-portrait: 'There had been in Wilfred's face something which suggested that he had been cast out of happiness . . . That was only two years after the Armistice, and she knew now what utter disillusionment and sense of wreckage he had suffered after the war.' This emptiness and despair inside him makes it in the end impossible for him to stay with Dinny; he is running away from himself as much as from her: 'You'll laugh, but I feel like bleeding to death inside. I want to get to where nothing and nobody remind me.' 'Ironical isn't it? I was driven to Dinny by loneliness. I'm driven away from her by it.'

This picture of a man suffering was the strongest, most brutally drawn character that Galsworthy had depicted since his Richard Shelton in *The Island Pharisees*. But where Shelton's hate is directed at the world outside himself, Desert hates the world within himself. It cannot be chance that Galsworthy named him Desert.

Inevitably he has to leave Dinny and return to the East and his spiritual isolation. The pain of broken love that Dinny then has to experience must recall the anguish that Galsworthy and Margaret Morris had gone through nearly twenty years earlier. 'She lay on her back, quivering and dry-eyed, wondering for whose inscrutable delight she was thus suffering. The stricken do not look outside for help, they seek within. To go about exuding tragedy was abhorrent to her. She would not do that! But the sweetness of the wind, the moving clouds, the rustle of the breeze, the sound of children's voices, brought no hint of how she was to disguise herself and face life afresh.'

Over the River is once again concerned with unhappy marriage; this time it is Dinny's sister Clare who is ill-treated by her husband Gerald Corven. (We are told he horse-whips her.) She escapes from her marriage and is happily united to her new lover Tony Croom. A sub-plot of the novel tells how Dinny, having heard of the death of Wilfred in the East, settles for the steady but unexciting Eustace Dornford.

There are passages in *Flowering Wilderness* and *Over the River* that show that Galsworthy could still write with great power and imagination, but almost only when he allowed himself to write of characters whose problems were not dissimilar to his own. How truly could he have said of himself that 'The stricken do not look outside for help, they seek within', and if only he had allowed himself to write more often of what was 'within'. Wilbur Cross in his book *Four Contem-*

porary Novelists has quoted Galsworthy as saying: 'It might be said of Shaw's plays that he creates characters who express feelings which they have not got. It might be said of mine, that I create characters who have feelings which they cannot express.' Galsworthy spoke of his own tragedy as a creative writer.

Chapter 34

Death

It is impossible not to see in Galsworthy's last writings his pre-occupation with the death he now felt to be so near. Two characters, both playing apparently small roles, dominate *Over the River* and his play *The Roof.* Wilfred Desert, the despairing lover of Dinny Cherrell, does not appear in *Over the River*, but his absence from Dinny's life and his death in the East are in a strange way the key incidents of the novel. In a letter which reaches Dinny after the news of his death, he writes: 'I am at peace with myself at last . . . I've gained some of the Eastern conviction that the world of other men does not matter; one's alone from birth to death, except for that fine old companion, the Universe – of which one is the microcosm.' Lennox in *The Roof*, a middle-aged writer with a fatal heart condition, is unable to find a philosophy that will resign him to his approaching death:

> L. 'Nurse, forgive an awkward question – but you must have seen a lot of death. Is it, or isn't it?'
> N. 'The end? I don't know, Mr. Lennox; I don't think so.'
> L. 'I'm afraid it *is*.'

> L. '. . . Nothingness! There's no realizing that one won't be! . . . I funk dying; and I'm afraid of showing that I funk it.'

Galsworthy, who had all his life admired courage, did now, like Lennox, 'funk dying'. In the first place he was conscious that, despite outward appearances, he was unfulfilled as a writer; subtly, in their own way, the Forsytes, his rich uncles, had got their own back on their wayward nephew. 'I don't want my son to be a famous author,' Blanche Galsworthy had commented petulantly to her son-in-law, Georg Sauter.[1] And now two tragedies had struck deep into Galsworthy's life, tragedies that were for him beyond expression: his personal betrayal of Ada in having loved Margaret Morris, and the world tragedy of the war. A writer less inhibited by his past could have used these experiences to write with greater depth, but Galsworthy had been brought up according to a certain code of behaviour, which dictated that a gentleman hides rather than expresses what hurts him most. As a young man he had fought against the taboos of his class, and his early novels, particularly *Jocelyn* and *The Island Pharisees*, had earned him the strong disapprobation of the older generation; many eyebrows were raised, many drawing-rooms were closed to him, not only because he wrote, but because, with Ada, he acted as he wrote. Now, in the latter half of his life, he had become a conformist, and his writing had become thinner and less truthful where it needed to be deeper and more personal. The result was books that were immediately pleasing and popular, but lacking that core of truth that might have given them a permanent place in literature.

A secondary result of these tragedies was to make him frighteningly dependent on Ada. Had his association with Margaret Morris developed it might have given him the mental freedom that he so badly needed. But there was something almost childish in the way he always needed Ada's presence; as the Sauters have said, his immediate question on seeing them about the house at Bury was always 'Where's Auntie?' Having once earned her displeasure he never wished to do so again; it had been like an eclipse of the sun. However much he had longed for the stimulation and youthfulness of Margaret Morris, this longing was as nothing compared with the loss of Ada. The two were knotted in an inextricable, claustrophobic relationship. But this knot would be broken by death.

Not unnaturally they both longed for some hope that they might be reunited in another world, and, lacking any sort of religious conviction, the only avenue open to them was the faint possibility that the dead might still be able to communicate with those they had left behind. Rudolf Sauter has said that they discussed trying to establish some contact after death, even suggesting that a certain hour of the day should be put aside for this purpose. Before his death they had taken part in seances, but John remained sceptical.

During those last years at Bury Galsworthy was a tired man. It was with increasing difficulty that he wrote his last three novels, and with enormous relief that he finished *Over the River* on 13 August 1932, the day before his sixty-fifth birthday. Dorothy Easton seeing him at a PEN dinner said, 'he looked paler, laced-in and rather like a lion in a cage; for a shy man to be the focus of a crowd is an ordeal.'[2]

'Most of us would now prefer to have our lives blown out as a man blows out a candle; choose to burn steadily to a swift last, instead of with a flickering sorrowful dwindling of our flames into darkness that we can see creeping round us,' Galsworthy had written in an essay entitled 'Burning Leaves' in 1922. Now the darkness was literally creeping round him; even before that pernicious spot appeared on his nose he had been conscious of his dwindling strength. It was in August 1931 according to Rudolf Sauter that he was first overcome by an attack of speechlessness; his old friend J. W. Hills was spending the weekend with the Galsworthys and the attack occurred during dinner. These attacks continued to occur from time to time; a fall from his horse, which normally would have caused little concern, worried him. When he rode, he no longer rode alone, but always accompanied by his nephew or a groom. Nevertheless, he resolutely attempted to ignore the symptoms of his failing health. He refused to see doctors; as he told Vi Sauter at the beginning of his illness, 'I don't want to get into the hands of doctors. If you once get into doctors' hands, Vi, you never get out . . . never get out . . . never get out.'[3]

But though he refused medical help, the conviction that he was very seriously ill, in fact that he was a dying man, obsessed him. Far more tragic than the details of Galsworthy's final illness, harrowing though they were, was his inability to accept his situation or to communicate his mental distress to those around him.

The American tour during the winter of 1930–31 did something to restore his health and spirits, and the spot on his nose appeared to have healed. But a few months later there was a recurrence of the poison, and this depressed him enormously.

> He [Galsworthy] who always liked a room well lighted began to shun the light, to insist that the lights be dimmed and to manoeuvre that the right side of his face only should be presented to people.
>
> Finally, though the spot really looked no more than a passing blemish, he grew to avoid people altogether. He would have no mention of his health, and, for six months, lived the life of a recluse, working unhappily, self-conscious even in our company – but no efforts would induce him to have a medical opinion.[4]

Galsworthy did in fact consult a Dr Darling in November 1931, and subsequently underwent a course of radium treatment from December 1931 to May 1932, though this was not advocated, or approved of, by the doctor. J. W. Darling, writing to Rudolf Sauter, made this revealing and perceptive comment about his patient: 'My opinion, from the only time I saw him about his present illness, was that something evil and final had got a firm grip and that the head symptoms were secondary and subsequent – that the trouble did not originate there.'[5] This view is borne out by his strange behaviour and gloomily prophetic remarks to his family, *after* the spot had apparently been successfully cured by the radium treatment: 'There was that June day when, coming back from a short trip abroad, with summer just breaking her sails and that ache on the air, he remarked: "You had better look at me well now, because it's the last time you'll ever see me quite well again."'[6]

It was about this time that Ralph Mottram saw his old friend for the last time. He was spending the night at Grove Lodge on 25 May, and as he was stealing out of the house to catch an early morning train Galsworthy 'came running downstairs in his maroon silk dressing gown, unlatched the door for me and wrung my hand, exclaiming astonishingly, "God bless you, old man!" as if we were parting for some long journey.'[7]

His determination to complete his novel *Over the River* kept him going through the summer months of 1932, but it was only with tremendous resolution and effort that he accomplished this final piece of writing. 'Time and again to the question: "had a good morning, Uncle?" would come the reply: "not very good; only one page this morning" . . .'[8] And when at last the book was finished on 13 August he was for a short period happier than he had been for months.

But rapidly the symptoms of illness became more apparent and more debilitating: everything tired him; there were recurrent attacks of speechlessness; he made the strange complaint that his hats were becoming too large for him, and to counteract this Ada stuffed paper into the lining bands to make them fit more comfortably.

It was at this time, on 10 November, that the announcement came from Stockholm that Galsworthy had won the Nobel Prize for Literature. To have this greatest of all literary honours conferred on him gave occupation and distraction if not new hope to the dying Galsworthy; he and Ada methodically set to the task of personally answering the many letters of congratulation that poured in each day – though Vincent Marrot, lunching at Grove Lodge ten days later, wrote that 'he seemed little if at all elated by his Nobel Prize'. His chief concern, which was discussed at this lunch party, was a proposed deed of trust for the Nobel Prize money in favour of P E N.[9]

Galsworthy was still fighting hard against the onset of illness, determinedly continuing to live the life of a healthy man. He was playing croquet at Bury when the news was phoned through to him that he had won the Nobel Prize; the day after, he was thrown from his horse, Dhu, an accident which caused considerable concern to his household, though he appears only to have received minor injuries; two days later he was riding again. Above all he was determined to honour his literary commitments – he was to go to Paris for an International P E N Congress on 23 November, and to Stockholm to receive his Nobel Prize early in December. But on the day he was due to travel to Paris he was unwell and running a slight temperature, and the journey had to be abandoned at the last minute.

Similarly he fought against any idea that he would be unable to travel to Stockholm in December, but to his family the symptoms of his deteriorating health were painfully obvious: the attacks of speechlessness and stuttering were more frequent, his limbs were weak and his walking shaky. 'Looks tragically ill,' Rudolf wrote in his notebook on 2 December. Galsworthy visited Dr Darling, mainly with the intention of getting a doctor's letter should he have to cancel Stockholm; the doctor advised a complete overhaul and prescribed a tonic. But 'J.G. won't hear of examination', and the next day refused even to take the medicine.[10]

It was as if by refusing to admit illness he would escape being ill; with all the determination of which he was capable he rejected the symptoms of his failing health. It was a tragic and appalling struggle and one that was bound to end in failure. At last, finding that he could not even read the speech that he was writing without stumbling and stuttering, he told Rudolf what had been obvious to his family all along, that he could not go to Stockholm. This was on 3 December; on the 5th he retired to his bedroom, a man totally beaten and exhausted, and seldom after that came downstairs at all.

The speech on which he had been working almost obsessively during those last few weeks of November, and which he had believed he would deliver in Stockholm at the Nobel Prize Ceremony, was to him almost what a final confession is to a dying Christian; it was an assessment and appraisal of his life and achievement, an assessment which in the end he found wanting. 'Mine indeed was a deep, dark youth, an apprenticeship cheered on by some driving quality within me, and by the belief that I would some day be a real writer. And as I read to you these melancholy reminiscences, it seems to me as little true now that I shall ever be a writer worthy of the name.' And he ended his speech: 'I am not afraid of the vanishing civilization. I am more afraid of that moment when I shall have said all I have to say, and must just wait till life slips behind me, says, "Time, sir," and I answer, "You have been long in coming. Here is my pen – the ink in it is dry. Take it and give it to some other who will serve you better."'

'Time, sir,' it was, and it had not been long in coming. Galsworthy had now no alternative but to accept illness, but he did so with a poor grace. After a lifetime of such exceptional goodness, of such self-effacing gentleness, it is frightening to read the day to day account in Rudolf Sauter's diary of the transformation of Galsworthy's character that took place during those first weeks of complete invalidism. He became bitter and resentful, seeming almost to hate all those who were trying so painstakingly to do everything they could to alleviate his suffering. Again and again Rudolf writes, 'V. and R. hardly dare to go in [to his room]'; 'more depressed-looking and views everything and everyone with a "hostile eye",' he wrote on 7 January.[11]

Early in the illness Sir Douglas Shields had tried to persuade Galsworthy that he must go into a clinic for a full medical examination, and at last, with extreme reluctance and misery, he agreed to this. The examination took place at a clinic in Park Lane on 14 November and lasted for two days. The results were inconclusive, four badly abscessed teeth and a duodenal ulcer, scarcely enough to account for the extremely low physical and mental condition from which Galsworthy was so evidently suffering. The teeth were extracted at Grove Lodge – Galsworthy obstinately refusing to return to the clinic for the minor operation. The treatment that the doctors prescribed in order to improve his general condition was pathetically amateurish: 'massage, sunlight, electricity, rest and injections and baths.'[12]

The scene round Galsworthy's deathbed was one of almost medieval horror. Ada, panic-stricken, was hardly able to control her despair: it had been so much assumed between herself and John that *she* was the weak and ailing partner, he the strong one, the constant support, and now the roles were reversed. Undoubtedly John, as far as was possible in his condition, was concerned for Ada; in fact Rudolf Sauter believed that this was one of the main reasons for his distress. That something was troubling the sick man is certain, and his inability to communicate added enormously to this.

> J.G. tries all day to get out something without avail; none of us can make out what; so in desperation, after dinner, R. tries. R:- 'Would you like me to help?' J.G.:- 'Yes.' R: 'Is it about money?' J.G.: 'No'. R: 'Business?' J.G.: 'No'. R: 'Is it about Auntie?' J.G.: 'Yes' then cannot get any further. Eventually J.G. clambers out of bed and walking up and down in great agitation mumbles a few phrases, like '. . . jump! . . . a spring! . . .' and finally comes up to R. shakes hands hard three times saying, 'goodbye! . . . goodbye! . . . goodbye!'[13]

The next day he tried to write out some message on the page of a minute pocket book; with immense labour and difficulty, crossing out more than he wrote, he at last achieved a few words, one short sentence: 'I've enjoyed too pleasant circumstances . . .' These few words convey much more than is at first apparent; Rudolf Sauter, present when they were written, is still haunted by the despair that Galsworthy tried somehow to convey in his last coherent message. 'I've enjoyed too pleasant circumstances . . .'[14] Ada, money, large houses, foreign travel, success and literary awards. But these things had in the end cheated him of the one thing he longed for, the one thing he lived to do, to write really well, to have written books that would not only please his own generation but that would have a place for ever in the literature of his country. Now he was dying, and deep inside he felt the gnawing pain of failure.

New medical opinions were summoned almost daily: Dr Dunn, Sir Farquhar Buzzard, Dr Gordon Holmes, Dr Hurst, Sir Douglas Shields. No one seemed to agree as to diagnosis or treatment, whether there was a brain tumour or not, or possibly a secondary growth or virulent anaemia. New tests were carried out, new treatments ordered, all adding immeasurably to the suffering of the sick man. The room was a battlefield of discordant opinions. Mabel Reynolds urged homoeopathic treatment; Lady Rothenstein described an identical illness of Sir William, which had in the end been found to be caused by poisoned teeth; letters arrived by almost every post urging new treatments and theories. It was not an atmosphere in which to die, and yet Galsworthy had almost certainly been convinced from the very beginning what the outcome of his illness must be; his first doctor,

Dr Darling, seems to have been the most perspicacious when he wrote, 'something evil and final had got a firm grip'.[15]

Though during the first weeks he was bitter and hostile, resenting everything that was done for him, loathing his own increasing helplessness, half way through December a change was observed: he, Galsworthy, 'really smiles (such a sad smile but really a smile all the same) and waves a kiss, with hand only half way up . . . so tired . . . but almost as if he didn't resent things quite so much.' And on the 17th: 'the face is so drawn as to be hardly recognizable, with sunken temples and cheeks, and the great hollow eyes of a deeper than physical and mental, a spiritual tragedy.'[16]

As the month drew to its close, the doctors and Rudolf and Vi began to realize with a fearful certainty that Galsworthy was dying, that nothing that anyone could do could help him now. There was nothing left but to alleviate his suffering as much as could be, by nursing and if necessary by drugs.

But for Ada it was different; if John died, how could she survive? There would be nothing in life without him. Her distraught condition became a considerable additional worry to the household. On the 26th Dr Dunn suggested that injections of morphia would relieve Galsworthy's agonizing struggle for breath, and the pain from the heart attacks that were now becoming frequent, but he had to warn them that once morphia was given it was unlikely that Galsworthy would ever regain consciousness. Such a decision Ada could not make; she turned desperately for more medical help. Sir Douglas Shields was contacted once again. Unfortunately he was reassuring: he was not convinced that there was a tumour; all avenues, he told Ada, who was clutching at every possible straw, had not yet been explored. To those who were watching at Galsworthy's bedside such hopes were plainly ridiculous, though it was apparent to them that the doctors were in considerable disagreement with each other, and furthermore had never discussed the case together, or with Shields. Such a conference was now convened at Shield's Park Lane nursing home, at which he was finally convinced that the diagnosis of the brain tumour must be correct. Still Ada could not accept their verdict; she wanted an entirely new opinion, and on the recommendation of Lady Rothenstein suggested Dr Arthur Hurst. Hurst came on the 29th, and again her hopes were falsely raised; there was a possibility, Hurst told her, that Galsworthy was suffering from anaemia which was affecting his nervous system, and he ordered a blood test the following day. But by now Galsworthy's temperature had begun to rise dramatically, and by the morning of 31 January it had reached 107. At last he was allowed the relief of morphia, and went into a final coma.[17]

These last two terrible months had been a painful microcosm of his life; his efforts to die had been as frustrated as his efforts to live, frustrated by the cushioning love and care of Ada, by his family, and by the wealth that could buy everything, even unlimited medical care. Whether his illness was in fact caused by a brain tumour, or, as Dr Darling suggested, by some fatal malaise of the spirit, must still remain uncertain. Now at last even Ada began to realize that John, *her* John, was dying. He, who she had always assumed would outlive her, would be there to nurse her through her own final illness when it came, was going to leave her. It was for Ada the last most galling betrayal of her life; to so great an extent did she feel this that anger and bitterness were her first emotions rather than grief.

John too had seen it as a sacred charge that he should care always for Ada; he never forgot how deeply life had wounded her, as a child, as a young woman, even he had added to these wounds. This love of his had been protective; for nearly forty years he had shielded her from the world, often at the expense of his own life and writing. Now, helpless and dying, he must leave her. He knew, as probably no one else did, that Ada could not survive without him, though she did 'live' on for more than twenty years. His first prayer for her might well have been his last:

> 'God of the dark defend her,
> And keep well in thy sight
> Her happy feet and send her
> The kiss of sleep at night.'

On the morning of 31 January, at 9.15, after a final agonizing struggle, John Galsworthy was dead. Ada knew that she was alone once more, and her protector was gone. At first she would neither accept nor believe it; how could she hurt this man, even beyond the grave? With a mind sorely disturbed her first reaction was to destroy everything that was his; even his beloved horses Ronald and Primrose she ordered to be shot (though mercifully they were reprieved by John's nephew, Hubert). Poor Ada, one must weep for a woman who had now so agonizingly to reap the reward of possessiveness; he whom she had possessed to too great a degree had gone beyond possession.

John Galsworthy was cremated privately at Woking on 3 February, and a memorial service was held in Westminster Abbey on the 9th – though permission for an Abbey burial, which was requested by E. V. Lucas and the Society of Authors, was refused by the Dean, Dr Foxley Norris.

On 25 March, as he had specifically desired, his ashes were scattered by his nephew Rudolf Sauter on the hills above Bury. At last the man was free, his remains blown over the hills and the countryside he had loved.

> Scatter my ashes!
>   Hereby I make it a trust;
>   I in no grave be confined,
>   Mingle my dust with the dust,
>   Give me in fee to the wind!
>   Scatter my ashes.

Appendix

Works by John Galsworthy

Novels and short stories

1897 From the Four Winds
(John Sinjohn)
1898 Jocelyn
(John Sinjohn)
1900 Villa Rubein
(John Sinjohn)
1901 A Man of Devon
(John Sinjohn)
1904 The Island Pharisees
1906 The Man of Property
1907 The Country House
1909 Fraternity
1911 The Patrician
1913 The Dark Flower
1914 Memories
1915 The Freelands
1917 Beyond
1918 Five Tales
1919 The Burning Spear
(A.R. P-M Pseudonym)
1919 Saint's Progress
1920 In Chancery
1920 Awakening
1921 To Let
1922 The Forsyte Saga
(Man of Property,
In Chancery, To Let)
1924 The White Monkey
1925 Caravan
The Assembled Tales
of John Galsworthy
1926 The Silver Spoon

1927 Two Forsyte Interludes
1928 Swan Song
1930 On Forsyte Change
1931 Maid in Waiting
1932 Flowering Wilderness
1933 Over the River
(posthumous)

Plays (Dates of Production)

1906 The Silver Box
1907 Joy
1909 Strife
1910 Justice
1911 The Little Dream
1912 The Eldest Son
(written 1909)
1912 The Pigeon
1913 The Fugitive
1914 The Mob
1915 A Bit o' Love
1917 The Foundations
1920 The Skin Game
1921 The Family Man
1921 The First and the Last
The Little Man
Hall Marked
Defeat
The Sun
Punch and Go
(*not produced
published as
Six Short Plays 1921*)

1922	Loyalties
1922	Windows
1924	The Forest
1924	Old English
1925	The Show
1926	Escape
1929	Exiled
1929	The Roof

Essays etc.

1908	A Commentary
1910	A Motley
1912	The Inn of Tranquillity
1915	The Little Man and Other Satires
1916	A Sheaf
1919	Another Sheaf
1919	Addresses in America
1920	Tatterdemalion
1923	Captures

1924	Memorable Days (*privately printed in July*)
1927	Castles in Spain
1935	Forsytes, Pendyces and others
1937	Glimpses and Reflections

Poetry

1912	Moods, Songs & Doggerels
1921	The Bells of Peace
1926	Verses New and Old
1934	The Collected Poems of John Galsworthy

Works by Ada Galsworthy

1935	'The Dear Dogs'
1937	Over the Hills and Far Away

Bibliographic Note

Manuscript Sources
The Diaries of John Galsworthy 1910–1918
Notebooks of Ada Galsworthy
The Diary of Lilian Galsworthy (Sauter)
Elstree Memories: The Lancelot Sandersons in the Eighties,
    Agnes Ridgway.
E. L. Sanderson and John Galsworthy in Fiji, 1893
Memoirs of Dorothy Easton.

Published Sources
The 'official biography' of John Galsworthy was written immediately
after his death by H. V. Marrot with the assistance of Ada Galsworthy.
It was published in 1935. This work, *The Life and Letters of John Galsworthy*,
contains an immense amount of material and letters. It is a source book and
does not profess to contain any criticism of the literary work; of the man it
is totally eulogistic. Nevertheless it is the book, containing much material
that now no longer exists, to which anyone studying the life of Galsworthy
will be bound to refer. In the text of my book I have referred to this work
simply as 'Marrot'. The other principal works consulted are listed as follows:

R. H. Mottram	For Some We Loved 1956
M. E. Reynolds	Memories of John Galsworthy 1936
Rudolf Sauter	Galsworthy the Man 1967
Margaret Morris	My Galsworthy Story 1967
Edward Garnett (Edited by)	Letters from John Galsworthy 1900–32
H. V. Marrot	A Bibliography of the works of John Galsworthy 1928
R. H. Mottram	John Galsworthy (Writers and their Work, No 23) 1953
H. L. Ould	John Galsworthy 1934
Leon Schalit	John Galsworthy, A Survey 1929
Dudley Barker	The Man of Principle, A View of John Galsworthy 1963
David Holloway	John Galsworthy. International Profiles 1968

Sheila Kaye Smith	John Galsworthy 1916
Ford Madox Ford	It was the Nightingale 1933
Arthur Mizener	The Saddest Story, A Biography of Ford Madox Ford 1972
Jocelyn Baines	Joseph Conrad 1960
Rupert Hart-Davis	Hugh Walpole 1952
Cynthia Asquith	Portrait of Barrie 1954

Notes on Text

Chapter 1

1 J. G., 'Note on My Mother',
quoted in Marrot.
2 ibid.
3 ibid.
4 J.G., 'A Portrait',
from *A Motley*.
5 ibid.
6 ibid.
7 J.G., 'Note on My Mother'.
8 Lilian Galsworthy's
(later Sauter) diary.
9 J.G., 'Note on My Mother'.

Chapter 2

1 J.G., 'Memorable Days'.
2 ibid.
3 ibid.
4 M. E. Reynolds,
Memories of John Galsworthy.
5 ibid.
6 Quoted in Arthur Mizener,
The Saddest Story, p. 10.
7 Reynolds, op. cit.
8 ibid.
9 A.G., *Over the Hills
and Far Away*.
10 J.G. to Frank Harris,
April 1921.

Chapter 3

1 J.G., *Addresses in America 1919*.
2 Horace Vachell, *The Hill*.

3 J.G. to his mother,
22 May 1881.
4 J.G. to his mother,
4 February 188–.
5 Quoted in Marrot, p. 37.
6 Quoted in Marrot, p. 48.
7 M. E. Reynolds,
Memories of John Galsworthy.

Chapter 4

1 Quoted in Marrot, p. 66.
2 ibid.
3 Ford Madox Ford,
It Was the Nightingale.
4 Agnes Ridgway, *Elstree
Memories of the Lancelot
Sandersons in the Eighties*.
5 ibid.
6 M. E. Reynolds,
Memories of John Galsworthy.
7 Ridgway, op. cit.
8 Lilian Galsworthy's diary.
9 ibid.
10 ibid.
11 ibid.
12 ibid.
13 Quoted in Marrot, p. 64.
14 Lilian Galsworthy's diary.

Chapter 5

1 J.G., 'A Portrait',
from *A Motley*.

2 Letter dated 18 May 1911, published in *Glimpses and Reflections*.

3 Rudolf Sauter, *Galsworthy the Man*.

4 ibid.

5 J.G.'s diary, 1891.

6 ibid.

7 Quoted in Marrot, p. 70.

8 J.G. to his family, quoted in Marrot, p. 70.

9 Quoted in M. E. Reynolds, *Memories of John Galsworthy*.

10 J.G. to his family, quoted in Marrot, p. 70.

Chapter 6

1 Agnes Ridgway, *Elstree Memories of the Lancelot Sandersons in the Eighties*.

2 ibid.

3 ibid.

4 ibid.

5 ibid.

6 ibid.

7 ibid.

8 Letter from J.G., 27 December 1892, quoted in Marrot, p. 75.

9 Letter from J.G., 22 December 1892, quoted in Marrot, p. 74.

10 E. L. Sanderson, *E. L. Sanderson and John Galsworthy in Fiji*.

11 ibid.

12 ibid.

13 J.G. to his mother, 20 January 1893.

14 Sanderson, op. cit.

15 ibid.

16 ibid.

17 ibid.

18 J.G. to Lilian Galsworthy, 14 February 1893.

19 J.G., 'Reminiscences of Conrad', *Scribner's Magazine*, 1924.

20 Letter from J.G., 8 April 1893, quoted in Marrot, p. 85.

21 ibid.

22 J.G. to Monica Sanderson, 8 September 1894.

Chapter 7

1 R. H. Mottram, *For Some We Loved*.

2 The will of Emanuel Cooper, 1876.

3 Marrot, p. 101.

4 Dudley Barker, *The Man of Principle*.

Chapter 8

1 Quoted in Marrot, p. 65.

2 A.G. to R. H. Mottram, 21 July 1902.

3 A.G. to R. H. Mottram, 3 January 1903.

4 A.G. to R. H. Mottram, 18 January 1904.

5 Ford Madox Ford, *It was the Nightingale*.

6 Preface to Manaton Edition Vol. IV, *Villa Rubein and Other Stories*.

7 Draft speech for Nobel Prize ceremony.

8 J.G. to Fisher Unwin, 29 January 1898.

9 Joseph Conrad to J.G., 16 January 1898.

10 Ford, op. cit.

Chapter 9

1 Preface to Manaton Edition Vol. IV, *Villa Rubein and Other Stories*.

2 Ford Madox Ford to J.G., n.d., quoted in Marrot, p. 123.

3 Preface to Manaton Edition Vol. IV.

4 Preface to Manaton Edition Vol. IV.

5 J.G., *Man of Devon*, 1901 edition.

Chapter 10

1 R. H. Mottram, *For Some We Loved.*

2 ibid.

3 ibid., p. 30.

4 David Garnett, *The Golden Echo*, p. 3.

5 Quoted in Arthur Mizener, *The Saddest Story*, p. 107.

6 David Garnett, op. cit.

7 Introduction to *Letters from John Galsworthy* by Edward Garnett.

8 David Garnett, op. cit.

9 J.G. to Edward Garnett, 18 September 1910.

10 J.G. to Edward Garnett, 12 February 1902.

11 J.G. to Edward Garnett, 10 May 1902.

Chapter 11

1 R. H. Mottram, *For Some We Loved*, p. 32.

2 Mottram, op. cit.

3 J.G., 'Reminiscences of Conrad', *Scribner's Magazine* 1924.

4 Jessie Conrad, *Joseph Conrad and His Circle.*

5 Joseph Conrad to J.G., 6 March 1901.

6 Quoted in Marrot.

7 A.G. to R. H. Mottram, 21 February 1904.

8 Joseph Conrad to J.G., 24 December 1905.

9 Joseph Conrad to J.G.

10 Joseph Conrad to J.G.

11 Joseph Conrad to J.G.

12 Joseph Conrad to J.G., 1 June 1902.

13 Undated letter, quoted in Marrot, p. 119.

14 Undated letter, quoted in Marrot, p. 127.

15 Ford Madox Ford, *It was the Nightingale.*

16 Quoted in Arthur Mizener, *The Saddest Story*, p. 87.

17 J.G. to Ford Madox Ford, 14 April 1904.

18 Violet Hunt, *The Flurried Years*, p. 18.

Chapter 12

1 Draft speech for the Nobel Prize ceremony.

2 Preface to Manaton Edition Vol. V, *The Island Pharisees.*

3 'If I only knew', first published in *The Triad*, 1924; reprinted *Glimpses and Reflections*, 1937.

4 Preface to Manaton Edition Vol. IV, *Villa Rubein and Other Stories.*

5 Edward Garnett to J.G., 20 May 1903.

6 J.G. to Edward Garnett, May 1903.

7 Joseph Conrad to J.G., 8 October 1902.

8 Joseph Conrad to J.G., 1 November 1902.

Chapter 13

1 J.G. to Edward Garnett,
   11 December 1929.
2 Introduction to *Letters from
   John Galsworthy* by Edward
   Garnett.
3 J.G. to St John Hornby,
   10 December 1904.

Chapter 14

1 J.G. to R. H. Mottram,
   December 1904.
2 A.G., *Over the Hills and
   Far Away*, p. 90.
3 Draft speech for
   Nobel Prize Ceremony.
4 J.G. to Edward Garnett,
   1 February 1905.
5 ibid.
6 A.G. to R. H. Mottram,
   9 April 1905, from Florence.
7 Edward Garnett to J.G.,
   8 May 1905.
8 A.G., op. cit., pp. 43–4.
9 J.G. to Edward Garnett,
   16 May 1905.
10 Edward Garnett to J.G.,
   27 May 1905.
11 ibid.
12 J. G. to Edward Garnett,
   1 June 1905.
13 Edward Garnett to J.G.,
   27 May 1905.
14 J.G. to Edward Garnett,
   1 June 1905.
15 ibid.
16 J.G. to Edward Garnett,
   Tuesday, n.d.
17 J.G. to Constance Garnett,
   14 June 1905.
18 J.G. to Edward Garnett,
   2 June 1905.

19 J.G. to Edward Garnett,
   13 July 1905.
20 Edward Garnett to J.G.,
   26 July 1905.
21 J.G. to Edward Garnett,
   6 January 1906.

Chapter 15

1 J.G. to Edward Garnett,
   24 July 1905.
2 J.G. to Edward Garnett,
   n.d. (June 1905).
3 J.G. to R. H. Mottram,
   22 July 1905.
4 A.G. to Mrs Mottram,
   23 September 1905.
5 J.G. to R. H. Mottram,
   23 September 1905.
6 A.G.'s notebook.
7 J.G. to Lilian Galsworthy,
   11 September 1905.
8 M. E. Reynolds,
   Memories of John Galsworthy.
9 J.G. to Lilian Galsworthy,
   11 September 1905.
10 A.G. to Rudolf Sauter,
   11 February (no year).
11 J.G. to R. H. Mottram,
   7 April 1906.
12 Quoted in Arthur Mizener,
   The Saddest Story, p. 120.
13 Joseph Conrad to J.G.,
   quoted in Marrot, p. 187.
14 Joseph Conrad, 'John
   Galsworthy', *Outlook*,
   31 March 1906. Reprinted
   Last Essays, 1926.

Chapter 16

1 A.G. to R. H. Mottram,
   29 September 1905.
2 R. H. Mottram,

For Some We Loved, p. 97.

3 ibid., p. 74.

4 ibid.

5 A.G., *The Dear Dogs*, p. 10.

6 A.G. to R. H. Mottram,
30 October 1905.

7 J.G. to R. H. Mottram,
19 December 1905.

8 Edward Garnett to J.G.,
8 March 1906.

9 J.G. to Edward Garnett,
30 September 1906.

10 Edward Garnett to J.G.,
8 March 1906.

11 J.G. to Edward Garnett,
10 March 1906.

12 A.G. to R. H. Mottram,
28 September 1906.

13 J.G. to R. H. Mottram,
(?) October 1906.

14 A.G. to R. H. Mottram,
28 January 1906.

15 A.G. to R. H. Mottram,
11 June 1906.

16 A.G. to R. H. Mottram,
12 July 1906.

Chapter 17

1 J.G. to Edward Garnett,
25 August 1906.

2 J.G. to Mrs Mottram,
(?) July 1904.

3 J.G., 'Disquisition on
Joseph Conrad', 1910.

4 J.G. to Edward Garnett,
25 August 1906.

5 A.G.'s notebook.

6 Edward Garnett to J.G.,
14 June 1901.

7 J.G. to Thomas Hardy,
27 March 1916.

8 Joseph Conrad to J.G.,
Friday (August 1908),
quoted in Marrot, p. 234.

9 Leon Schalit, *John
Galsworthy, A Survey.*

Chapter 18

1 E. F. Benson, *As We Were.*

2 Arnold Bennett, *Journals,*
9 April 1909.

3 J.G. to Edward Garnett,
30 September 1906.

4 J.G. to Edward Garnett,
17 February 1907.

5 J.G. to Edward Garnett,
20 February 1907.

6 A.G. to R. H. Mottram,
(?) January 1907.

7 Violet Hunt, *The Flurried
Years.*

8 Edward Garnett to J.G.,
4 November 1906.

9 H. G. Wells to J.G.,
n.d. quoted in Marrot, p. 206.

10 E. V. Lucas to J.G.,
n.d. quoted in Marrot, p. 207.

11 Arnold Bennett to J.G.,
5 September 1909.

12 J.G. to R. H. Mottram,
5 November 1906.

13 A.G. to R. H. Mottram,
29 September 1907.

14 J.G. to Edward Garnett,
10 February 1907.

15 A.G. to R. H. Mottram,
29 September 1907.

16 A.G. to R. H. Mottram,
18 September 1907.

17 Joseph Conrad to J.G.,
n.d. quoted in Marrot, p. 212.

Chapter 19

1 List quoted in Marrot, p. 215.
2 Note quoted in Marrot, p. 240.
3 J.G. to Edward Garnett, 16 July 1907.
4 J.G. to Edward Garnett, 22 July 1907.
5 J.G. to Edward Garnett, 26 July 1907.
6 J.G. to Mrs Dawson Scott, 17 December 1931.
7 J.G. to correspondent, unnamed, 10 December 1931. Quoted in Marrot, p. 802.
8 J.G. to Edward Garnett, 19 August 1907.
9 A.G. to R. H. Mottram, 28 August 1907.
10 'On Prisons and Punishment. 1. Solitary Confinement', published in *A Sheaf*, 1916.
11 J.G. to Edward Garnett, 19 December 1909.
12 J.G. to Winston Churchill, 15 May 1910.
13 *Weekly Dispatch*, 27 February 1910.
14 *Pall Mall Gazette*, quoted in Marrot, p. 256.
15 J.G. to W. L. George, n.d. quoted in Marrot, p. 266.
16 John Masefield to J.G., n.d. quoted in Marrot, p. 257.
17 J.G. to Gilbert Murray, 23 July 1910.
18 Gilbert Murray to J.G., quoted in Marrot, p. 267.
19 Christopher Hassell, *Edward Marsh*.
20 J.G., 'Note on Edward Garnett', 1914. Published in *Forsytes, Pendyces and Others*.
21 J.G. to anonymous correspondent, 10 October 1912.
22 J.G. to Liberal agent at Moretonhampstead, 14 January 1910.
23 J.G. to Gilbert Murray, January 1911.

Chapter 20

1 A.G. to R. H. Mottram, 3 May 1908.
2 A.G. to R. H. Mottram, 22 April 1908.
3 J.G. to Edward Garnett, 20 May 1908.
4 A.G. to R. H. Mottram, 3 May 1908.
5 A.G. to R. H. Mottram, 17 June 1908.
6 ibid.
7 A.G. to R. H. Mottram, 5 October 1908.
8 A.G. to R. H. Mottram, (?) August 1908.
9 J.G. to Edward Garnett, 20 May 1908.
10 J.G., Note on *Fraternity*. Birmingham Collection. J.G. 472.
11 ibid.
12 Joseph Conrad to J.G., Wednesday (August 1908), quoted in Marrot, p. 230.
13 J.G., Note on *Fraternity*. Birmingham Collection. J.G. 472.
14 A.G.'s notebook.
15 A.G. to Mrs Mottram, 26 April 1909.

Chapter 21

1 A.G.'s notebook.
2 A.G. to R. H. Mottram,
20 January 1909.
3 A.G. to R. H. Mottram,
11 July 1909.
4 A.G. to R. H. Mottram,
30 July 1909.
5 A.G. to R. H. Mottram,
19 June 1909.
6 A.G. to R. H. Mottram,
28 November 1909.
7 Preface to Manaton Edition
Vol. XV, *The Inn of
Tranquillity.*
8 Letter 24 July.
Glimpses and Reflections,
p. 116.
9 J.G.'s diary, 15 July 1910.
10 A.G.'s notebook.
11 R. H. Mottram,
For Some We Loved.
12 A.G. to R. H. Mottram,
10 January 1910.
13 A.G. to R. H. Mottram,
31 March 1910.
14 J.G. to Edward Garnett,
24 April 1910.
15 J.G. to Edward Garnett,
12 May 1910.
16 A.G. to R. H. Mottram,
6 June 1910.
17 A.G. to R. H. Mottram,
18 June 1910.
18 Note quoted in Marrot, p. 285.
19 Gilbert Murray to J.G.,
n.d. quoted in Marrot, p. 286.
20 Edward Garnett to J.G.,
(1910) quoted in Marrot, p.
288.

Chapter 22

1 J.G. to M. E. Reynolds,
5 April 1911.
2 A.G. to R. H. Mottram,
2 April 1911.
3 J.G.'s diary, 22 June 1911.
4 A.G. to R. H. Mottram,
1 March 1911.
5 J.G.'s diary, 27 May 1911.
6 J.G. to Margaret Morris,
1 January 1912.
7 Margaret Morris,
My Galsworthy Story, p. 49.
8 ibid., p. 53.
9 ibid., p. 54.
10 ibid., p. 121.
11 ibid., p. 57.
12 ibid., p. 59.
13 ibid., p. 62.
14 A.G. to R. H. Mottram,
8 February 1912.
15 ibid., p. 63.
16 ibid., p. 66.

Chapter 23

1 J.G., *The Dark Flower.*
2 J.G.'s diary, 24 February 1912.
3 J.G. to Gilbert Murray,
28 February 1912.
4 J.G.'s diary, 3 March 1912.
5 J.G. to Gilbert Murray,
20 March 1912.
6 A.G. to M. E. Reynolds,
20 March 1912.
7 A.G. to M. E. Reynolds,
23 March 1912.
8 A.G. to M. E. Reynolds,
23 April 1912.
9 J.G.'s diary, 26 March 1912.
10 J.G. to Margaret Morris,
26 March 1912.

11 J.G. to Margaret Morris,
6 April 1912.

12 J.G., *Memories.*

13 A.G., *Over the Hills and Far
Away.*

14 ibid.

15 ibid.

16 J.G.'s diary, 26 April 1912.

17 J.G.'s diary, 30 April 1912.

18 J.G.'s diary, 9 May 1912.

19 J.G. to Margaret Morris,
3 March 1912.

20 J.G. to Margaret Morris,
13 March 1912.

21 J.G. to Margaret Morris,
23 March 1912.

22 J.G. to Margaret Morris,
12 April 1912.

23 J.G. to Margaret Morris,
31 March 1912.

Chapter 24

1 A.G. to R. H. Mottram,
31 May 1912.

2 A.G. to R. H. Mottram,
1 July 1912.

3 A.G. to R. H. Mottram,
31 May 1912.

4 J.G.'s diary, 8 April 1912.

5 J.G.'s diary, 12 June 1912.

6 J.G. to Margaret Morris,
12 June 1912.

7 J.G. to Margaret Morris,
17 June 1912.

8 J.G. to Margaret Morris,
8 July 1912.

9 J.G. to Margaret Morris,
n.d., quoted in Margaret
Morris, *My Galsworthy Story,*
p. 113.

10 J.G. to Margaret Morris,
9 November 1912.

11 J.G.'s diary, 3 September 1910

12 J.G.'s diary, 12 July 1912.

13 J.G.'s diary, 13 July 1912.

14 'Record of a month at
Cortina', quoted in Marrot,
p. 342.

15 J.G.'s diary, 16 October 1912.

16 A.G. to R. H. Mottram,
11 November 1912.

17 ibid.

18 Joseph Conrad to J.G.,
1 November 1910.

19 J.G. to Margaret Morris,
n.d., quoted in Morris,
op. cit., p. 113.

20 J.G. to J. W. Hills,
11 January 1913.

21 A.G. to R. H. Mottram,
25 November 1912.

22 A.G. to R. H. Mottram,
4 December 1912.

23 ibid.

24 A.G. to R. H. Mottram,
31 May 1912.

25 J.G.'s diary,
'Record of work this year'
(1912).

Chapter 25

1 A.G., *Over the Hills and Far
Away.*

2 J.G.'s diary, 8 March 1913.

3 J.G.'s diary, 1 March 1913.

4 A.G.'s notebook.

5 J.G.'s diary, 9 January 1913.

6 J.G.'s diary, 11 February 1913.

7 J.G.'s diary, 20 March 1913.

8 J.G.'s diary, 22 March 1913.

9 J.G.'s diary, 4 April 1913.

10 J.G.'s diary 9 April 1913.

11 J.G.'s diary, 6 April 1913.

12 J.G.'s diary, 6 May 1913.

13 J.G.'s diary, 31 May 1913.
14 J.G.'s diary, 9 May 1913.
15 J.G.'s diary, 23 January 1911.
16 J.G.'s diary, 27 July 1913.
17 Gerald du Maurier to J.G.,
   3 June 1913.
18 J.G. to Dorothy Easton,
   19 September 1913.
19 J.G. to F. L. Lucas,
   7 August 1913.
20 A.G. to R. H. Mottram,
   14 August 1913.
21 Quoted in Marrot, p. 376.
22 A.G.'s notebook.
23 ibid.
24 Marrot, p. 377.
25 Marrot, p. 378.
26 A.G. to R. H. Mottram,
   5 November 1913.
27 J.G.'s diary,
   18 December 1913.
28 A.G.'s notebook.
29 ibid.
30 ibid.
31 J.G.'s diary, 8 January 1914.
32 J.G.'s diary, 31 January 1914.
33 J.G.'s diary, 2 February 1914.
34 J.G. to F. L. Lucas,
   21 January 1914.
35 J.G.'s diary, 5 February 1914.
36 A.G., *Over the Hills and Far
   Away.*
37 J.G. to F. L. Lucas,
   21 January 1914.

Chapter 26
1 J.G.'s diary, 10 May 1914.
2 J.G.'s diary, 16 May 1914.
3 J.G.'s diary, 28 June 1914.
4 J.G.'s diary, 11 July 1914.
5 J.G.'s diary, 15 July 1914.
6 J.G.'s diary, 21 July 1914.

7 J.G.'s diary, 20 July 1914.
8 J.G.'s diary, 28 July 1914.
9 A.G. to R. H. Mottram,
   12 September 1914.
10 J.G.'s diary,
   25 September 1914.
11 J.G.'s diary, 7 November 1914.
12 J.G.'s diary, 6 May 1915.
13 A.G. to R. H. Mottram,
   24 December 1914.
14 J.G.'s diary, 9 November 1914.
15 J.G. to Hugh Walpole,
   2 February 1915.
16 A.G. to R. H. Mottram,
   1 November 1915.
17 A.G. to R. H. Mottram,
   24 November 1915.
18 J.G.'s diary, 25 May 1915.
19 A.G. to R. H. Mottram,
   7 April 1915.
20 J.G.'s diary, 24 June 1915.
21 J.G.'s diary,
   27 September 1915.
22 J.G.'s diary, 6 October 1915.
23 J.G.'s diary, 17 October 1915.
24 J.G.'s diary,
   16 December 1915.
25 J.G.'s diary,
   31 December 1915.
26 'Novelists in Profile', 1925.

Chapter 27
1 A.G. to R. H. Mottram,
   10 December 1915.
2 J.G.'s diary, 22 March 1916.
3 A.G.'s notebook.
4 J.G.'s diary 1 April 1916.
5 J.G.'s diary, 1 May 1916.
6 A.G. to R. H. Mottram,
   26 May 1916.
7 A.G. to R. H. Mottram,
   27 May 1916.

8 J.G.'s diary, 23 May 1916.

9 J.G.'s diary, 25 June 1916.

10 A.G. to R. H. Mottram,
12 June 1916.

11 A.G. to R. H. Mottram,
3 October 1916.

12 A.G. to R. H. Mottram,
19 October 1916.

13 J.G. to Dorothy Allhusen,
15 September 1916.

14 J.G. to André Chevrillon,
3 October 1916.

15 A.G. to R. H. Mottram,
1 November 1916.

16 ibid.

17 J.G., 'France 1916–1917'.

18 J.G.'s diary,
15 November 1916.

19 J.G.'s diary,
16 November 1916.

20 J.G., 'France 1916–1917'.

21 J.G.'s diary,
18 November 1916.

22 J.G. to M. E. Reynolds,
26 November 1916.

23 A.G. to R. H. Mottram,
22 August 1616.

24 A.G. to R. H. Mottram,
17 December 1916.

25 J.G., 'France 1916' (MS.
draft of essay referred to in
notes 17 and 20).

26 A.G. to R. H. Mottram,
3 March 1917.

27 J.G. to Dorothy Allhusen,
3 January 1917.

28 ibid.

29 J.G.'s diary, 28 March 1917.

Chapter 28

1 A.G.'s notebook.

2 J.G.'s diary, 7 September 1917.

3 J.G.'s diary, 9 September 1917.

4 A.G. to Rudolf Sauter,
3 June 1917.

5 J.G.'s diary, 2 November 1917.

6 A.G.'s notebook.

7 A.G. to Rudolf Sauter,
13 November 1917.

8 A.G. to R. H. Mottram,
7 January 1918.

9 Arnold Bennett, *Journals*,
30 January 1918.

10 J.G.'s diary,
13 November 1917.

11 *Scrutinies* 'John Galsworthy',
by D. H. Lawrence.

12 J.G.'s diary,
31 December 1917.

13 ibid., and A.G.'s notebook.

14 A.G. to R. H. Mottram,
7 January 1918.

15 A.G. to R. H. Mottram,
2 February 1918.

16 Preface to Manaton Edition
Vol. XII, *Saint's Progress*.

17 A.G.'s notebook.

18 Preface to Manaton Edition
Vol. XII.

19 J.G.'s diary, 10 April 1918.

20 A.G. to R. H. Mottram,
5 September 1918.

21 A.G. to Rudolf Sauter,
6 June 1918.

22 R. H. Mottram,
For Some We Loved.

Chapter 29

1 J.G. to Hugh Walpole,
3 March 1918.

2 A.G.'s notebook.

3 R. H. Mottram,
For Some We Loved.

4 A.G. to R. H. Mottram,
   (?) December 1918.
5 Siegfried Sassoon,
   Siegfried's Journey 1918–1920.
6 Quoted in Marrot, p. 443.
7 J.G. to Dorothy Easton,
   28 September 1918.
8 J.G., 'Note on W. H.
   Hudson, 1924'.
9 J.G. to Dorothy Easton,
   14 October 1918.
10 A.G. to Rudolf Sauter,
   7 February 1919.
11 Ada Galsworthy,
   Over the Hills and Far Away.
12 A.G. to R. H. Mottram,
   1 March 1911.
13 J.G. to Hugh Walpole,
   28 June 1919.
14 A.G.'s notebook.
15 J.G., *Addresses in America*, 1919.
16 A.G., *Over the Hills and Far
   Away*, p. 199.
17 Rudolf Sauter,
   Galsworthy the Man.
18 ibid.

Chapter 30
1 Quoted in Rupert Hart-
   Davis, *Hugh Walpole*, p. 165.
2 J.G. to Dorothy Easton,
   23 July 1919.
3 A.G.'s notebook.
4 J.G. to Gilbert Murray,
   18 May 1919.
5 J.G. to Dorothy Easton, n.d.
6 Mrs Thomas Hardy to A.G.,
   17 November 1919.
7 A.G.'s notebook.
8 ibid.
9 J.G., lecture to Young P E N.

(unpublished. Birmingham
Collection).
10 Rudolf Sauter,
   Galsworthy the Man.
11 Dorothy Easton, Unpublished
   Memoir of John Galsworthy.
12 A.G.'s notebook.
13 ibid.
14 Marrot, p. 486.
15 A.G., *Over the Hills and Far
   Away*, p. 48.
16 J.G. to Rudolf Sauter,
   2 January 1920.
17 A.G., *Over the Hills and Far
   Away*, p. 133.
18 A.G.'s notebook.
19 ibid.
20 *The Daily Telegraph.*
21 Thomas Hardy to J.G.,
   19 May 1920.
22 J.G., 'Note on Maggie
   Albanesie.'
23 Joseph Conrad to J.G.,
   20 May 1920.
24 J.G. to H. Granville Barker,
   20 January 1921.

Chapter 31
1 A.G.'s notebook.
2 ibid.
3 J.G. and A.G. to Rudolf
   Sauter, 11 February 1920.
4 A.G.'s notebook.
5 R. H. Mottram,
   For Some We Loved, p. 233.

Chapter 32
1 Marrot, p. 525.
2 ibid.
3 Herman Ould,
   John Galsworthy.
4 Marrot, p. 541.

5 Quoted in Marrot, p. 542.
6 J.G. to Dorothy Easton,
   18 September 1923.
7 Quoted in Marrot, p. 546.
8 J.G. to Mrs Chichester,
   17 December 1924.
9 Mrs Thomas Hardy to A.G.,
   3 November 1924.
10 Diary of Rudolf Sauter, 1924.
11 Diary of Rudolf Sauter,
    quoted in Marrot, pp. 567–8.
12 J.G. to Dorothy Easton, n.d.
13 J.G. to André Chevrillon,
    18 July 1925.
14 J.G. to H. Granville Barker,
    1 March 1926.

Chapter 33
1 Rudolf Sauter,
   quoted in Marrot, p. 584.
2 Dorothy Easton,
   Memoir of John Galsworthy.
3 Quoted in Rupert Hart-
   Davis, *Hugh Walpole*, p. 306.
4 Rudolf Sauter,
   Galsworthy the Man.
5 Quoted in Reginald Pound,
   Arnold Bennett.
6 Quoted in Rupert Hart-
   Davis, *Hugh Walpole.*
7 Quoted in Marrot, p. 604.
8 J.G. to H. Granville Barker,
   8 April 1927.
9 R. B. Cunninghame-Graham,
   to J.G., 19 July 1928.
10 Gilbert Murray to J.G.,
    23 August 1928.
11 J.G. to Leon M. Lion,
    1 February 1929.

12 Quoted in Marrot, p. 621.
13 J.G. to André Chevrillon,
    2 November 1930.
14 J.G. to M. E. Reynolds,
    8 February 1931.
15 Cynthia Asquith,
    Portrait of Barrie.

Chapter 34
1 Rudolf Sauter,
   Galsworthy the Man.
2 Dorothy Easton,
   Memoirs of John Galsworthy.
3 Rudolf Sauter,
   John Galsworthy's Last days
   and hours. Notes made at the
   time by his nephew.
4 Account given to Marrot
   by Rudolf Sauter, Marrot,
   p. 645.
5 J. W. Darling to Rudolf
   Sauter, 23 January 1933.
6 Quoted in Marrot, p. 646.
7 R. H. Mottram,
   For Some We Loved, p. 259.
8 Quoted in Marrot, p. 646.
9 Preface to H. V. Marrot,
   *Life and Letters of John
   Galsworthy.*
10 Rudolf Sauter, *Last days* . . .
11 ibid.
12 ibid.
13 ibid.
14 ibid.
15 J. W. Darling to Rudolf
    Sauter, 23 January 1933.
16 Rudolf Sauter, *Last days* . . .
17 Rudolf Sauter, *Last days* . . .

Index